RELIGION, ETHNICITY AND SOCIAL CHANGE

Religion, Ethnicity and Social Change

Liz Fawcett
Lecturer in Media Studies
University of Ulster
Northern Ireland

Foreword by Eileen Barker
Professor of Sociology
London School of Economics

Consultant Editor: Jo Campling

First published in Great Britain 2000 by
MACMILLAN PRESS LTD
Houndmills, Basingstoke, Hampshire RG21 6XS and London
Companies and representatives throughout the world

A catalogue record for this book is available from the British Library.

ISBN 0–333–72047–4 ✓

 First published in the United States of America 2000 by
ST. MARTIN'S PRESS, INC.,
Scholarly and Reference Division,
175 Fifth Avenue, New York, N.Y. 10010

ISBN 0–312–22567–9

Library of Congress Cataloging-in-Publication Data
Fawcett, Liz, 1961–
Religion, ethnicity and social change / Liz Fawcett ; foreword by
Eileen Barker ; consultant editor, Jo Campling.
p.   cm.
ISBN 0–312–22567–9
1. Ethnicity—Religious aspects.   I. Campling, Jo.   II. Title.
BL65.E75F39   1999
306.6'618348—dc21   99–26811
                                                      CIP

This book is printed on paper suitable for recycling and made from fully managed and
sustained forest sources.

10   9   8   7   6   5   4   3   2   1
09   08   07   06   05   04   03   02   01   00

Printed and bound in Great Britain by
Antony Rowe Ltd, Chippenham, Wiltshire

For my parents and my sister, Kathy

Contents

List of Figures

List of Abbreviations

ANC	African National Congress
APK	Afrikaanse Protestante Kerk
AWB	Afrikaner Weerstandsbeweging (Afrikaner Resistance Movement)
BBC	British Broadcasting Corporation
CODESA	Convention for a Democratic South Africa
DRC	Dutch Reformed Church
DRCA	Dutch Reformed Church in Africa
DRMC	Dutch Reformed Mission Church
DUP	Democratic Unionist Party
FAK	Federasie van Afrikaanse Kultuurvereniginge (Federation of Afrikaans Cultural Associations)
IRA	Irish Republican Army
PCI	Presbyterian Church in Ireland
PUP	Progressive Unionist Party
SACP	South African Communist Party
SDLP	Social Democratic and Labour Party
UDP	Ulster Democratic Party
UUP	Ulster Unionist Party
UVF	Ulster Volunteer Force
WARC	World Alliance of Reformed Churches
WCC	World Council of Churches

Foreword

Why might people who share a religion kill each other if they have different coloured skins? Is it for the same reasons that people with the same coloured skins might kill each other if they have different religions? And the 'why?' question implies a 'how?' question: How do people come to recognise and then either maintain, reinforce or alter their recognition of the other, who is 'the same', as the Other who is to be feared and despised, controlled and, sometimes, killed because he or she 'is different'?

These are questions that lie at the heart of this important study of the conflicts in Northern Ireland and South Africa during the early to mid-1990s. In both societies a section of the population which had long enjoyed a position of privilege with respect to social status, economic and political power had come to fear, with justification, that their erstwhile privileges were being eroded.

It is primarily to the Presbyterian Church in Ireland (PCI) and the Dutch Reformed Church (DRC) in South Africa that Liz Fawcett turned in her attempt to understand the processes of continuity and change. The picture that emerges is of two Churches deeply concerned to look after their interests and preserve their status as best they can by, to mix metaphors rather horribly, keeping a foot in the past and an eye on the future.

In their role as preservers of the threatened status quo, both Churches have reassured their members that they shared a common identity which is rooted in a culture with a unique historical heritage that accords them certain rights – despite, perhaps because, their land and their power had been taken from the Other. Finding themselves unable to continue to dominate in reality, Afrikaners and Ulster Protestants have had to rely increasingly upon symbolic domination in the discourse they employ. Complementing the myths which support claims that 'we' are superior, are strategies that define the Other as inferior, not really civilised – perhaps not really human. By using their own criteria to define the boundaries of civilised society, they can place the Other as inevitably beyond the pale. Thus, blacks can be described as illiterate when 'illiterate' is defined as unable to read or write in English or Afrikaans; and Catholics can be described as non-Christians or, simply, as unbelievers when 'real religion' is defined as Protestant religion. The verbal distinctions can, furthermore, be reinforced by symbolic actions that also draw boundaries which exclude – we are told of a Protestant minister who explained that members of his congregation attend church 'because they are not Catholics'.

But the separation is not merely symbolic. A social pillarisation has been effected both culturally and structurally – and legally through the apartheid system in South Africa. Geographical separation has been maintained by strong opposition to selling 'our' land to Catholics or to blacks. Cultural separation is maintained as children are differentially socialised not only in different families but also through the provision of different schools – and, of course, intermarriage is almost unthinkable. Although, theologically and historically the Church to which the whites and blacks in South Africa both belong is the same Church, this has not meant that those with different coloured skin would worship together. Successful missionising in the early part of the nineteenth century led to the development of separate congregations which had evolved into separate Churches by the latter part of the century – the Dutch Reformed Mission Church for 'coloureds' and the Dutch Reformed Church in Africa for 'blacks'; when these two came together in 1994, they deliberately decided to call themselves the Uniting (rather than the United) Reformed Church until such time as DRC had joined the merger.

In Northern Ireland, attempts at ecumenical cross-community discussions on theological issues have enjoyed little enthusiasm from either side, with Catholics suspicious of what they may have rightly construed as little more than evangelical outreach. And it did little to bridge the Protestant and Catholic divide when the PCI's General Assembly determined not to follow the Presbyterian Church in Scotland's decision to remove references to the Pope as 'the Anti-Christ' from the 450-year-old Westminster Confession of Faith, which all new ministers and elders have to sign.

But at the same time, the Churches have proclaimed the need for a peaceful resolution of the conflicts, and have, indeed, contributed to some not insignificant extent to the very changes that have eroded the boundaries that separate the Other. That is, not only have the Churches maintained their position in society through their reinforcement of the status quo, they have also tried to ensure that they are not excluded from the approaching order – an order in which the erstwhile Them is part of the emergent Us.

This is certainly not a book that paints a simple picture of a single, clear dichotomy in either of the two societies it describes. Concentrating on the mainstream rather than the extremes (such as Paisley's Free Presbyterian Church or TerreBlanche's Afrikaner Weerstandsbeweging), Dr Fawcett reveals internal (rather than purely external) dynamics and tensions, and explores the differences within the communities. Among the many variables she examines, the most consequential are those related to the urban/rural distinction. But there are several other significant differences, such as those between the clergy and the laity; between the politically conservative and the politically liberal; between the working and the middle classes; and between those who found themselves facing unemployment and those who were relatively secure in their economic position and social status.

It is the ordinary people rather than the elite who are the key players in this story, and Dr Fawcett reveals plenty of ambiguities within the individuals whom she talked to and observed, with a person expressing one view in one social context and an apparently contradictory view in another. We are of course all aware that people, including ourselves, are more than capable of transposing or translating principles that we hold at a general, theoretical level into apparently opposing beliefs and/or actions when it comes to a more immediate context that directly affects us or our families. But tensions and *prima facie* contradictions can also be found within the official statements of the Church. Take, for example, the DRC's *Church and Society 1990: A Testimony of the Dutch Reformed Church*, an important document which clearly states that apartheid 'is in conflict with the Bible', but which also declares that the Church 'must testify against ... racism, *integrationism* and all other unchristian ideologies (emphasis added)'.

While Dr Fawcett is careful not to generalise beyond the confines of the two societies which she has studies, her work has a significance that extends well beyond the contemporary situations of Northern Ireland and South Africa. And, on a practical note, we are offered insights that could be of significance in understanding other situations in other times and other places. On a more theoretical note, we are led to question the claims of certain theorists who have not themselves ventured into the field, or who have rashly generalised from limited knowledge.

Religion, Ethnicity and Social Change presents us with a sensitive and perceptive understanding of some of the processes by which human beings create, maintain and negotiate their identities. Having read the book, not only do we become considerably more informed about what has been going on in two tragically divided countries, we are also given the opportunity of gaining a deeper insight into the human condition. This, in my opinion, is an example of the sociological enterprise at its best.

London School of Economics EILEEN BARKER

Acknowledgements

There were many, many people who gave of their time, help, advice and support during the production of this book and the research on which it is based. All I can do is single out a few and apologise to those whose names are not mentioned. First and foremost, I owe a special debt for his invaluable guidance to Liam O'Dowd, who supervised the PhD thesis on which this book is based. I am also indebted to Richard Jenkins and Mike Smuts, who read the manuscript in its entirety, and to John Dunlop, who read portions of it. They provided many useful comments. I would also like to thank Pieter Meiring at the Dutch Reformed Church, and both Ruth McConnell and Stephen Lynas at the Presbyterian Church in Ireland, who all patiently dealt with countless requests for information. Needless to say, any factual errors which remain are mine, as are the views I express in this text.

I would also like to thank the ministers in the congregations in which I did my fieldwork for devoting a great deal of time and effort to facilitate my research. My thanks too to the many other individuals whom I interviewed, nearly all of whom gave of their time very willingly, despite the fact that a study such as this was of no immediate or obvious benefit to them.

There are certain other individuals to whom I owe a special debt. Johann Groenewald was extremely generous with his time, his advice and the provision of his departmental facilities. Anne-Marie Nel came to my rescue in Louis Trichardt by very kindly allowing me to use her home as an office while I was there. I would also like to thank Eileen Barker for being kind enough to write the preface to this book, and my consultant editor, Jo Campling, for her support and encouragement.

My thanks to the Central Community Relations Unit of the Northern Ireland Civil Service, and the BBC World Service Alexander Onassis Trust. Without the generous funds they provided, this study would not have been possible.

Finally, I would like to thank both my friends and my family for their patience and support – and a special thankyou to Angela Versari, whose friendship while I was in South Africa and since has been something I treasure.

LIZ FAWCETT

Introduction

I have lived in Northern Ireland for many years now but every time I visit my parents just across the water in Scotland, my father asks me the same question. 'Tell me,' he says, looking genuinely perplexed, 'What is it all about? Why can't they just get on and live with each other?' For my father, and for so many other British people, the conflict in Northern Ireland is tribalism writ large. It defies explanation in 'rational', 'civilised' terms and that is troubling to those who like to feel that western society has progressed and that we are 'rational', 'civilised' people.

The outbreak of bitter ethnic conflict in the former Yugoslavia has challenged the notion that 'tribal' allegiances have been put to one side in the west, and exchanged for more 'sensible' concerns. Indeed we are fooling ourselves if we think this is the case. One only has to look at the patriotic fervour whipped up over the Gulf War in the United States and over the Falklands War in Britain. National and ethnic identities may lie latent in more 'civilised' countries most of the time. However, they can be mobilised quickly and are often signalled in more mundane ways.[1]

Religion is another phenomenon which refuses to lie down and rest in the 'civilised' west. The persistence of belief in God, the popularity of so-called New Age religions, the publicity accorded to many fundamentalist and evangelical groups, and the continued significance of the mainstream churches as moral authorities are all testimony to the fact that religion is very much alive in the west. Yet religion is like ethnicity in that it too defies rational explanation. What is intrinsic to both these phenomena is their appeal to the emotional rather than the rational side of our nature.

At a worldwide level, there has been a proliferation of high-profile and often violent expressions of ethnic and religious identity. However, in western academic literature, there has been a much greater focus on ethnicity than on religion, and relatively few attempts to examine the relationship between the two phenomena in any great depth. Religion and ethnicity often go hand in hand where there is ethnic conflict, as in the former Yugoslavia, the Middle East, India and Sri Lanka. Yet religion has received surprisingly little attention, given the wealth of writing on ethnicity.

Moreover, where its role has been examined, religion tends to be characterised as 'fundamentalist', 'extreme', 'radical' or 'militant' in the context of ethnic conflict.[2] This is misleading because it constructs a dichotomy between those 'extreme' brands of religion portrayed as being caught up in, or even fermenting, bitter violence elsewhere, and the cosy mainstream denominational religions which form part of the cultural backdrop for those of us in the west who watch these 'tribal' outbreaks on our TV screens from the safety of our living-rooms.

This book focuses on two situations of ethnic conflict in which religion has played a part. However, the form of religion involved has been the cosier mainstream variety and the two ethnic groups in question are westernised in their lifestyle and in most aspects of their culture. One of the conflict situations is Northern Ireland, the other South Africa. The two groups in question, Afrikaners and Ulster Protestants, enjoyed a dominant position in these territories for much of their history. Religion played a key role in sustaining that position, particularly in South Africa. This study focuses on the role of religion during the early to mid-1990s, a period in which the power and privilege of these two groups came under threat.

My central concern is the interrelationship between the political and religious spheres, and the links between these spheres and the symbolic aspects of ethnicity during this period. The book shows how religious institutions which formed pillars of the ethnic establishment adjusted their official pronouncements to accommodate the new political order as the balance of power began to shift. My argument is that the churches on which this study focuses relied on the collective cultural power of a number of institutions which formed what I call the *cultural mainstream* of their respective ethnic groups.[3] Once it became clear that the political order was changing, there was a need for these churches to reposition themselves so that they could benefit from the cultural power of the emerging mainstream which would underpin the new order. In the process, the churches became sites of struggle between discourses of continuity and discourses of change. There were also conflicts of interest between their role as churches representing their particular ethnic group, and their professed role as conciliator, reaching out to the external ethnic Other.

It is vital to examine the way in which these processes manifested themselves at the micro- as well as the macro-level. At the macro-level, denominational religion could no longer take for granted the symbolic and discursive authority it had been able to wield. However, at the micro-level, within individual congregations, clergymen were still granted a certain amount of power and authority.[4] This had important consequences for the way in which various conflicts of interest were played out. There was also a notable difference between the way in which these struggles manifested themselves in urban and in rural settings. There were strong parallels between rural congregations in South Africa and Northern Ireland, suggesting a sociogeographical divide between rural and urban areas that, in many ways, was as significant as the ethnic divisions which concerned politicians at the time.

RELIGION AND ETHNICITY

The ethnic elements of identity are very important when one is examining Afrikaners and Ulster Protestants. The French term *ethnie* fits both these groups very well. A. D. Smith has defined it as describing a community:

> which unites an emphasis upon cultural differences with the sense of an historical community. It is this sense of history and the perception of cultural uniqueness and individuality which differentiates populations from each other and which endows a given population with a definite identity, both in their eyes and in those of outsiders.[5]

Smith stresses that what matters is not the extent to which this common history and cultural distinctiveness exist in 'reality', but that the *sense* of it exists. Ethnicity, then, is an extremely malleable social construct. Yet, it is an aspect of identity which clearly meets a profound need in many people. George A. De Vos and Lola Romanucci-Ross eloquently sum up the appeal of ethnicity:

> to know one's *origin* is to have not only a sense of provenance, but perhaps more importantly, a sense of *continuity* in which one finds the personal and social *meaning* of human existence to some degree. It is to know *why* one behaves and acts in accordance with custom. To be without a sense of continuity is to be faced with one's own death.[6]

This desire is one that is often used by politicians for their own ends, as was the case in the drive for political power by Afrikaner nationalists in South Africa in the earlier part of this century. The construction of an Afrikaner cultural identity and the mobilisation of ethnic senti-ment were vital factors in the National Party's victory in 1948. Until that project began, 'Afrikaners' would not have labelled themselves as 'Afrikaners' as they had no sense of a collective identity. They were persuaded by intellectuals and other elites to adopt both an 'Afrikaner' identity and an 'Afrikaner' culture. Yet, although this sense of identity could be seen as an artificial creation, its mobilisation would not have succeeded it if had not tapped into a deep need for some sense of collective identity.[7]

The constitution of ethnic identity revolves around features which are perceived as being shared by all members of the group. Typically, these include a collective name, a common myth of descent, a shared history, a distinctive shared culture, an association with a specific terri-tory and a sense of solidarity.[8] However, as Fredrik Barth has pointed out, the process of defining what lies within the collectivity also involves specifying what lies without.[9] One of the most important debates within the field of ethnic studies has centred on whether it is the 'cultural stuff' inside the collectivity or the process of constructing and maintaining the boundaries around it that is most significant from a social-anthropological point of view.[10] The analysis of Ulster Protestants and Afrikaners set out in this book suggests that it is the process of boundary creation and maintenance which should form the starting-point of any examination of ethnicity.

The process of boundary maintenance can be seen in countries throughout the world with regard to both national and ethnic identity. Michael Billig has drawn our attention to the way in which nation-hood is constantly 'flagged' in the news media so that even those who would claim to have no interest in their ascribed national identity are constantly reminded that they 'belong' to a particular nation.[11] From newspaper articles which refer to 'the government', assuming readers will regard it as their national government, to political rhetoric which talks of 'the British people' or 'the American people', we are continu-ally reminded in a subtle way that we have – or, at least, should believe that we have – a national identity.

Through these subtle means, we come to see our national or ethnic identity as something to be taken for granted rather than questioned. The more we are reminded of our ethnic or national identity, the less we are likely to view it as a relative and ideological construction which could be substituted by other identities, such as social class or gender. In situations of *ethnic conflict*, however, newspapers can also be used to remind people that their ethnic or national identity is most certainly not something to be taken for granted. This happens in Northern Ireland, where the nationalist *Irish News* generally refers to 'the British government' and 'the British army', while the unionist *News Letter* refers simply to 'the government' or 'the army'. In this way, the *Irish News* constantly reminds its predominantly Catholic readership that their imposed 'British' identity is something to be contested.

In addition to the cultural power of discourse, Benedict Anderson makes the point that there is also an ideological function attached to the actual act of consuming the news media.[12] He stresses the significance of the shared ritual of reading a 'national newspaper' in constituting and reconstituting a sense of national identity. This generally happens in a mundane fashion of which readers remain unconscious. Yet, when one nation goes to war with another, the ritual of reading the newspaper or watching a television bulletin is performed with much greater engagement than usual; 'banal' nationalism suddenly becomes 'hot' nationalism. This was very evident in America and Britain during the Gulf War; the news media were consumed with a frantic appetite for every scrap of information about 'our boys' in the Gulf.

This analysis helps us to identify one of the most important ways in which religion can contribute to the maintenance of a sense of ethnic identity. In countries where ethnic and religious boundaries happen to converge, there is a parallel between the ritual of reading a 'national' or 'ethnic' newspaper, and the ritual of collective worship. This is true where religion is an ethnic marker, as in Northern Ireland. However, it is equally true where worship is organised along ethnic or racial lines, as has been the case in the Dutch Reformed Church in South Africa. Thus, in Christian denominations in such situations, attendance at church quietly 'flags' the fact that its members belong to Group A, which can worship in their church, rather than Group B, which is either not permitted to do so or which chooses to worship elsewhere.

In the case of Afrikaners and Ulster Protestants, it must also be remembered that both groups had enjoyed a position of dominance which was originally obtained through the usurpation of land from the native Other. The original Afrikaner and Ulster Protestant settlers lived in fear of reprisal from those they had dispossessed. As we shall see in the next chapter, that fear and insecurity seemed to shape the collective mind-set of both groups throughout their respective histories. As the twentieth century drew to a close, that fear was intensified by the prospect of radical political changes which posed a serious threat to their privileged position.

Thus, in both cases, the ethnic boundary underpinned a concentration of power which was becoming ever more insecure. For members of the dominant group, this lent a particular significance to ritual acts which flagged identity and, in so doing, symbolised the balance of ethnic power. This meant that the act of joint worship with the Other represented an encroachment of the boundaries which delineated the privileged position of the dominant group. It is not surprising, therefore, that there were heated debates over mixed worship in the two churches on which this book focuses; the Presbyterian Church in Ireland (PCI) and the 'white' Dutch Reformed Church (DRC) in South Africa. In the PCI, the issue was religiously mixed worship while, in the DRC, there was controversy over racially mixed services. Thus, in both Northern Ireland and South Africa, the act of worship effectively acted as a symbolic boundary marker of both ethnic identity and ethnic dominance.

The appeal of the ritual element in worship is its apparently unchanging nature, giving those who participate in it a sense of continuity. The symbolic power of the ritual is derived from the firm link its participants believe it to have with the past.[13] In addition to this weekly flagging of identity, there were other, less frequent, rituals which inspired particular passion within the ethnic groups we are examining. In Northern Ireland, the colourful and controversial Orange Order parades on the Twelfth of July are the obvious examples of this type of occasion. Here an explicit link is made with the past through the commemoration of the victory of King William of Orange at the Battle of the Boyne in 1690, an event which forms the chief focus of the symbolic element of Ulster Protestant identity.

Neil Jarman has observed that this particular ritual feeds into the process of constructing identity through the constitution of boundaries between the ethnic group and the Other: 'The parade is the cultural medium for constructing that collective Other that at other times is largely invisible.'[14] Jarman contends that the world of Ulster Protestants tends to consist of encounters with individual Others, who may be regarded in a positive light, but that the collective Other remains a distant entity which, partly through ignorance, is cast in negative terms. Parading enables people on both sides of the 'divide' in Northern Ireland to constitute the sense of difference from the Other which is so essential to their sense of collective identity.

I would take issue with Jarman when he talks about the 'invisibility' of the Other in Northern Ireland. What became evident from my own research was the acute and often unpleasant *visibility* of the symbolic Other for Ulster Protestants. The threat of the Other was discursively symbolised by them in the form of the twin institutions of the Irish government and the Catholic Church. Inter-party talks and the loosening of the British government's commitment to the constitutional union between Britain and Ireland were both seen as enabling these two negative signifiers to encroach on the freedom of Protestants. The appearance on television of the Sinn Fein leader, Gerry Adams, was another negative signifier guaranteed to raise the hackles of many Protestants I interviewed.

These encounters with the symbolic Other were another vital aspect of the process of constituting difference. Like attendance at church, they were more akin to the low-level flagging of identity discerned by Billig than the special ritual of the annual Twelfth parade.[15] Similar processes could be seen at work within the Afrikaner community in South Africa. Here, the black Other was discursively symbolised by many Afrikaners in the form of the ANC, Nelson Mandela and Archbishop Desmond Tutu. Both these men were often viewed as individuals whose real agenda was the overthrow of whites and who, therefore, could not be trusted.

The important point to note, however, is the significance of the Other in the making and remaking of collective identity. We can only construct our own sense of identity by contrasting ourselves with others; identity is *relative* to the Other. In both the cases we are examining, that process of constituting identity *vis-à-vis* the other had been underscored by the power to institutionalise ethnic divisions. As we shall see, the removal of much of the dominant group's enforced authority to define boundaries gave added significance to the symbolic and ritualistic modes of constituting identity which are examined in this book.

RELIGION AND THE MOBILISATION OF ETHNIC SENTIMENT

Ethnic sentiment does not simply arise spontaneously. Its appearance is related to the material interests of those mobilised by it and, most importantly, the economic and political interests of those who take the lead in awakening ethnic consciousness. A. D. Smith has

highlighted the role of the intelligentsia and other elites in constructing or reconstructing an ethnic culture and in mobilising ethnic sentiment.[16] This ability to authoritatively define culture and identity stems
from the amount of cultural power which such elites are able to wield;
in other words, the extent to which they are able to exercise influence
and to command prestige and authority through the use of different
cultural means, such as education, the media and the church.[17]

Smith contends that, throughout the world, the authority to dissem-
inate and reinforce ethnic identity has tended to shift from religious
leaders and priests to secular, university-trained intellectuals.[18] He
does concede that there are exceptions, including Ireland, Poland,
Iran and Pakistan. Indeed, more recently, he has drawn attention to
the revival of religious sentiment around the world.[19] However, it is
questionable whether it is a useful exercise to try to isolate one type of
elite grouping as the catalyst for ethnic mobilisation. After all, no elite
group or institution operates in a vacuum. Their ability to exercise cultural power is dependent on other elites. It seems more fruitful to
conduct one's analysis by examining the interdependent nature of
powerful interests within an ethnic group.

As the next chapter shows, a number of different elite groups were
jointly responsible for mobilising ethnic sentiment at key periods in the
history of both Afrikaners and Ulster Protestants. These groups tapped
into a collective cultural conscience or at least a deep need for some
form of ethnic identity. In this sense, they exercised collective cultural
power. In such situations, religion can play an invaluable role because
it possesses a special type of cultural power. Where the religious and
secular spheres are perceived as separate arenas, religion is seen as
transcending the secular world. The authority or weight which it carries
as a result is viewed as being of a different order to that accorded to
secular elites such as academics or politicians. This special competence, which is claimed by and bestowed on religious groups and
institutions, is referred to by Pierre Bourdieu as 'religious capital'.[20]

In addition, denominational religion is also able to offer a ready-
made organisational structure through which the ethnic message can
be disseminated.[21] This is precisely what happened in the case of the
DRC in South Africa, which took on the role of a *volkskerk* ('church
of the people') in the Afrikaner nationalist movement in the 1930s
and 1940s, playing a pivotal part in the promotion of Afrikaner culture
and ethnic allegiance. I have already referred to the symbolic
significance of the act of worship where ethnic and religious boundaries converge. Likewise, the opportunity and, to some extent, mass

demand for a church to play a leadership role within that ethnic group is clearly more likely to be present where this convergence occurs.

The appeal of religion for ethnonationalists also lies in the sense of continuity which religion provides. Smith makes much of the 'chosen people' narratives employed by many religions but that is not a necessary prerequisite in order for religion to play a significant role in mobilising ethnic sentiment.[22] In the cases examined in this study, the 'chosen people' theme was not a particularly significant factor. However, religion did provide discourses which reinforced the notion of the innate superiority of the dominant ethnic group. In the DRC, there was a discourse of 'mission' which was used to refer to church activities which involved black South Africans. This dated back to the work of the missionaries who accompanied the first colonial settlers in Africa. They set out to convert the 'natives' to Christianity, convinced that western religious beliefs were superior to those of the indigenous people. This was done on the assumption that the ways of black Africans were inferior to those of white westerners. The continued use of the term 'mission' and frequent talk of 'civilising' blacks in South Africa incorporated this implicit assumption. In the PCI, there was a not dissimilar discourse of 'evangelicalism' which suggested that one brand of Christian belief was superior to others.

CIVIL RELIGION

The type of religion we have discussed so far is 'religion' in the conventional sense. However, sociologists of religion also sometimes refer to a more secular form of religion, which they term 'civil religion' – in other words, symbols which resonate at some level in the cultural consciousness and which have a motivational force similar to religion. Robert Bellah, the American writer who popularised this term, saw civil religion as helping to reinforce a sense of national, collective consciousness in the United States.[23] American civil religion included symbols such as the national flag and various national monuments, as well as patriotic references in political speeches. In Britain, the monarchy has been the central focus of the nation's civil religion, although the symbolic authority of this particular institution has been damaged by national media which have become bolder and more antagonistic in their attitude towards the Royal Family.

Civil religion generally forms a vital part of the mobilisation and the maintenance of ethnic identity. This can be seen clearly in the case of both Ulster Protestants and Afrikaners. However, the pool of civil religion symbols within a particular ethnic group can be a contested resource. In both the cases studied in this book, we shall see how different interest groups competed for definitional authority over the meaning attached to certain symbols. At the same time, civil religion can take on institutionalised forms, as with the Orange Order in Northern Ireland and the Broederbond in South Africa. These have formed an integral part of the cultural mainstream of Ulster Protestants and Afrikaners. We can see here the mutual dependence of the different elements of the mainstream; just as civil religion institutions have benefited from the enhanced credibility provided by their close relationship with denominational religion, so denominational religion has gained from its links with civil religion. However, shifts in the balance of political power can cause strains in this relationship. This was particularly evident in Northern Ireland during the violent flare-ups over certain controversial Orange Order parades in the mid-1990s.

At the same time, both denominational and civil religion have provided symbolic resources for politicians in each of the ethnic groups. Civil religion supplied a source of potent symbols for the right-wing Afrikaner Volksfront in South Africa. It also provided an opportunity to gain political credibility for two leading unionists, Ian Paisley and David Trimble, in Northern Ireland.[24] Moreover, there has been a close relationship between denominational religion and politics in each territory. Denominational religion has an additional benefit for politicians; it not only gives them symbolic resources, but can also provide them with the moral authority they need to influence the values which underpin the way in which politics is debated and carried out.

RELIGION IN THE CULTURAL MAINSTREAM

It is in its role as a fund of potent symbolic and authoritative moral resources that organised religion possesses religious capital within the public sphere. That power is enhanced when ethnic and religious boundaries converge. In such situations, where a denomination operates as a *volkskerk*, it draws on what we could call *ethnoreligious* capital. However, a church cannot take for granted its possession of ethnoreligious capital or its ability to wield cultural power. The influence of religious institutions is interwoven with those of the other elites which possess other forms of cultural power. Together, these groups occupy what can be called the *cultural mainstream* of their particular society; that is, the ideas, institutions and values which have greatest hegemonic weight and centrality within the public sphere. If centres of political and economic power are to retain their influence without resorting to coercion, they need to draw on the power of the cultural mainstream. At the same time, the capacity of the mainstream to influence both our behaviour as individuals and the course of events at a societal level depends on the degree of legitimacy and authority which we accord elite symbolic producers.[25]

In a society ruled by coercion, that authority may be accorded out of fear. Certain values and ideas are imposed by those who hold power. However, in societies where there is at least some semblance of democracy, the legitimacy and authority of political, economic and symbolic producers is maintained through hegemony: the widespread, taken-for-granted acceptance of a set of ideas about the way in which society should be ordered.[26]

Hegemony is a dynamic rather than a static phenomenon. Its success lies in its ability to incorporate ideas which challenge it. Thus, hegemony constantly shifts ground but always to the advantage of those who hold political and economic power, although the centres of these types of power can change. The cultural mainstream plays a vital part in this process by providing the collective cultural power which helps maintain the ideological dominance of the centres of political and economic power. It shapes the values which underpin the way society is run. It acts as a reference point in constituting our sense of identity. It enables us to construct meaning, and it motivates our actions. It also defines the parameters within which public debate on various issues takes place.

At times, however, there are major shifts in the balance of political or economic power. During such periods of transition, the cultural mainstream becomes both the arena on which the contest between different axes of political or economic power is played out, and a reflection of that struggle. The benefit of being in the mainstream is that one can draw on the combined cultural power of the whole. This means, however, that members must have an eye to future shifts in this alliance of interests in presenting their current standpoint on various issues. One consequence of an abrupt change in the balance of political power of the type examined in this book is the formation of a new mainstream which, to some extent, transcends ethnic boundaries.

In the two cases examined here, the emerging mainstream was based around a plurality of ethnic identities, and was more secular in its ethos than its predecessors. Thus, the churches studied had to convert ethnoreligious capital into more straightforward symbolic or cultural capital; in other words, they could no longer take their position within the mainstream for granted on the basis of their ethnoreligious standing.[27] This study illustrates the way in which denominational religion had to keep in mind the likely parameters of the new discursive order in making its public pronouncements in such situations.

The resulting tensions between the discourses of continuity and change within the DRC and the PCI illustrate the strain under which this process can place churches. While public statements may reflect the 'new thinking', many clergy and laity remain firmly wedded to the old order. Denominational religion effectively becomes a site of struggle between competing discourses. This same tension can be seen at an individual level; I often observed interviewees employing different, contradictory discourses in the course of one interview. This was part of the process of attempting to grapple with the momentous changes taking place at a wider level.[28]

In addition to this conflict between discourses of change and discourses of continuity, there was also a conflict within the Churches between their traditional role as a *volkskerk* or church of the people, and their self-proclaimed role as conciliator between their own ethnic group and the Other. While research suggests that churches can be very effective in promoting better understanding between different groups, their ability to do so in practice was clearly limited by this unresolved tension within both the DRC and the PCI.[29]

Such discursive struggles do not take place in a freeform fashion but are themselves structured by history and social context. Orthodox and conservative discourses have great power to influence the parameters of such debates because they represent the *status quo* and because they tend to have their own *internal* logic which has an appeal which goes beyond those who would claim to subscribe to them.[30] There is a parallel here with political debates in Western Europe over immigration and race issues. The xenophobic rhetoric of right-wing politicians influences the discourse and policies of mainstream politicians; while they fear the ability of the extremists to gain votes, they also see how they can turn a 'moderate' version of such rhetoric to their own advantage. The crude internal logic of racist discourse has wide appeal.[31] Right-wingers have been able to help ensure that the immigration 'problem' is seen as being one which is centred around the numbers allowed into Western European countries, rather than

the racist attitudes of those who live in these nations. Similarly, orthodox discourses were able to structure the debates within the DRC and
the PCI on such issues as ecumenism and mixed worship.

As we shall see in the next chapter, the persuasiveness of versions of
these orthodox discourses led to the creation of fundamentalist-style
religious movements which challenged the intra-ethnic religious hegemony of the mainstream churches. The best-known of these movements is the Free Presbyterian Church, founded by the Reverend Ian
Paisley, leader of the more hardline of the two main unionist parties.
The similarity in the denomination's name has led many people
outside Northern Ireland to identify Paisley with mainstream Ulster
Presbyterianism. However, the two are distinct entities.

While the membership of the 'Free Ps' has remained relatively
small, it has undoubtedly exercised a constraining influence on the
approach taken within the PCI towards cross-community initiatives.
However, the 'Free Ps' have never been embraced wholeheartedly by
the elites who have formed the cultural mainstream in the Ulster
Protestant community. As we shall see, Ian Paisley is viewed with contempt by many Protestants; while he has been a potent figure-head for
a sizeable proportion of unionists, he could not be viewed as a 'mainstream' figure within the Protestant community because he does not
have elite support. Yet in academic analyses of Northern Ireland,
there has been a focus on Paisley, and on the 'fundamentalist' and
'evangelical' aspects of Ulster Protestantism, at the expense of
sufficient investigation into the religious denominations to which most
Protestants belong and which are at the heart of their cultural
mainstream.[32]

This brings us back to the point made at the beginning of this
chapter – that religion and ethnicity are capable of arousing great
passion, even in mainstream churches which form part of 'civilised',
'westernised' communities. Mainstream churches derive great cultural
power from being part of the alliance of elite interests which exercises
collective cultural power within their own communities. It is not surprising, therefore, that the two denominations examined here took on
a *volkskerk* role within their own ethnic groups, prior to the period
covered by this study. Neither is it surprising that tensions within the
churches were heightened when the shift in the balance of political
power made it inevitable that a new mainstream, underpinning the
new political order, was on the horizon. At a denominational level,
the churches were operating in an increasingly secular climate where
elites within the mainstream saw the value of religious capital but did

not defer to it to the extent that they would have done previously. Within the denominations themselves, religious authority was nominally devolved to both clergy and laity. However, as we shall see, the clergy retained a large amount of religious capital within their congregations. This gave them a key role as symbolic agents in the contest between competing discourses within their churches.

All these issues are examined in some depth in the rest of this book. The first part provides some background on both Afrikaners and Ulster Protestants, and on the two churches on which this study focuses, the main Afrikaner church, the DRC, and the largest Protestant denomination in Northern Ireland, the PCI. The reader is introduced to the congregations in which fieldwork was carried out, and to the sense of fear and alienation which existed in the congregations. The second part of the book examines the different roles of the two churches, and the conflicts of interest which they faced. There is an analysis of the relationship between the churches and the political sphere, and their relationship with the institutionalised forms of civil religion. Civil religion was a much stronger social force in rural areas, and the book examines some of the differences which emerged between rural and urban congregations. Finally, the book draws together its different strands to underline the main arguments it puts forward, and to consider the significance of this analysis for other situations, both those where there is ethnic conflict and those where ethnicity and religion are less visible phenomena. This study is underpinned by an emphasis on the perspective of ordinary people. Too often comparative studies focus on the analysis of texts and interviews with elite individuals. While such material is drawn on in this book, much of the data is concerned with the views of the clergy and laity of both churches. It thus provides what I hope will be an illuminating record of the opinions of ordinary Afrikaners and Ulster Protestants during a highly significant period in the histories of both groups.

1 Under Siege: A Brief History of Afrikaners and Ulster Presbyterians

In southern Africa, the white settlers who trekked into uncharted territory used to form up their wagons into a circle when they stopped for the night, as a defensive measure against attack. This formation was called the *laager* and writers still speak of the *laager* mentality of Afrikaners. It is a label which could equally well be applied to Ulster Protestants. Both groups have frequently been characterised as being defensive and rigid, viewing difference and change as a threat. This characteristic is sometimes said to stem from their settler past.[1] In terms of both history and stereotype, there are clear parallels between Ulster Protestants and Afrikaners. However, there are also differences. In this chapter, I shall examine these differences before outlining what I consider to be the most important aspects of the respective histories of each group, and then drawing out the common themes from those histories and experiences.

Until recently, many academics and observers were very wary of the comparisons made between Northern Ireland and South Africa. Perhaps it was a way of explaining the lack of progress in finding a solution to the conflict in Northern Ireland, when measured against the success of the inter-party talks in South Africa which led to non-racial elections and the introduction of democracy. However, slowly, politicians and academics in Northern Ireland have begun to realise they can learn a great deal from the South African experience. In 1995, the former South African President and leader of the National Party, F. W. De Klerk, addressed the Forum for Peace and Reconciliation which was set up to examine a range of options and measures which might help to achieve peace in Northern Ireland. Mr De Klerk cautioned that the South African experience might not be applicable to Northern Ireland, but there was media interest in his comments on the issue of the decommissioning of arms, which dogged the start of inter-party talks in Northern Ireland.[2] Firmer recognition of the relevance of the South African experience came in May 1997, when a group of Northern Ireland politicians flew out to South Africa to meet some of those involved in that country's negotiations and to find out what lessons might be learned.

However, those who have cautioned against making facile comparisons do have some strong arguments. As with any comparative study, there are significant differences. The most obvious contrast relates to what is at the heart of the conflict in each situation. In South Africa, the conflict has centred around discrimination along racial lines, while in Northern Ireland, the dividing line has been a religious one. Some would argue that this nullifies any attempt to compare the two situations. I do not share this view.

RACE AND RELIGION AS ETHNIC MARKERS

A very simple argument can be made against the validity of the comparison between divisions based on race and those which centre on religion; one's race is instantly recognisable and cannot be changed, while one's religion is not instantly manifest and can be altered.[3] This argument presupposes that there is some element of reality to race. Clearly, there is indeed a reality about the fact that one person has black skin and another white. However, there is also a reality about the fact that some white people have blonde hair while others have dark brown. From a sociological point of view, what is important is whether that difference in skin or hair colour is institutionalised in terms of difference in opportunities and material resources, and whether people categorise each other on the basis of that difference in a way which has significant consequences. Race is important in these terms in many countries, while hair colour generally is not.

Yet, race has not always been a means of categorisation in this way. Indeed, the concept of 'race' is a relatively recent invention in the English language. It first appeared in the early seventeenth century and was used as a means of scientific categorisation in Europe and North America from the late eighteenth century.[4] As David Mason points out, the fact that race is far from an 'obvious', objective category 'is demonstrated by the fact that in all the most rigidly stratified societies in which "race" is the principal criterion of social placement, it has been necessary to develop complex procedures for classifying the phenotypically ambiguous.'[5] This is precisely what happened in South Africa.

However, even though it may be difficult for those involved in the process of assigning racial categories to label everyone, there can be little doubt that the extreme differences in terms of race are visible. Most of us would agree that some people are undoubtedly 'white' while others clearly fall into the category 'black'. To some extent, then, race is visible in a way that religion is not. Or is it?

In fact, one can argue that religion is every bit as visible in Northern Ireland. The small size and intimate nature of the place mean that one's religion rarely remains secret. People can discover what religion you are with relative ease, using clues such as the area you come from, your name or the school you attended. Moreover, they frequently make it their business to find out because such social significance is attached to religious background.

In theory, of course, one can change one's religion whereas changing one's skin colour is much more difficult. Yet, in practice, the rate of conversion from Protestant to Catholic and vice versa in Northern Ireland is relatively low. The one occasion when conversion is quite common is when two people from different religions marry. However, such marriages are far from the norm.[6] Just as there has been a considerable stigma attached to interracial marriages in South Africa, mixed Protestant–Catholic unions in Northern Ireland tend to be frowned on or at least discouraged.[7]

The negative attitude towards intermarriage in both territories is not surprising; mixed marriage represents a threat to the ethnic boundary. In South Africa, such marriages result in children who blur the colour line, while in Northern Ireland, they result in changes of denomination or simply a loss of interest in religion among those involved.[8] *The stigmatisation of* intermarriage is thus an essential part of the process of boundary maintenance in both societies.

It is the role of race and religion as boundary markers which makes the religious label in Northern Ireland comparable to racial labelling in South Africa. The significance attached to this categorisation means it affects the way people interact with each other. At a wider structural level, it influences access to material resources. This differential access to resources has been institutionalised in both territories, in terms of patterns of discrimination in Northern Ireland and in terms of the ultimate form of insitutionalised racism, apartheid, in South Africa.

Yet, although one can draw parallels, it must be emphasised that one cannot equate the discrimination which has been practised in Northern Ireland with the awful reality of apartheid. Apartheid institutionalised racism through legal sanction, regulation, state-sponsored violent repression and a rationale which was accepted uncritically by most whites. In Northern Ireland, the former unionist government also supported institutionalised discrimination for many years. Here, however, there was no grand, carefully articulated project in the manner of apartheid. The scale of institutionalisation of discrimination through legal means in Northern Ireland is dwarfed by the panoply of laws which existed under apartheid in South Africa. The embeddedness of the structures put in place there is deeply rooted and its effect will be felt for many years to come. The racism which flourished as a result has by no means disappeared. Moreover, the scale of economic inequality left by apartheid is far greater than the more modest material differences between Protestants and Catholics in Northern Ireland.

Nevertheless, there are parallels. Many of the effects of apartheid are echoed in Northern Ireland, albeit in more subtle ways. Catholics are still more likely to be unemployed than Protestants.[9] A large proportion of the population of Northern Ireland lives in an area which is segregated along religious lines.[10] Most children attend a school which is religiously segregated. A vast security apparatus has been used by the British government to maintain control. Most importantly, there is still a legacy of ignorance, bitterness and hatred between Protestants and Catholics.

The stark nature of the unfairness and discrimination in South Africa had repercussions in terms of the amount of international pressure for change exerted on the South African government. While the British government has come under pressure from the United States, from time to time, to come up with a solution to the Northern Ireland conflict, there has never been the sustained, heavy level of pressure that was placed on South Africa by the international community. Moreover, the major players in South Africa were brought together by the very real prospect of complete economic collapse and the escalation of civil war. These factors lent an urgency to the task of finding a solution which did not exist in Northern Ireland.

However, while these factors undoubtedly help to account for the contrast in the speed with which change has taken place in South Africa and Northern Ireland, both these territories have undergone rapid social change. It is perhaps most accurate to talk about *transformation* in the South African case and *transition* in the case of Northern Ireland during the period on which this book focuses, the early to mid-1990s. In South Africa, this period saw a transformation in political structures which began to shape the rest of the social structure. At the same time, Northern Ireland was undergoing a transitionary phase which held the prospect but not the certainty of radical transformation.

One further, important contrast between the two territories relates to the nature of Afrikaner and Ulster Protestant identity. On the face of it, Afrikaners have a much stronger sense of cultural and ethnic identity than Protestants; Afrikaners have their own language, sports and cultural activities. However, this identity was constructed as part of a political project aimed at securing political power for Afrikaner nationalists. It was created very much in relation to what it was not. The significance of the Other in defining identity applies to both Afrikaners and Ulster Protestants.

As we shall see below, both the DRC and the PCI have played their part in the constitution of that identity. I have examined the significance of race and religion as ethnic boundary markers. However, I have not discussed how denominational religion fits into this picture. Can one really argue that it has performed exactly the same role in both Northern Ireland and South Africa? In both territories, the respective ethnic markers are of great significance to many within the churches I examine. The churches have formed an important part of the process of the institutionalisation of those ethnic boundaries and of the consequent social and economic divisions. It is true that, for the members of the PCI, there has been no point in its history when it has considered uniting with the Roman Catholic Church; theologically, this has always been a non-starter. Thus, the development of Presbyterianism in Northern Ireland has always taken place within the boundaries of one ethnic group. On the other hand, as we shall see below, there was a period in the history of the Dutch Reformed Church in southern Africa when it did straddle the racial divide. However, during the nineteenth century, the church institutionalised the racial boundaries within its own denomination which had been unofficially observed for some time. In so doing, it became part of the process by which racial difference was labelled as significant and was institutionalised into the structures of society. Until recently, for most people within the white DRC, the need for racial boundaries was as obvious and natural as was the necessity for theological boundaries to members of the PCI. From a sociological viewpoint, it is important to unpick the taken-for-granted and investigate why such assumptions exist. In both the cases examined here, the churches have played a major role in the naturalisation and institutionalisation of ethnic divisions. In order to appreciate the significance of this role, it is important to examine it in its historical context. I do not pretend that the brief histories which follow amount to more than a selective review of some key events and trends. However, for those not acquainted with Ulster Protestants or Afrikaners, the remainder of this chapter does provide some important background material.

THE AFRIKANER EXPERIENCE

The Development of Afrikaner Nationalism[11]

The construction of a cohesive political and cultural Afrikaner identity began after the Anglo-Boer War of 1899–1902. The movement behind the campaign eventually succeeded in bringing to power its own political grouping, the National Party, in 1948. Two factors played a big part in precipitating this mobilisation of Afrikaner nationalism. One was the bitterness of Afrikaners at the humiliation they suffered at the hands of the British; the war had been fought over control of territory and the final settlement left the two South African republics which had 'belonged' to the Boers as British colonies. Furthermore, some 26 000 Afrikaner women and children died in British concentration camps, a fact many Afrikaners are still extremely bitter about. (14 000 black African internees also lost their lives in the British concentration camps; a statistic rarely referred to by Afrikaners or English-speaking white South Africans.)

From the mid-nineteenth century, attempts had been made to try to mobilise a sense of Dutch-Afrikaner identity. These efforts met with limited success; it would seem this was largely because of both regional and class-based rivalries. However, the Anglo-Boer War left many Afrikaners in an extremely grim position economically and it was this unfavourable economic situation that provided the impetus for extensive support for Afrikaner nationalism among all sections of the Afrikaner community.

After the war, there was a mass exodus of impoverished Afrikaners from rural areas to the cities. This move was prompted by various catastrophes, including the burning of farms by the British army during the war and a five-year drought which began in 1903. Many tenant farmers were evicted from their farms and had no choice but to migrate to urban areas. Yet, they rarely possessed the qualifications needed to get a job. In 1932, an investigation by the Carnegie Commission found that some 20 per cent of adult Afrikaner males were unable to secure a proper means of livelihood. The Commission termed them 'poor whites'; in such straitened circumstances, any movement which could provide a collective sense of worth was bound to prove popular.

The Afrikaner nationalist movement had various different strands to it: economic, cultural, religious and political. It was spearheaded by members of the Afrikaner middle class; in particular, intellectuals, teachers, clergymen and financiers. The campaign was supported by both the white DRC and the influential but secretive fraternity known as the Afrikaner Broederbond. The nationalist movement encouraged economic and cultural allegiance to the Afrikaner cause. Probably the single most successful means of mobilising support for the campaign was a large-scale re-enactment of the Great Trek, a move which captured the imagination of ordinary Afrikaners across the country.

The original Great Trek remains the centrepiece of Afrikaner history; it took place in the 1830s when thousands of settlers loaded up their wagons and headed off into the interior of Africa. Those involved in the journey were dubbed the 'Voortrekkers'. It was a difficult and dangerous journey; the Voortrekkers had to contend with hostile terrain and Zulu warriors. The most dramatic confrontation took place on 16 December 1838, when 464 Voortrekkers killed 3000 Zulu warriors and won what became known as the Battle of Blood River.

During the battle, the Trekkers vowed to celebrate the day each year to the glory of God, if God gave them victory. It subsequently became known as the Day of the Vow and celebrations were held in all four provinces on the appropriate day. However, according to the historian, T. Dunbar Moodie, little was made of these celebrations from the formation of the Union in 1910 until 1928 in either the Transvaal or Cape Afrikaans press. It was the huge re-enactment of the Great Trek (known as the Oxwagon Trek), staged to mark the centenary in 1938, which really revived interest in the symbolic significance of the Battle of Blood River and the Great Trek:

> At night folks would gather around the campfires of the trekkers in their hundreds and thousands to sing traditional Afrikaans liedjies ('folk songs') and the old Dutch psalms, to watch scenes from the Voortrek enacted in pantomime, and to thrill to inspired sermons culled from the depths of the civil faith.[12]

The DRC, the largest Afrikaner church, played a pivotal role in this movement. Its willingness to become involved was precipitated by its concern with the plight of 'poor whites'. As this coincided with the strengthening of Afrikaner national consciousness and the language movement, the Church soon became dubbed the *volkskerk* ('church of the people'). DRC ministers played an important part in the re-enactment of the Great Trek, appointing reception committees in every town and hamlet to welcome the 'Trekkers'. The Church also became involved in education at a local level to try to counteract the effects of the government's policy of 'anglicisation' of state educa-tion. Moreover, local ministers came out in strong support of the Reddingsdaadbond (RDB), one of the key economic organisations in the Afrikaner nationalist movement. John W. De Gruchy comments:

> quite apart from any direct involvement in political activity, the DRC held the key to the birth of Afrikanerdom. In every town and village, the DRC and its sister Afrikaner churches provided conti-nuity with the traditions of the Afrikaner. They provided educated and articulate leadership, and offered a moral and spiritual basis for personal and social life.[13]

In 1933, the DRC supplied a further boost to the nationalist move-ment with the provision of a Bible in Afrikaans, the language of the Afrikaner. The Afrikaans language was central to the nationalist movement and undoubtedly made it much easier to create a sense of a tangible, solid Afrikaner culture. Originally, it was very much the lan-guage of the rural and less well-educated Afrikaner; educated Afrikaners tended to speak English while Dutch was used in church and in schools. However, the moving work of certain Afrikaner poets who wrote in Afrikaans about the Boer heroism and suffering during the Anglo-Boer War began to alter the image of the lesser status of the language. The educated classes began to view it as a language of worth. This, combined with fears of British attempts to 'anglicise' Afrikaners, ensured that the Afrikaner nationalist movement had a firm linguistic base on which to build.

The real fusing of religious, cultural, political and business interests rested in the Broederbond, however. The Bond was formed in 1918 by a small group of Afrikaners who were concerned about the threat posed by cultural anglicisation and worried about the domination of the economy by non-Afrikaner organisations. In 1922, the Bond went underground. It was divided into cells which met once a month to discuss 'how the ethnic life of the Afrikaner might be enriched'. According to the historian, Dan O'Meara:

The vital significance of the Bond ... lay in the fact that through it the intellectual cream of the Afrikaner petty bourgeoisie was independently organised into a militant, highly disciplined body. Through the coordination and direction of the disparate individual talents of this class, and their 'systematic infiltration' into all 'key bodies in national life' where they could exercise 'quiet influence', the Bond provided a superb vehicle for the discussion, elaboration, adoption and eventual execution of what ... amounted to the independent programme of the Afrikaner petty bourgeoisie.[14]

Alongside the mobilisation of a sense of common Afrikaner cultural interests lay the promulgation of a common economic consciousness. A campaign to dissuade Afrikaner workers from belonging to English-dominated trade unions and to establish alternative Afrikaner labour associations had some, albeit limited, success. Moreover, the Afrikaner business community began to build its own source of capital for those attempting to develop their own businesses. O'Meara sees this latter mobilisation of funds as serving to get the message across to all Afrikaners that their economic interests would only be served in exclusively Afrikaner and Christian-national organisations.[15]

There was a distinctly 'sacred' nature to this economic movement, according to O'Meara:

Malan [the Afrikaner nationalist leader who became Prime Minister in 1948] himself termed the economic struggle the Tweede Trek (Second Trek), and a major series of ideological publications appeared under the same title. The economic struggle itself was cast in terms of yet another stage in the heroic struggles of a united volk against the overwhelming weight of 'imperialism' on the one hand and the engulfing tide of African barbarism on the other. This was rooted firmly in the belief in the divine calling of the volk. The ideological elaboration was cast likewise in a rigidly Calvinist framework – it was both Christian and nationalist.[16]

The DRC and Apartheid

The Afrikaner nationalist campaign culminated in 1948 in the victory of the National Party, which remained in power until South Africa's first non-racial election in 1994. The new government swiftly began enacting a series of laws based on the policy of apartheid – the supposed desirability of keeping different races separate. The ugly bedrock of apartheid was to ensure that whites reaped the largest share of the benefits of economic growth at an extremely heavy social and economic cost to the majority black community. It also meant Afrikaners were able to go some way towards 'catching up' with their English-speaking white counterparts. The former 'poor whites' saw a great leap in their standard of living. By the mid-1970s, at least 70 per cent of Afrikaners enjoyed a secure, middle-class existence.[17]

In the public sector, the government instigated blatant job discrimination in favour of Afrikaners and against blacks. Most cruelly of all, there was an enormous programme of residential segregation which entailed the enforced movement of millions of people to specified 'group areas'. This process caused untold suffering for black and so-called 'coloured' (mixed-race) people. However, whites remained in blissful, if distinctly incurious, ignorance as apartheid separated them physically from the misery it had created.

Moreover, the worth of apartheid was upheld by the DRC partly for practical reasons and partly on biblical grounds, although there were differing views within the church on the religious justification.[18] The theological argument rested largely on an adaptation of neo-Kuyperian Calvinism which took Abraham Kuyper's idea of the God-ordained separate spheres of church, state and so on, and applied them to the different races. Thus the concept of God-willed 'separate development' or apartheid was born – the races were to be kept apart because that was the way God wanted it.[19]

Indeed, such was the enthusiasm of the Church for 'separate development' that it actually lobbied the government on certain apartheid proposals. According to Cecil Ngcokovane, this happened before the National Party came to power. He contends that, as early as 1942, the Church urged the outlawing of racially mixed marriages and the legal underpinning of racially segregated areas, two measures which the National Party quickly enacted when it came to power. The Church itself has more recently admitted that it campaigned for such measures when the National Party took office.[20]

This concept was doubtless all the easier to follow, given that *de facto* separation of the races already existed within the DRC. The origins of this policy lay in a dilemma faced by the DRC in the 1820s; missionary efforts among the 'natives' had proved far more successful than anyone had imagined and soon racial prejudice was manifesting itself among white worshippers who did not wish to share their church with blacks. By 1857, the DRC Synod had decided that, owing to the 'weakness' of some (in other words, whites), separate services for blacks and whites were permissible. This was partly influenced, also, by the belief among some that missionary work should be carried out in ways appropriate to different cultures.

Separate congregations eventually developed into completely separate churches. The Dutch Reformed Mission Church (DRMC) – designed for 'coloured' people – was the first to be established, in 1881. It was followed by the Dutch Reformed Church in Africa (DRCA), for blacks, and the Indian Reformed Church. In April 1994, the 'mission' and 'black' churches joined together into one unified institution. It has been the stated intention to establish one multi-racial umbrella structure for all four different churches. However that goal has been taking longer to achieve than its proponents would have wished. While other difficulties have emerged more recently, opposition to the proposal within the DRC was initially a major problem.

Early attempts to persuade the Church to acknowledge the oppression and misery produced by apartheid failed. In 1961, the DRC's regional synods rejected a declaration which Church delegates had supported at a conference organised by the World Council of Churches. This statement condemned unjust discrimination, recognised each race as part of the population, and asked for a review of low wages and unjust conditions for blacks.[21] The Church's failure to stand by the conference resolutions greatly disillusioned one of its leading members, Beyers Naudé. In 1963, he formed an organisation called the Christian Institute, dedicated to reconciliation with blacks. The DRC immediately disowned the Institute and prominent clergymen demonised it, warning Afrikaners to counter the Institute's 'liberalistic' and 'Communistic' tendencies.[22]

The DRC's trenchant support for apartheid was immensely valuable to the government. In 1974, the government demonstrated its recognition of the Church's propaganda value by secretly offering to fund an ecumenical office for its General Synod. The DRC accepted the money but only a few leading members of the Church were aware of this transaction. The Church maintains that the DRC did not cede autonomy in return for this funding. When the deal was revealed in 1978, the Church admitted it had made an error of judgement.

During the 1970s, relations between the DRC and other Reformed churches around the world became increasingly strained. Finally, in 1982, the World Alliance of Reformed Churches (WARC) produced a statement condemning apartheid and the DRC's support for it. It suspended the DRC's membership of the Alliance, highlighting the gulf that now existed between the DRC and the international Christian community.[23]

The Move Away from Apartheid[24]

In 1979, P. W. Botha became President and soon embarked on a process of piecemeal reform of the constitutional measures and laws which underpinned apartheid, under the slogan 'adapt or die'. At first, Botha seemed sincerely convinced of the need for radical reform of the apartheid system, but his stance changed abruptly as black protests grew in scale. Black South Africans were particularly angry that constitutional reforms extended electoral representation in Parliament to include mixed-race 'coloureds' and Asians, but not blacks, who were deemed to be represented within their own government-imposed 'homelands'. As black resistance intensified, Botha's government adopted increasingly repressive measures in a fruitless attempt to quell it. International protests against South Africa also increased, and economic sanctions began to have an effect. However, Botha refused to heed pleas from the international community and from within his own party for more fundamental reform of the apartheid system.

In 1989, Botha resigned under pressure from his Cabinet and F. W. De Klerk took over as President. In his opening address to Parliament in February 1990, De Klerk announced the unbanning of the African National Congress (ANC), the Pan Africanist Congress and the South African Communist Party (SACP). Shortly afterwards, he released many political prisoners, including Nelson Mandela. The following year, the government repealed major pieces of apartheid legislation. It then began talks with a range of parties, including the ANC, on establishing a new constitution which would provide democratic rights for all.

The DRC had already begun to alter its view of apartheid. This change was signalled in a DRC document entitled *Church and Society*, published in 1986, which stated:

> the conviction has gradually grown [within the DRC] that a forced separation and division of peoples cannot be considered a biblical imperative. The attempt to justify such an injunction as derived from the Bible must be recognised as an error and rejected. The Dutch Reformed Church is convinced that the application of apartheid as a political and social system by which human dignity is

adversely affected, and whereby one group is detrimentally suppressed by another, cannot be accepted on Christian-ethical grounds ...[25]

Its publication produced uproar and a significant exodus of members from the Church. However, this did not stop the DRC printing a somewhat stronger repudiation of apartheid four years later:

> The Dutch Reformed Church had not sufficiently perceived that apartheid as a system had inter alia in its struggle against integration also received an ideological and ethnocentric basis. The right and freedom to remain true to one's own cultural heritage, was extended to become a political ideology of apartheid as a system for the protection of the white minority's own interests to the detriment of others ... Apartheid began to function in such a way that the largest part of the population of the country experienced it as an oppressive system which through the forced separation of peoples was in reality favouring one group wrongfully above the others ... Any system which in practice functions in this way, is unacceptable in the light of Scripture and the Christian conscience and must be rejected as sinful. Any attempt by a church to try to defend such a system biblically and ethically, must be seen as a serious fallacy, that is to say it is in conflict with the Bible.[26]

Moreover, the DRC also rejected the idea of the church as a *volkskerk*:

> it must be maintained that the indigenization of the Gospel must never mean that church and nation become so interrelated that the church loses its character as a confessional church and becomes an exclusive church of a particular nation, which serves that nation and chiefly has the function to grant religious sanction to that nation's values, ideals and ambitions.[27]

The decision to review the Church's stance towards apartheid was taken at its General Synod in 1982.[28] It paralleled a major shift in the Broederbond's approach towards constitutional issues. In 1983, Pieter De Lange, a man committed to constitutional reform, took over as chairperson of the Bond. He claims that the Bond was well ahead of the National Party in its reformist thinking.[29] According to De Lange, by 1984, the Bond had accepted that black South Africans should be given the vote. Two years later, the Bond's members voted for full citizenship rights for blacks.

In reality, it is impossible to separate the processes of liberalisation which were taking place in the DRC, the Bond and the National Party at this time. All three organisations had a very close relationship. In his book, *The Afrikaners*, the BBC's former Southern Africa Correspondent, Graham Leach, is quite adamant that the DRC was doing no more than catching up with government policy, arguing that *Church and Society* could have been much bolder in explicitly calling for repeal of the most repressive pieces of apartheid legislation:

> the NGK [DRC] had committed itself in the religious field to no more than the government had undertaken in the political arena: it had removed the basis for the more hurtful and humiliating aspects of racial discrimination. Like the government though, the church had been unable to consign apartheid to the dustbin lock, stock and barrel. Arguing that its role was not political, the NGK had pulled back from the brink; it had failed to denounce all aspects of racially motivated policy and call instead for a democratic society for all.[30]

In adopting such a position, the church was falling in line with the National Party and those other organs of Afrikanerdom which were inching away from 'grand apartheid' but were not quite certain which path to follow.

Nevertheless, by issuing the document, the Church was playing its part in helping to ensure that Afrikanerdom continued to 'inch away' from apartheid. One leading DRC clergyman has argued that *Church and Society* made a vital contribution to debate in the National Party and that the Church was not simply 'catching up' with the government as Leach suggests.[31] Certainly, it must be remembered that the 1986 version was issued at a time when Botha had become more hardline. While many in the government were anxious to press ahead with reform, their case could only have been strengthened by the DRC's stance. However, the most serious opposition to reform of apartheid lay outside the government. In 1982, one of its senior figures, Andries Treurnicht, left the National Party in disgust at Botha's power-sharing proposals and set up his own Conservative Party. Other disillusioned hardliners joined him and the party succeeded in making significant inroads into the National Party's vote during the 1980s. In 1987, it became the official opposition party in Parliament, and there were real fears among Nationalists and liberals that it could become the party of government. The publication of *Church and Society* probably played its part in helping to ensure that that did not happen. The

Conservative Party undoubtedly had strong appeal within the DRC. One estimate suggests that as many as a third of the Church's membership had joined the party by 1990.[32] Had the Church not changed its position on apartheid, the Conservative Party's pro-apartheid stance would have had even greater credibility among the DRC's members.

The need to prevent a further exodus of white voters from the National Party became all the more crucial when De Klerk began to push through his radical reforms. P. Eric Louw argues that De Klerk's government used 'the deep religiousness of most whites as a basis for arguing that a common South African value system did exist which cut across racial and cultural differences.'[33] Without the DRC's qualified repudiation of apartheid, this task would have been very difficult. We shall see in the chapters which follow how many church members draw a sharp demarcation line between the spheres of 'religion' and 'politics'. Church statements may not directly change their views in terms of what they regard as straightforwardly 'political' issues. However, the DRC's shift on apartheid had implications for the language used by church leaders and clergy with regard to the 'religious' or 'moral' sphere; this shift in discourse was bound to affect the way in which church members perceived and articulated their underlying moral values. This was perhaps the most significant contribution the DRC made towards the gradual abandonment of apartheid. At the same time, it is important to note that the DRC's move ensured that the Church retained its status and credibility. Had the DRC not acted thus and had the National Party still succeeded in retaining sufficient electoral support for its reforms, the Church would have looked outdated and irrelevant. As we have seen, it had already become isolated within the international Christian community.

However, the publication of *Church and Society* came at a price for the Church, despite the fact that it was in tune with government thinking. In all, 30 000 members and 100 ministers departed from the DRC amid great bitterness. Some 2000 former members voted to form a whites-only Afrikaanse Protestante Kerk (APK).[34] According to the 1991 South African Census, its membership has grown to around 30 000.[35] While this is a tiny number in comparison to the 1.3 million-strong membership of the DRC, fear of further defections was bound to act as a constraining factor for liberal ministers in the Church. Many who did not leave the DRC had at least some sympathy with those who had departed.

Summary

This small-scale exodus was one of the most visible signs of the strains caused by the struggle between the conflicting discourses of change and continuity which reverberated in the DRC during the eighties. Prior to this time, liberal voices within the Church had been largely suppressed; a discourse which advocated change carried little authority within the church because those with power continued to support the status quo. The shift in the balance of *definitional authority* between these competing discourses reflected the shift which was occurring in the *cultural mainstream* of which the DRC was an important part.

The DRC's central position in the Afrikaner nationalist mainstream was originally secured when the nationalist movement was established. The vital role that the Church played illustrates the symbolic and motivational elements of cultural power which a church can bring to a process of ethnic mobilisation. By acting as a *volkskerk*, the DRC added to the collective cultural power of the Afrikaner nationalist project; the Church contributed ethnoreligious capital. At the same time, it benefited from being seen to be part of the mainstream. As political forces began to shift significant elements of the mainstream away from apartheid, the Church really had no option but to participate in that process if it wished to retain its cultural power. This is not to suggest that any cold-blooded calculation to that effect was made at the time. While it may not have been setting the pace in disengaging from apartheid, its role in the process was neither a passive nor a disinterested one. Its decision to renounce its support for apartheid added to the momentum for change. It probably helped to ensure that support for the Conservatives never reached the point where Treurnicht's party could take power. It certainly assisted in preparing the Afrikaner public for the dismantling of the apartheid system and the subsequent introduction of black majority rule. There was, therefore, a symbiotic and interactive relationship between church and government that was of mutual benefit to both parties.

THE ULSTER PRESBYTERIAN EXPERIENCE[36]

The Roots of Ulster Presbyterianism

At about the same time as the Dutch landed at the Cape in the seventeenth century, a large influx of English and Scottish settlers was arriving in the north of Ireland. A major reason for this population movement was the British plantation of Ulster, which effectively usurped all but the poorest land from the native Irish. Scottish settlers played a significant part in this colonial project.[37] Jonathan Bardon observes that, 'The English had more capital but the Scots were the most determined planters ...' The Scots, who were all Presbyterians, greatly outnumbered the English, who were Anglicans. By the early eighteenth century, the combined total of English and Scottish settlers in the planted areas had swelled to a slightly greater level than that of the native Irish.

According to David Hempton, with the possible exception of Bohemia, this concerted drive to usurp Irish land resulted in the greatest 'upheaval in the religious composition of [the] landowning elite' anywhere in Europe. The proportion of Irish land owned by Catholics dropped from 80 per cent in 1600 to a mere 14 per cent a century later. The impact of these changes was more painfully evident in Ulster than in any other part of the island.[38] The Irish were progressively pushed back onto the worst agricultural land which, in the north of Ireland, is the land that sits some distance above sea level:

> in the planted portions of Ulster, a pattern emerged locale by locale, whereby the native Irish, embittered but unbowed, lived on the heights and looked down on the fertile valleys possessed by the Scottish and English invaders.[39]

In the mid-seventeenth century, the Scottish settlers of Ulster were urged to sign the Covenant drawn up in 1638 by the opponents of the attempts by Charles I to impose a new liturgy on the Church of Scotland. D. H. Akenson interprets it as promising unconditional loyalty to God and conditional loyalty to the 'temporal monarch', loyalty to the latter being conditional on him showing loyalty to God.[40] As we will see, there is a parallel here with the 'Vow' of the Voortrekkers in that the symbolism of the Covenant was to be resurrected in the early part of this century to mobilise support for the unionists' anti-Home Rule campaign.

The drive to persuade Ulster Presbyterians to sign the Covenant got under way after the Scottish army was sent over in 1641 to quell an uprising by the native Irish in which many Protestants were killed. According to Akenson, the Church of Scotland General Assembly appointed four Presbyterian ministers to encourage both soldiers and settlers in Ireland to take the oath to support the Covenant. This was not always an easy task and Akenson admits that 'the reluctance of the people of Belfast and Londonderry was only overcome with effort'.[41]

Moreover, although another historian, David Miller, believes the clergymen were met with great enthusiasm, he suspects this sprang less from any sincerely held Presbyterian convictions than from a belief that the Covenant was a means of self-preservation with its emphasis on the Protestant as opposed to the Catholic religion.[42]

Nevertheless, Presbyterians quickly became treated as the 'poor relations' *vis-à-vis* Anglicanism. After Charles II was restored to the throne in 1660, the established episcopal churches were brought back and 61 Presbyterian ministers lost their livings and were evicted. However, the Crown realised it could not afford to alienate the Scots Presbyterian population in Ulster and so a compromise was reached by which Presbyterian ministers received a royal grant from 1672.[43] Despite this concession, Presbyterians remained second-class citizens compared with Anglicans; for example, Presbyterian marriages were not legally recognised as valid until 1845.

The Orange Order

However, while Charles II did not make himself popular with Presbyterians, they reacted with far greater horror when a Catholic king, James II, acceded to the throne in 1685. He was successfully challenged by the Protestant William of Orange in an attempt to wrest the throne. The victory of William over the Irish at the Battle of the Boyne in 1690 has become the most potent and widely celebrated symbol of Ulster Protestantism. Murals portraying 'King Billy' on his white steed can be found on gable walls in Protestant areas all over Northern Ireland. However, 'King Billy' really comes into his own on the Twelfth of July each year when the Orange Order holds a number of large parades, each characterised by great colour, pageantry and the sound of flutes and drums.

The Orange Order was founded in 1795 but Orangeism had already appeared by then. According to Tony Gray, 'Long before the Orange Order there were men describing themselves as Orangemen – loyal followers of William of Orange …'[44] Moreover, in Derry, clubs had already been established dedicated to commemorating the relief of the siege of Derry, another victory of great symbolic importance to Protestants.

The origin of the Orange Order itself is tied up with the tensions caused by the enormous economic and social change which accompanied industrialisation in the late eighteenth and nineteenth centuries. Protestants had fared much better than Catholics under the quasi-feudal rural-based economy which predominated until that point; they were quite simply favoured by the largely Anglican landowning class who judged them a better security risk than Catholics. However, the growth of the textile industry and reliance on paid employment for income gave Catholics a chance to start improving their relative economic position.

In County Armagh, economic rivalry erupted into violent sectarian rivalry where 'a bitter sectarian conflict between Protestant "Peep-of-Day Boys" and Catholic "Defenders" [rival gangs] raged intermittently from 1784 to 1795'.[45] This ongoing conflict culminated in a particularly fierce battle in 1795 at a crossroads called The Diamond near Loughall in County Armagh. It was won by the Peep O'Day Boys who, flushed with victory, established a more formal secret organisation which was originally called the Orange Boys but soon became known as the Orange Order.

The Protestant gentry were initially rather nervous of the Orange Order and its strange rituals and strong peasant roots. However, it was not long before the upper classes began joining the Order, lending it an air of respectability as they took over the leadership of many local lodges. Membership quickly expanded so that, within the first three years it had grown 'from an obscure agrarian Ulster Protestant society into the strongest single political force in Ireland and an organization unassailable in Ulster without the aid of troops brought in from outside the country'.[46] The historian David Miller observes that this new organisation represented an inter-class version of Protestant 'contractarianism': 'Orangeism sustained for Protestant workers in town and country the sense that the most important feature of the old structure – a special relationship between them and their Protestant betters – still obtained.'[47]

However, it was an openly provocative organisation. From around 1800, Orange Order lodges chose to march 'through predominantly Catholic villages or districts in the cities, carrying arms, shouting anti-papish slogans and singing offensive songs'.[48] This has been attributed to the fact that Protestants were very fearful of another Catholic rebellion. Writing about the situation almost two hundred years later, Frank Wright discerned a tendency for the Order to take care over where it put up Orange arches (temporary constructions over a street) or where it held its parades when relations between Protestants and Catholics were relatively relaxed; however, it tended to become insensitive during times of tension.[49]

The Presbyterian Church and Politics

One of the tensest periods in Irish history occurred at the beginning of this century with the campaign for 'Home Rule'; in other words, some form of self-government for Ireland.[50] Home Rule was bitterly opposed by many northern Protestants who were fearful that such a measure would enable Catholics to usurp Protestant land and wealth. They mounted a vigorous campaign against it. A leading role was played by an umbrella unionist body known as the Ulster Unionist Council. It recognised the symbolic value of the covenant, given the part that it had played in Protestant history. Hence, the anti-Home Rule campaign culminated in the drawing up of a new 'Covenant' to defend Ulster's position of equal citizenship in the United Kingdom. The new Covenant, which described the signatories as 'loyal subjects' of the King, echoed the Covenant of 1638 in its language. It was signed by 218 000 men. A similar number of women put their names to a separate 'Declaration'.

The Presbyterian Church played a part in the creation and legitimisation of this Covenant; the document was submitted to the main Protestant churches for comment before it was published and a few words were added at the suggestion of the Presbyterians. The Church was concerned that people might be confused at this new Covenant, given that the original Scottish Covenant was seen as binding in perpetuity; it thus suggested that the wording should make clear this new Covenant related to 'our time of threatened calamity'. Moreover, on the day appointed by the document's creators for the signing of the Covenant – Ulster Day, 28 September 1912 – a former Presbyterian Moderator, Dr William McKean, delivered the sermon at a service attended by the unionist leaders of this campaign, Captain James Craig and Sir Edward Carson.

This was not the first time the anti-Home Rule lobby had received public backing from the higher echelons of the Presbyterian Church. On Easter Tuesday of the same year, both the Presbyterian Moderator and the Church of Ireland primate had said prayers at the opening of a mass demonstration against Home Rule at the Balmoral show grounds in south Belfast. These gestures of support were for constitutional forms of protest. However, the Home Rule campaign quickly moved on to incorporate 'all means which may be found necessary' to fight Home Rule.[51] An army, known as the Ulster Volunteer Force (UVF) was formed in 1913. Its members met regularly to train, using mock rifles and wooden batons. By the end of the year, some

90 000 men had joined up. This militaristic movement was given an enthusiastic endorsement by the then Presbyterian Moderator, Revd James Bingham. He described it as 'a great and noble army of men … preparing to defend themselves and us from the dangers that threaten our citizenship, liberties and religion'.[52] This expression of support was the closest that the Presbyterian Church came to challenging the power of the state during the twentieth century.

In the event, while 26 counties of Ireland did achieve independence, unionists ended up with a form of Home Rule in six of the northern counties; this territory was to be run by a devolved Northern Ireland government within the UK. While unionists did not see this as the ideal solution, they accepted it in the realisation that 'a parliament of their own offered better security against rule by Dublin'.[53] The PCI journal, *Irish Presbyterian*, clearly saw a powerful role for the Church in this new regime:

> Our Church is now entrusted with great influence in the Ulster leg-
> islature and the new position has its perils as well as its advantages.
> It will demand much wisdom and singleness of purpose to establish
> on the right lines the relations of church and state in the province.[54]

The Church certainly made strenuous efforts to ensure that it did influence education policy in the new Northern Ireland state. Shortly after Partition, the Catholic Church refused to go along with the Stormont government's proposals for a system of lay control for schools; the result was the creation of a system of Catholic schools for Catholics and state schools which were attended largely by Protestants. This religious division was subsequently reinforced by the joint efforts of the three main Protestant churches in Northern Ireland (the PCI, the Church of Ireland and the Methodist Church) and the Orange Order. Together, they mounted a campaign which led to a reluctant decision by the Stormont parliament in 1930 to ensure that 'Protestant-style' Bible instruction was provided in certain categories of school.[55]

The main Protestant churches and the Orange Order continued to lobby vigorously on various aspects of education policy. There were sharp differences of opinion between the lobbyists and the government. Yet, while they did not always get their way, the Protestant lobby was not a force the government could simply ignore. There were differences between the government and leading figures within the PCI over certain other aspects of policy. One analyst of these events, Stewart Jones, believes these differences 'prevented the Presbyterian

Church from becoming, in a very uncritical fashion, the unionist party at prayer'.[56] At the same time, however, 'Presbyterians always drew back from any action that might seriously damage the Unionist Government.'[57] Indeed, writing just before the imposition by the British government of Direct Rule in the early 1970s, Martin Wallace suggests that the influence of the Protestant churches worked on a more subtle level than the clashes over policy might have suggested:

> While Protestants and Catholics live partly separate lives in Northern Ireland, the state to some extent imposes a Protestant ethos on the Catholic minority. In such matters as Sunday observance and liquor licensing laws, it is the more puritanical Protestant outlook which prevails; the Protestant churches are influential in this respect, but there is a wider Protestant feeling that a stand must be taken against Catholic values. At different levels of society, this instinctive attitude has always proved an obstacle to dealing justly and dispassionately with Catholic grievances.[58]

This 'instinctive' attitude was reflected in the systematic discrimination against Catholics which was evident in local government, in employment practices and in the allocation of housing. These institutionalised forms of unequal treatment lasted for the fifty-year life of the Stormont parliament. Although historians differ over the extent of this phenomenon, most observers agree that it was the eruption of Catholic anger over these discriminatory practices which led to the most recent period of violent conflict.[59]

During most of the lifetime of the Stormont administration, the issue of discrimination went unrecognised by the PCI. It was not acknowledged until the mid-1960s when a report on the subject was received by the General Assembly in 1966/67. The document was not an unconditional endorsement of all attempts to outlaw discrimination; indeed, it appeared to accept discrimination in certain circumstances. Thus, while it urged fair employment practices, it added that 'it is understandable that owners of small private concerns may prefer to employ "their own" people'.[60] While it opposed discrimination in housing, it did not accept that the limited franchise which then operated in local elections amounted to discrimination in favour of Protestants.

It was almost ten years before the Church produced an unequivocal statement on discrimination. This happened in 1976 when the General Assembly expressed support for legislation designed to eliminate discrimination in employment on various grounds, including religion.[61]

During that year, the British Parliament passed the Fair Employment Act which set up a Fair Employment Agency to tackle employment discrimination on the basis of religious and political beliefs. The General Assembly was thus in tune with, but certainly not ahead of, government policy on the issue.

This effort by the Church to keep pace with the 'modern values' generally recognised by the wider world has led to tensions within the PCI. Most of the Church's documents concerning 'topical' matters have been produced by a body called the Church and Government Committee. In 1993, it produced a major report entitled *Presbyterian Principles and Political Witness* which, like *Church and Society*, focused on the application of biblical principles. This represented the most definitive statement that the Church had yet made on its role in the troubled political affairs of Northern Ireland. The document contained a significant statement which echoed that made by the DRC over its support for apartheid:

> The Presbyterian Church shares the guilt of the majority community in Northern Ireland for tolerating the practice of discrimination in jobs, housing and voting rights which largely led to the Civil Rights Campaign of the 1960s. Such discrimination was acknowledged in a report received by the General Assembly in 1966/67. Albeit belatedly, the legitimate grievances of the minority community have been recognised.[62]

The same report suggested the Church was just as keen as the DRC to distance itself from a *volkskerk* role:

> We believe that amid conflicting cultures God is willing us to create a distinctively Christian counter-culture, in which we distance ourselves from the kind of Protestantism which closely identifies the reformed faith with particular political and cultural aspirations.[63]

The document reflected the way in which the political climate had changed since the early 1970s in Northern Ireland. In January 1990 the then Northern Ireland Secretary, Peter Brooke, launched an attempt to hold inter-party talks on reaching a political solution to the Northern Ireland 'problem'. These began the following year and faltered along on a stop-start basis. By late 1993, the negotiations had failed to make any significant progress, although politicians did achieve some useful groundwork in discussing the basis on which such talks might take place. During this period, church leaders frequently urged the politicians to keep talking and claimed that the public were anxious to see meaningful negotiations. *Presbyterian Principles* could be seen as an attempt by the Church to set out a consensual value system which might underpin such talks. This is apparent in the language used to describe the role of the government in a situation of conflict:

> All societies have minorities and vested interest groups competing, to some degree, for influence and power. Constitutional politics and the rule of law seek to manage such a situation fairly and peacefully. Where such diversity exists, government should seek consensus as far as possible, the guideline being justice and involvement for both minorities and majorities, with all accepting their due responsibility for society.[64]

This contrasts with the tone adopted in a statement made by the PCI's General Board in February 1972, shortly before the introduction by the British government of Direct Rule. The statement reflected the deep sense of hurt and anger felt by many Protestants at the time:

> The persistent lack of any real understanding of the position of the great majority of our people and, we believe, of Northern Protestants generally, shown not least by so many Government spokesmen and leaders of public opinion in the Irish Republic, must constantly be borne in mind. Nor is it just particular sectarian constitutional provisions in the Irish Republic, but also the general political and cultural traditions and claims, which are seen as a threat to their identity, associations, standards, and even their existence here.
>
> It still remains our first and most earnest aim that the tragic conflicts in our land should be resolved peacefully by persevering discussion between our contending communities, by painstaking recognition of the different interests and ideals among us, and by honest readiness for change. We consider this the way towards solving issues of internment, the role of the army, civil disobedience, etc.[65]

The publication of *Presbyterian Principles* followed a period during which the Church had enjoyed relatively little influence in the affairs of government. Its ability to bend the ear of government had rapidly diminished after the British government introduced Direct Rule.[66] Indeed, in 1977, the Church and Government Committee was moved to complain that the then Northern Ireland Secretary, Roy Mason, could not even find time to meet the Church's representatives!

Clearly, the British government did not feel that it was dependent on the support of the Church. However, as we shall see further on in this book, the government did send out signals that it saw the Church as a useful element of its 'public relations' strategy. This happened as the government began to develop a more directive line on inter-party talks.

Summary

While the term *volkskerk* was unknown in Presbyterian circles in Northern Ireland, the PCI undoubtedly took on a *volkskerk* role during the campaign over Home Rule. It retained a close relationship with subsequent Stormont governments, while differing on some matters of policy. Unionist administrations clearly felt they had to listen carefully to the PCI, while the Church seemed anxious to ensure that any criticisms it made did not seriously undermine the government. The British administration which took over the affairs of Northern Ireland in 1972 was not as interested in the views of the PCI. After the imposition of Direct Rule, the Church made its first full and unequivocal statement on discrimination against Catholics. However, this happened in the same year that the British government brought in legislation to tackle employment discrimination on the basis of religious and political beliefs. Thus, the Church was in tune with but by no means ahead of government policy on this contentious issue. As in the DRC, there were those in the PCI who would have liked the Church to have taken a bolder stand on the issue earlier on. Within the PCI, there was a contest between discourses of continuity and discourses of change. A watershed in that struggle was reached in 1993 with the publication of *Presbyterian Principles*. That document admitted that the Church had not spoken out sufficiently with regard to the problem of discrimination, and made it clear that the Church wished to distance itself from any *volkskerk* role.

AFRIKANERS AND ULSTER PRESBYTERIANS: THE PARALLELS

By now, the reader has probably been struck by a number of parallels between the histories of Afrikaners and Ulster Presbyterians. Let us examine some of the similarities a little more closely. In both cases, a sense of common cultural identity has developed over time. However, one can see a particular moment or moments in history when certain elites have mobilised mass support under an ethnic banner. This is most evident in the case of Afrikaner nationalism, where it is clear that a concerted effort was made to foster a sense of ethnic identity in the early part of this century. There is no precise equivalent in Ulster Protestant history. Yet, two of the events outlined above did play an important part in awakening a collective ethnic consciousness. These were the formation of the Orange Order and the campaign against Home Rule. The establishment of the Orange Order and the anti-Home Rule movement created and reinforced a sense of religio-cultural distinctiveness *vis-à-vis* Irish Catholics. Moreover, the anti-Home Rule protest promoted a sense of a common history among Ulster Protestants by invoking the symbolic myth of the covenant.

It is important to ask why these events happened at the point they did. Both the construction of an Afrikaner ethnic identity and the formation of the Orange Order clearly happened in response to social changes which were having an adverse material effect on those who got involved in these movements. The new collective consciousness which resulted provided a communal sense of self-esteem and held out the promise of a more secure economic future. In both cases, the involvement of elite groups was a significant factor in this process. In South Africa, the Afrikaner nationalist movement was spearheaded by intellectuals and members of the bourgeoisie. However, they would not have got very far if their drive had not resonated with the collective needs and consciousness of ordinary Afrikaners at that time. For them, the nationalist movement provided a way of making sense of social change. In Ireland, the Orange Order was established by ordinary Protestants. Elite involvement only came later. However, the role of the Protestant upper classes became important because it enabled Protestant workers to feel they had a special bond with their superiors not shared by their Catholic counterparts.

The same analysis applies to the campaign against Home Rule. In this case, Protestants from both the upper and lower social classes saw Home Rule as a threat to their economic interests. Most land and nearly all businesses in the north of Ireland were owned by Protestants. Protestant businessmen were worried that an Irish government would tax them heavily and pass measures which supported southern industry at the expense of the north. While Protestants and Catholics in Belfast had equal access to unskilled jobs in industry, Protestants had a distinct advantage when it came to skilled jobs. Naturally, they greatly feared that an Irish nationalist government would act to rectify the imbalance.[67]

Thus, these defining moments in the development of ethnic identity were very much underpinned by material interests. They illustrate how elites were able to join together to mobilise ethnic sentiment, thus establishing or reinforcing their position as part of the *cultural mainstream* of their ethnic group, and helping to secure a position of dominance for their particular ethnic group within the political sphere. In each case, we see the interrelationship between the religious (including civil religious) and the political spheres.

There is another important issue, however, and that is the extent to which ethnic identity was constituted in relation to what it was *not*. It will be obvious to the reader that, to a large extent, Ulster Protestants defined their identity in terms of *not* being Catholics or Irish. In South Africa, Afrikaners went through a similar process. As Aletta J. Norval argues:

> Afrikaner nationalism was an obsessional quest for a core of authenticity which could, however, not be found. It could only be produced, and, hence, constantly had to be reproduced, by differentiating itself from competing conceptions of ordering: an exclusive Afrikaner nationalism was what was left once British liberalism and imperialism, communism, doctrines of equality, and so forth, were all externalized as foreign to the traditions of the *volk*. It thus forged itself in terms of a series of negative operations in which the truly *volkseie*, while remaining invisible, could be inferred *a contrario* by the alleged visibility of the 'other': the non-true Afrikaner, the English, the Jew, the black, the coloured, and so forth.[68]

However, it can also be argued that, for both Afrikaners and Ulster Protestants, the construction of identity was underpinned by a settler mentality which deeply feared the Other. This fear led to the imposition by force of apartheid measures in South Africa. It also led to the widespread pattern of discrimination against Catholics in Northern Ireland. Jennifer Todd describes how this fear still affects many Ulster Protestants:

> The colonial resonances generate a sense of cultural unease. The native's very presence suggests another side of the story – a narrative of dispossession – which must be constantly repressed ... Catholics are a constant presence and contact with them must be limited so that the Protestant perspective can remain untouched by Catholic perceptions.[69]

This attitude was evident in the wish of many Protestants I interviewed to limit their contact with the collective Other. It helps to explain the Protestant fear of Catholics in Northern Ireland and the Afrikaner fear of blacks in South Africa. Indeed, Todd argues that Ulster Protestants still weave a narrative of attempts by the Catholic 'natives' to wipe out Protestant settlers. This is how Protestant farmers in areas bordering the Irish Republic used to view the IRA prior to its ceasefires. More recently, there has been much talk among Protestants in border areas of a republican campaign to 'ethnically cleanse' such districts by forcing the removal of Protestants, through threats and intimidation.

The desire to dominate is evident in the symbols of civil religion around which both the Ulster Protestant and Afrikaner ethnicities have been built; one can see this in the invocation of the *voortrekker* mythology and the Battle of Blood River by Afrikaners, and in the manner in which Orange parades in Northern Ireland symbolically stake out Protestant territory. In both cases, there has been a degree of institutionalisation of these symbols through organisations such as the Broederbond and the Orange Order. At the same time, civil religion has also been used as a *resource* to further political ends.

Clearly, the DRC played a central role in the development and promulgation of Afrikaner nationalism and undoubtedly earned its unofficial label of *volkskerk*. However, the PCI can also be viewed as having performed a *volkskerk* role in its symbolically significant espousal of the unionist cause during the campaign against Home Rule. The DRC also had a close and supportive relationship with the National Party government. While the PCI clashed with the unionist-controlled Stormont government on many issues, it did not embarrass the unionists and a Protestant ethos coloured that government's approach to policy. Neither the DRC nor the PCI was 'established' in terms of being accorded any special constitutional recognition. However, both were firmly positioned in the mainstream of their respective ethnic communities. With the exception of the PCI Moderator's support for the UVF in 1914, neither church directly challenged the state.

There are a number of other important parallels between the two churches. There are similarities in terms of theology. However, I make no apology for not exploring these in any depth, as, in general, the lay members I interviewed took little interest in the subject. What is important to me as a sociologist is the way in which that theology is used by the church to justify its stance on secular issues.

Theology has been held to be particularly significant in one respect; this concerns the contention that the notion of being a 'chosen people' has formed an important part of both Afrikaner and Ulster Protestant history. One of the proponents of this view is Akenson.[70] He stresses the enormous importance of Calvinism to the Scottish settlers who came to the north of Ireland in the seventeenth century, in terms of helping them carve out their own identity and instil a sense of discipline within their society. He contends that they saw themselves as 'God's People'. Yet, the facts contained in his own account of the settlers do not match his assertion. As noted above, the Scottish ministers sent over to whip up support for the Covenant of 1641 found little enthusiasm for it, according to Akenson. While Miller believes that they did, in fact, receive a reasonably warm reception, he suggests that the welcome sprang from a desire for self-preservation rather than any deep religious conviction.[71] This picture is hardly commensurate with a group of people truly fired up with the idea they were 'God's People'!

Akenson and others take a similar view of the significance of the 'elect' in the beliefs of the Voortrekkers as they staged their Great Trek northwards from the Cape. Yet that claim has been seriously questioned and does appear to lack convincing evidence to back it.[72] It seems more likely that this belief arises out of the myth surrounding the Great Trek that was subsequently created by the proponents of Afrikaner nationalism.

Thus, while there seems little basis for suggesting that theological credence has played a part in weaving myths of a 'chosen people', it is true that such a symbolic narrative formed part of the effort to construct a nationalist identity for Afrikaners. One can see parallels with the significance of the idea of a Covenant with God in the history of Ulster Protestants, a concept which is also important in Afrikaner mythology in the story of the Battle of Blood River.

There are other parallels. The Protestant Reformation was a reaction against the authoritarianism of the Catholic Church, and this tradition lives on in the devolved power structures which exist in both the DRC and the PCI. In both cases, much decision-making is devolved down to congregational level, where a committee of lay members, along with the minister, runs the congregation. At a higher level, policy changes and other important decisions have to be debated and approved by a democratic assembly; in the DRC, this is known as the General Synod, while in the PCI it is called the General Assembly.

The decentralised nature of the two churches has undoubtedly contributed to fairly open divisions within them. In the DRC, early attempts to criticise its support for apartheid were stymied. However,

its acknowledgement of the error of its ways in the mid-1980s precipitated the formation of the breakaway church, the APK, which acted as
a constraining influence on the DRC. The same pressure was applied
on the PCI by the Free Presbyterian Church, which was founded by
Ian Paisley, the leader of the Democratic Unionist Party, in 1951. The
Church now has some 13 000 members, which is small by comparison
with the 350 000-strong membership of the PCI. Nevertheless, by
virtue of having the charismatic figure of Paisley at its helm, it
achieved a much higher profile than numbers alone would have war-
ranted. Paisley used to delight in attacking the PCI, sometimes turning
up at its General Assembly to protest.[73] Many observers feel the 'Free
Ps' played a significant part in discouraging ecumenism in Northern
Ireland.[74]

At the same time as both the DRC and the PCI faced conservative
pressures within and without their own denominations, they were also
coming under pressure from the international Christian community.
The DRC was severely criticised for its stance on apartheid, which
looked outdated and oppressive to the outside world. In a 'modern'
world which espoused liberal values such as equality and freedom, the
very idea that apartheid could be biblically justified seemed quite
incredible.

The relationship between the PCI and the rest of the Christian
world was somewhat different. Again, however, it spoke in a language
which most of its international counterparts did not share. This led it
to withdraw from the World Council of Churches (WCC) in 1980. The
move was made in protest at an alleged link between the WCC's
Programme to Combat Racism and certain liberation and paramilitary groups. However, Dr Paisley's anti-ecumenical drive undoubtedly
played a part.[75] The PCI also elected not to join the Council of
Churches of Britain and Ireland, which replaced the British Council of
Churches. The former Presbyterian moderator and committed
ecumenist Dr John Dunlop described these two decisions as 'the most
painful and divisive of my life'.[76]

With both the DRC and the PCI, the tension between these
churches and the international Christian community was mirrored by
tensions within the churches themselves. In both cases, there has
always been a liberal wing, however small, which has been open to the
idea of adaptation and change. On the other side of the fence have sat
the conservatives who stress the importance of continuity and stability.
These divisions, which echo those seen in American churches in
recent times, continue to this day.[77]

Moreover, both churches have had to wrestle with another, related conflict of interest – between their traditional *volkskerk* role and their self-professed role as conciliator attempting to build bridges and heal the divide. What makes it particularly difficult to reconcile these roles is that the churches play a vital part in reinforcing the ethnic boundary markers of religion and race, respectively. The act of worship takes on a special symbolic significance in this regard; it serves as a haven of certainty in uncertain times and as a refuge from a world in which the boundaries are being gradually dissolved. Great passion is aroused among Afrikaners over the maintenance of racial perimeters within the church, and among Ulster Protestants over the preservation of theological boundaries.

CONCLUSION

While one must recognise that there are important differences between the situations in South Africa and Northern Ireland, the parallels are significant. In both cases, religion and ethnic identity are woven together tightly. The churches have performed a significant role in terms of reinforcing the ethnic boundary markers and in acting as *volkskerks*. In recent years, both churches have acknowledged the role they played in institutionalising the boundaries, through support for apartheid on the part of the DRC and a failure to recognise the oppressive nature and extent of discrimination in the case of the PCI. However, it must be remembered that they have also contributed to the maintenance of those boundaries in a wider and less obvious sense in terms of their institutional structures and the belief-systems which have predominated within the churches. The PCI is effectively a curator of the theological boundary between Protestants and Catholics in Northern Ireland. Likewise, the DRC has been a curator of the racial divide in South Africa.[78] In performing this role, each church has been part of the process of naturalising the ethnic boundary so that its existence is taken for granted by both clergy and laity.

The symbols of civil religion have also played a vital role in the evolution of an ethnic identity in both cases. These symbols have taken on institutionalised forms such as the Orange Order, the Broederbond and the Day of the Vow celebrations. As we shall see, both the DRC and the PCI have had close links with these institutions of civil religion. They have also had a close and supportive relationship with the state, although this link was stronger in the case of the DRC. At the same time, politicians have drawn on both denominational religion and civil religion as a resource to further their political ends. Thus, in both cases, a symbiotic relationship has existed between the religious sphere, the political sphere and the symbols and institutions of civil religion. These three have all formed part of the respective main-streams of the two ethnic groups in question.

Moreover, in both cases, periods of rapid social change have proved to be a watershed in the development of a sense of ethnic identity. This study examines the impact of the latest period of rapid change for both Afrikaners and Ulster Protestants, focusing on the relation-ship between religion and ethnicity, and between the religious and secular spheres. Both these groups have faced a situation where their traditional dominance over the Other has been threatened. Given the strong parallels that have been identified, one would expect that some common patterns would emerge in the way that each group grappled with these transitions, which can help us understand the way in which religion works in other similar situations.

However, there is another important aspect to this study. While most of the previous research on the issues we are examining has drawn on documentary sources, the data for this investigation were gathered primarily through fieldwork interviews and surveys. This tells us a great deal about the way in which the discursive struggles and processes to which we have referred manifest themselves at grassroots level. In the next chapter, I shall provide a sketch of each of the six congregations in which that 'grassroots' investigation was conducted.

2 Setting the Scene: Afrikaners and Ulster Presbyterians in the Early 1990s

One of the curious things about carrying out research in both South Africa and Northern Ireland was the stereotyped notions the inhabitants of South Africa had about Northern Ireland and vice versa. The highly selective, skewed worldview offered by television news had ensured that each thought the other's territory to be a dreadful place, full of violence. Other than this calamitous image, they neither knew nor greatly cared about the complexities of life in what they regarded as a faraway, troubled 'hotspot'. From a personal perspective, my extended stay in South Africa gave me a much deeper understanding of life from an Afrikaner perspective. My great regret is that it was not possible to spend an equivalent amount of time finding out about the South African situation from the perspective of the majority black population. Likewise, while I learnt a tremendous amount about the Protestant perspective in Northern Ireland, the Catholic side of the story remains untold in this study. Nevertheless, I did achieve a much greater understanding of one situation with which I had been relatively unfamiliar and one on which I had reported as a journalist but in which I was still, as an English person, viewed as an 'outsider'. This chapter aims to give a flavour of the political context which prevailed while the research was carried out, the different congregations in which the fieldwork was undertaken, and the role that the church played in the lives of my interviewees.

SOUTH AFRICA

The Political Context

For an English person, used to towns that have no rhyme or reason to their layout, South Africa's towns and cities form a sharp contrast and none more so than Pretoria. There is a bland orderliness about the nation's administrative capital. From the grand buildings which stand as reminders of colonial times to the lush and repetitive suburbs, from the shopping malls to the bleaker poverty of the poorer white areas and the black townships, the layout never changes. As in so much of the United States, a uniform grid system of roads has been adopted, which is at once reassuring and yet utterly depressing in its relentless lack of character.

I spent a great deal of time in Pretoria while carrying out the research for this study in 1993. I hope any citizens of Pretoria who read this book will forgive me for admitting that I did not fall in love with their city. It would appear, however, that many inhabitants of Pretoria are fairly scathing themselves. The regimented and regulated nature of the place seemed to me to be an apt reminder of the apartheid era. The fact that most black citizens were still living outside the city in shabby, anonymous townships, well removed from white eyes, reinforced the message that apartheid was far from dead. The social structures and patterns that it had created lived on.

During my stay, I shared a house with eight Afrikaners, all young professionals or students. Most were relatively 'liberal' in the sense that they supported the National Party or even the relatively radical Democratic Party, rather than the right-wing Conservatives. Like young people everywhere they were messy, leaving washing-up piled high and beds unmade. The difference was that these young people had a black maid. It was the maid who picked up off the floor the plates with half-eaten food, the dirty glasses and cups, and the clothes which these fun-loving youngsters, had carelessly discarded secure in the knowledge that somebody else would do the clearing up.

Thus, apartheid lived on but, while I was in South Africa, a series of historical events was unfolding which would ensure that its demise would be hastened. I had first travelled to the country in August 1992. At the time, there was tremendous fear and uncertainty among both blacks and whites. It was only two and a half years since the ANC had been unbanned and Nelson Mandela released from jail. This watershed in history had been followed, in 1991, by the removal of three of the legal pillars of apartheid – the Group Areas Act, the Land Act and the Population Registration Act. That same year, the Convention for a Democratic South Africa (CODESA) was formed to tackle the mammoth and difficult task of negotiating a democratic constitution for South Africa.

In March 1992, President F. W. De Klerk risked his political neck by staging a referendum among whites on the desirability of the constitutional talks. A majority supported the move, greatly strengthening De Klerk's hand in dealing with the critics of negotiations both inside and outside his own party. However, it also encouraged him to take a tougher stand in the talks against the ANC, which fuelled the organisation's suspicions about the government's real agenda.[1] In May 1992, the talks broke down amid acrimony, although efforts continued to try to get them restarted.

Events overtook these endeavours, however. The following month South Africa was shattered by a grim massacre in the township of Boipatong, near Johannesburg: 38 people were killed by supporters of the Inkatha Freedom Party, which drew its support base from Zulus and was a bitter enemy of the ANC. Local residents claimed that police had also been involved in the massacre and that it was part of an attempt by the government to undermine the ANC. In response to widespread anger amongst its supporters, the ANC announced its formal withdrawal from the constitutional negotiations.

It was shortly after this massacre that I first visited South Africa. The climate of fear was palpable and many people believed a military coup was imminent. South Africa seemed very far from the goal of democracy. However, by the time I returned to begin my research, in May of the following year, events had moved on swiftly. The soured relationship between the ANC and the National Party had thawed. A new set of negotiations had begun. There had been further tragedy; in April 1993, Chris Hani, the general secretary of the SACP had been shot dead by a white racist who had links with the far right. However, this atrocity merely strengthened the determination of both the National Party and the ANC to achieve progress in the talks as quickly as possible.[2]

The momentum that was building up in the talks was regarded with deep suspicion by right-wingers. Shortly after I began my research in South Africa, the right-wing Afrikaner Volksfront was formed. The Volksfront was an umbrella group of right-wing organisations which attempted to exert as much pressure as possible on the government and the ANC to include an Afrikaner homeland in the 'new South Africa'. It was led by a former chief of the South African Defence Force, General Constand Viljoen. During the period of my research, it remained unclear how much support the Volksfront really commanded, but the organisation received a great deal of coverage in the South African media.

The Volksfront had the support of the Afrikaner Weer-standsbeweging (AWB) – the Afrikaner Resistance Movement, led by Eugene TerreBlanche. The AWB was the most fanatical of the main right-wing groups and claimed to have 40 000 'trained and armed' supporters ready to fight if necessary. At the time, journalists suspected the AWB's true level of support to be but a fraction of that figure but, again, no one knew for sure. Like the Volksfront, the AWB had achieved a high media profile. It captured international headlines on 25 June 1993, when heavily armed AWB members stormed the World Trade Centre, the building in which the negotiations on a political settlement for South Africa were taking place. While the Volksfront was not involved in this attack, General Viljoen refused to condemn it.

There were other setbacks throughout that winter.[3] Nevertheless, by the time I left South Africa in October, a date had been set for the country's first non-racial election. Agreement was finally reached on the new constitution on 18 November. The negotiations that achieved this settlement took place in the World Trade Centre, a mere forty-minute drive from Pretoria. While some of the proceedings were reported in the media, much of the most important debate took place behind closed doors. Thus, despite the fact that these events were happening so close to Pretoria, there was little sense of direct involvement by those I interviewed.

The Northern Transvaal Congregations

In both South Africa and Northern Ireland, I selected three congregations in which to conduct my fieldwork.[4] Each represented a different type of location: a congregation in a middle-class city suburb, a congregation in a working-class urban district, and a rural congregation in an area which was close to a symbolic 'border'. In South Africa, I conducted my research in the Northern Transvaal region. This area intrigued me because it was seen as the 'heartland' of support for the right-wing Conservative Party and yet it also included relatively 'liberal' districts, particularly in the middle-class parts of Pretoria. The urban congregations were known as Queenswood and Wespoort, while Louis Trichardt in the north of the region was chosen as the rural congregation.

The North Pretoria district of Queenswood was not one of the city's most affluent suburbs; contrary to the impression that foreigners often form, the neighbourhoods in which every house has a swimming pool and half an acre of garden are beyond the pockets of all but a relatively small elite in Pretoria. In socio-economic terms, Queenswood was fairly representative of a middle-class district in Pretoria. The modern Dutch Reformed church was a prominent feature. Situated in the centre of the suburb, it conveyed the immediate impression that it formed the focus for community life.

The DRC church in Wespoort was less central and also played a less significant role in local life. Wespoort, in the industrial west of Pretoria, formed a stark contrast to the contented blandness of Queenswood. In Wespoort, the skyline was dominated by the local steel plant and power station and the noxious-looking fumes they belched out. At one time, big employers like the steel plant and the power station provided a source of employment that whites could rely on. More recently, economic recession had forced a number of firms to cut their workforces. Although there appeared to be no evidence that the claims were true, many people in the Wespoort congregation were convinced they were being thrown out of work to make way for blacks. The impression undoubtedly contributed to a widespread negative attitude towards the 'new South Africa' and towards blacks.

Wespoort was made up of two suburbs, Danville and Elandspoort. Danville had been built by the government in the earlier part of this century to provide low-cost housing for the many poor white families who were moving from rural areas to Pretoria in search of work. Many people in Danville were unemployed or survived on what were often inadequate medical or old-age pensions.

A world away from this tough and depressing environment was the town of Louis Trichardt. It was located in the sort of idyllic rural setting that many of the inhabitants of Pretoria must have dreamt about; indeed, many city-dwellers had sold up and moved there. It was about four hours' drive north of Pretoria, not far from the border with Zimbabwe and right by the border with the black 'homeland' of Venda.[5] As in Queenswood, the DRC church was a prominent landmark.

The town itself was named after a famous Voortrekker leader who camped in the area in 1836, during the last stage of the Great Trek. Initially, those whites who tried to settle there were driven back south by the local Venda tribesmen. However, in 1889, 2000 white soldiers forcibly regained the area. The evening before the attack, the Boer general in charge of troops vowed to build a church if God gave them victory. His prayers were granted and the Church of the Vow, as it is now known, remained the largest church in the town.

The Voortrekker mentality was still evident among many whites in Louis Trichardt, who regarded blacks as little better than some barbarian tribe living in the Stone Age. It was not surprising, then, that in a town still trying to catch up with the ending of apartheid, the prospect of non-racial elections and an ANC-dominated government was regarded with deep foreboding. Many of those I interviewed owned or rented farms and were very worried that their land would be handed over to blacks once the new government was in power.

NORTHERN IRELAND

The Political Context

As I observed in the Introduction, during the period of my research in South Africa, the nature of change there could be characterised as *transformation* or wholesale change. However, in Northern Ireland, events were moving at a slower pace. When I carried out my fieldwork in Northern Ireland, in 1994, the shift in the political climate amounted to *transition* rather than transformation, but a transition which carried with it the very real prospect of more radical change.

As negotiations on the South African constitution were moving to their conclusion, hopes began to rise in Northern Ireland that a similar set of talks could begin there. John Hume, the leader of the 'moderate' nationalist party, the Social Democratic and Labour Party (SDLP), held a series of meetings with the Sinn Fein leader, Gerry Adams, which made considerable progress in laying the ground for the commencement of such talks. However, the political climate was shaken by two atrocities. In October 1993, an IRA bomb on the Protestant Shankill Road in Belfast left ten people dead. A week later, loyalist paramilitaries retaliated by killing seven people in a gun attack on a bar in County Derry.[6]

I arrived back in Northern Ireland shortly before these two incidents, profoundly moved by the way a seemingly hopeless talks process had moved forward in South Africa and convinced the same thing could happen in Northern Ireland. People in Northern Ireland did seem optimistic that perhaps, after all, a political solution to Northern Ireland's problems was achievable. The two attacks shattered the hopes of many ordinary Protestants and Catholics. For a few weeks, many stayed at home in the evening, fearing to go to their local pub lest it become the paramilitaries' next target.

However, the atrocities did not dent the determination of the British and Irish governments to add some momentum to the search for political progress. At the end of November, it was revealed that, contrary to its stated policy, the British government had had a 'channel of communication' with the IRA for a number of years. This was followed, in December, by a Joint Declaration by the British Prime Minister, John Major, and the Irish Taoiseach, Albert Reynolds. In this document, the British government reaffirmed that it would not stand in the way of a united Ireland if that was the wish of a majority of people in Northern Ireland. At that point, it was the most emphatic statement made by the British government on this issue, to date. The Declaration was designed to provide a broad framework for a political settlement and to woo republicans to lay down their arms to take part in talks leading to that end. It was given a very cautious welcome by the Ulster Unionist Party (UUP) but was greeted with disgust by the more hardline Democratic Unionist Party (DUP), which viewed it as 'the Anglo-Irish Accord Mark 2'.[7] Many interviewees saw it in similar terms and its existence undoubtedly contributed to a fairly common feeling among them that Northern Ireland was on an unstoppable path towards Irish unity.

The Northern Ireland Congregations

While each of the congregations in which I carried out my fieldwork had a distinct character, the parallels between the congregations in South Africa and those in Northern Ireland were quite striking. I selected two Belfast congregations, Stormont and Seaview, and a rural congregation, Second Newtownhamilton (referred to in this text as 'Newtownhamilton' for the sake of simplicity).[8] The similarities with South Africa were most marked in the case of Stormont, a middle-class suburb in East Belfast. The standard of living and sense of an ordered, comfortable lifestyle which pervaded Stormont reminded me strongly of Queenswood. As its name suggests, Stormont bordered on the estate which had housed Northern Ireland's own parliament prior to Direct Rule and, at the time of writing, was about to fulfil this function again for the new Northern Ireland Assembly. During the period in which the fieldwork was conducted, Stormont was used by British government ministers and Northern Ireland Office civil servants. The modern Presbyterian church building was a prominent feature on the busy Upper Newtownards Road which bisected the Stormont district.

Like Stormont, the largely working-class district of Seaview in North Belfast was dominated by a busy road. Again, the church was a conspicuous building. A number of interviewees lamented the fact that the area had gone 'downhill'; it certainly had the feel of a place which had seen better days. However, communal pride asserted itself around the Twelfth of July when red, white and blue kerbstones were repainted in some of the streets. While I was conducting my interviews, a UVF slogan appeared on a wall at the entrance to one of the more modern estates in the district. It vanished again, soon after July the Twelfth, however.[9]

Seaview was a predominantly Protestant district. While the level of sectarian violence was relatively low by Belfast standards, Seaview was not far from the bitterly divided areas for which the north of the city was best known. There had been sectarian incidents in Seaview; in the summer of 1993, a Catholic woman was shot dead by loyalist terrorists and, two weeks later, two Catholics were injured in another sectarian shooting. Many local people worked for employers which, prior to the introduction of fair employment legislation, had drawn most of their workforce from Protestant areas. These firms included the Belfast shipbuilders, Harland and Wolff; the plane-makers, Shorts, and a number of other engineering companies in Belfast. A few of the interviewees were unemployed, but others were on short-term contracts and had experienced periods of unemployment, or were in low-income jobs.

The inhabitants of Newtownhamilton also knew about hard times. Newtownhamilton is a small town just four miles from the border. Trade in the town was badly affected by the erection of permanent security checkpoints in the early 1970s. These were removed in 1990. Some effort had been made to spruce up the town. However, it still had the air of a place which had once been a hive of economic activity but was no longer. The town's population of just over 1000 was about 60 per cent Catholic and 40 per cent Protestant. In parts of the town, Protestants and Catholics lived side by side. However, there was an acute awareness of who was from which community. Accounts varied of the extent to which people mixed socially, depending on who one spoke to. One community group had succeeded in starting up two cross-community facilities, a playgroup and a senior citizens' club. However this had only been achieved with a great deal of persuasion and patience at the outset. The Protestant and Catholic churches had been unable to organise any similar initiatives. One of the ways in which it was evident that the boundary between Catholic and

Protestant was still deeply entrenched was in the collective possessiveness which surrounded the sale of land; most of the Presbyterians interviewed said they would not sell land to a Catholic.

THE SIGNIFICANCE OF THE CHURCH IN THE FIELDWORK CONGREGATIONS

I have already described the way in which, where religious and ethnic boundaries converge, the act of attending church quietly flags ethnic identity. This was particularly evident in Newtownhamilton where one third of those I interviewed said they would term themselves first and foremost 'Protestant', rather than 'Northern Irish' or 'Ulsterman/woman'. Newtownhamilton was the only one of the three PCI fieldwork congregations where 'Protestant' was a popular label. The ethnoreligious aspect of identity was clearly very important to many Presbyterians in Newtownhamilton and suggested that they were quite consciously involved in the process of flagging ethnicity. While Revd Wade believed many of his congregation went to church out of habit, rather than religious fervour, a minister in another Presbyterian congregation in South Armagh felt his flock attended church for what he termed 'political' reasons. 'They go to church because they are not Catholics,' he told me. When I asked him to elaborate, he said he felt that a sense that Protestants were of a different quality than their Catholic neighbours was woven into the attitude of many rural Protestants towards Sunday:

> Protestants don't shop on a Sunday.... They treat themselves, I won't say superior, but slightly different. They don't play games on a Sunday. They don't farm on a Sunday. Though, that to a certain extent is changing, but from the previous generation [that is their point of view], it would still be a great shame if their sons who are now working the farm worked on a Sunday. To do more than the minimum, that would be regarded as a very Catholic thing to do.

However, the differences in approach to Sunday between Protestants and Catholics in Northern Ireland have narrowed as Sunday has become less sacred and more secular, particularly in urban areas where many people have easy access to shops and leisure facilities which are open on Sunday. In Seaview, a third of those interviewed said they had not been to church in the previous twelve months. Indeed, most of these members had stopped going more than five years previously. This lack of active participation was mirrored, to a lesser extent, in the working-class congregation of Wespoort in Pretoria where one fifth of those interviewed said they had not attended a service in the past year.

In both cases, a number of interviewees said they found the services too formal. Others said they found the services boring or that they lacked relevance. One woman in Seaview said:

> I just didn't feel comfortable... I didn't feel welcome... I don't like going on my own. When you go in, you don't know where to sit... Although there's a man at the door, I think it could be his duty to tell you where to sit...

This drift away from the church fits in with a wider picture in Northern Ireland. The evidence suggests that the level of religious involvement among urban working-class Protestants is declining and is lower than that in other sections of Protestant society.[10] The PCI has been concerned about a decline in numbers in many of its churches in Belfast. Ministers in various parts of the city told me that there had been a drift of the Protestant population out from inner city areas to the suburbs. Many inner city churches seemed to keep going only through the continued patronage of some of those who had moved out, and often remained relatively irrelevant within the actual communities in which they were situated. These congregations appeared to be located largely, although not exclusively, in working-class districts.

In Seaview, if people stopped attending church, they did not generally try others. Not far away, a strikingly grandiose pentecostal church had opened its doors just a few years previously but had attracted little interest from members of the congregation. By contrast, 'shopping around' for a church was a phenomenon in Wespoort. Social workers there told me that many people were also put off going to the DRC church because they felt they were not smartly enough attired. One of the ministers took a cynical view of this excuse, however, telling me that people were simply apathetic.

Nevertheless, the DRC church in Wespoort did play a more prominent part in the life of the community than its Seaview counterpart. In both Wespoort and Louis Trichardt, the churches were involved in the distribution of food parcels to congregation members in need. They also offered programmes on 'life skills' for the less well-off. These schemes were subsidised by the South African government which offered much less in terms of direct welfare assistance than was provided by the British government in Northern Ireland. Thus, it is perhaps not surprising that Seaview supplied nothing similar for its unemployed members, although it did run schemes designed to provide some support for pensioners and mothers with young children. Indeed, although the PCI did run government-funded work experience schemes for the unemployed, a Church survey, published in 1994, found that no individual congregation ran any specific scheme targeted at the unemployed.[11]

The working-class congregations in Belfast and Pretoria can also be seen as examples of a phenomenon Grace Davie describes as 'believing without belonging'.[12] She discerns this tendency in working-class areas of Britain where she says many people believe in God but have no need to express their religiosity in an institutional form. Certainly, among the congregations I studied, the church was a more significant part of life in the urban middle-class and rural districts rather than in the urban working-class areas. Active participation in the church was greatest in the South African congregations. The highest levels of regular attendance were in both Queenswood and Louis Trichardt; nearly three-quarters of those interviewed claimed to attend church at least once a week in Queenswood, while just over half said they went on a weekly basis in Louis Trichardt. In the other congregations, between a third and half of the members attended church at least once a week. A number of people in Stormont and Seaview said they were only going to church so that their children or grandchildren could attend Sunday school.

In both the DRC and PCI middle-class congregations, the church also provided a wide range of social activities for its members. Stormont, for example, offered specialist clubs for gardeners and amateur artists, as well as sports clubs, a youth club and various scouting organisations. To a greater or lesser extent, each of the congregations responded to the social as well as the spiritual needs of its members. In so doing, they helped to maintain their social significance within their particular district.

CONCLUSION

If one measures the significance of the church in terms of regular attendance, it clearly played a more important part in the lives of those in Queenswood and Louis Trichardt than in the other congregations. However, attendance at church is only one measure of the significance of religion. In all the congregations, the church also responded to the social needs, in the broadest sense, of its members. It is clear that, in both the urban working-class congregations, many members did not feel moved to express their religious belief through the act of going to church. This raises the question of the usefulness of my argument that attendance at church was a means of flagging ethnicity. It undoubtedly was for those who did go to church. For some of those who did not, the church played a different role in the constitution of their identity. The church represented the formidable Other and was actually an institution from which they felt alienated. This mirrored a sense of alienation from the political process which existed, to a greater or lesser degree, in all six congregations. This aspect of identity is explored in the next chapter.

3 Fear, Insecurity and Alienation

Looking back on my time in South Africa, one of the most vivid pictures that comes to mind is of one of the many visits I paid to farms owned by Afrikaners in the area round Louis Trichardt. This particular farm was a bustling hive of activity with several black farm labourers working intently on a welter of different tasks. The lush, abundant garden round the farmhouse indicated that this 60-acre farm enjoyed plentiful supplies of piped water. However, just beneath it, obscured by trees, was a stark reminder of the social hierarchy left by apartheid. For, if one peered downwards through the foliage, one saw below a broad, barren-looking expanse of plain, dotted with townships. That land formed part of the black 'homeland' of Venda; land onto which blacks were eventually moved after much of their own territory had been taken away from them and given to white settlers.[1] The owner of this farm, Pieter De Wet, claimed the Vendas had failed to utilise the potential of the land they had had bestowed on them by whites.[2]

Others told a different story, however. They said that, in common with the policy of blatant usurpation of land followed in so many parts of South Africa, blacks had a raw deal. There was no irrigation and their attempts to farm had been affected by drought. Allegedly, some of them felt they had a right to reclaim the white land that was rightfully theirs and were looking forward to being able to do this once a democratically elected government was in place. This was the great fear of the white farmers in and around the town of Louis Trichardt, close to the border with Venda, and Mr De Wet was one of those full of anxiety.

He showed me the black farmholdings on the plain. 'They've been talking for a while now that they're going to take all these [the white] farms back', he told me. 'But this farm was bought by my grandfather and inherited by my father and it will be mine, and they'll have to drag my dead body away to take me off this farm … Shooting must be the last option … it's the very last resort but, if there's no choice, I'm not going to sit on my *stoep* [front step] while others are doing the job.'

Mr De Wet's lack of trust and his willingness to use physical force towards blacks was not just confined to those outside the bounds of his farm, however. 'This morning I shot a monkey' he told me, 'just so my workers can see I can shoot. It makes them afraid ...' He chuckled nervously as he spoke, aware that what he said must sound rather ridiculous to a foreigner such as myself. The implication of these words took a moment for me to digest; it seemed hard to believe they could emanate from such an apparently warm and courteous man.

Yet, for Mr De Wet, the threat of attack was no laughing matter. Throughout South Africa, there had been many reports in the white press of a spate of vicious attacks by blacks against white farmers. Naturally, this had provoked much alarm among the white farming community. In Mr De Wet's case, this anxiety was made all the more acute by the fact that a middle-aged relative of his had been brutally murdered on another farm in the same district. Her attackers poured poison down her throat, burned her face and strangled her with a tie. Mr De Wet was taking no chances. He had turned his house into a fortress: 'The rifles used to be lying around the house, but now they're locked up. Every night I put a rifle next to me on the floor. During the day, my wife locks both the front and the back door.'

The De Wets' trepidation encapsulates in a metaphorical way the very real sense of threat which pervaded both the Afrikaner and Ulster Protestant communities when I carried out my interviews. It was, of course, an entirely predictable reaction to the rapid change in the political landscape which was sweeping through both South Africa and Northern Ireland when I carried out my research. In his general manner, Mr De Wet was far from the stereotype of the arrogant, swaggering Boer perpetuated by English-speaking 'liberals' and the international media. However, his attitude towards his black fellow countrymen accorded perfectly with the *laager*-mentality stereotype of Afrikaners, as did the comments made by many other interviewees.

The BBC's former Southern Africa correspondent, Fergal Keane, has criticised the media's lazy use of such stereotypical images:

> Every day of life in South Africa produced encounters with people who seem to live up to one stereotype or another. Walk into a bar in any rural area and you will meet plenty of pot-bellied men with decidedly right-wing views. They are perfect fodder for visiting journalists because they can always be relied upon to deliver a racist quote and a blood-curdling warning of an apocalypse to come. But behind this racist haze there are surely people whose history and circumstances are more complicated than we, as journalists, often manage to convey.[3]

It is indeed vital to remember that there was genuine fear behind the insecurity and anger voiced by so many of my interviewees. Like Mr De Wet, the majority were kind, humane individuals who did not see themselves as bigots. They were, to a large extent, products of the manner in which history had unfolded and had shaped their collective lives and circumstances up to that point.

Keane remarks on the plethora of stereotypes which were employed by different groups of South Africans to describe each other. This range of clichéd images formed part of the variety of discourses which people drew on to make sense of change and of loss of power. This is why people in such a situation can be so horribly predictable in what they say. They are utilising certain discourses which have evolved in response to the changes taking place; in other words, they are drawing on a range of assumptions and beliefs which form a coherent discursive whole and enable them to explain what is going on.

These discourses do not emerge from nowhere. They are partly a product of history but, most importantly, they are closely related to power. Powerful institutions, such as the political sphere, the media and the church play a large part in shaping these discourses. In drawing out these ways of seeing the world, I too can stand accused of portraying a stereotypical picture of both Afrikaners and Ulster Protestants. However, in my defence, I would argue that it is as important to analyse these predictable patterns of talk as it is to try to understand the very real feelings and experiences of the individuals who express them. I hope I am able to do both in this book.

This chapter compares and analyses the uneasy atmosphere of threat, anxiety and uncertainty which permeated the congregations in which I conducted my fieldwork. At such a time, a sense of collective identity can provide a feeling of much-needed continuity. In this chapter, I also begin an examination of the way in which that sense of identity was constructed. Uncertainty and insecurity often produce a sense of collective powerlessness; this was evident in all the congregations. Thus, this chapter also analyses that alienation and the way in which it provided a means of coming to terms with change.

UNCERTAINTY, INSECURITY AND THREAT

It is important to bear in mind the precise point at which the research in each territory was carried out. As I have already observed, while

South Africa was effectively experiencing a wholesale *transformation* of the balance of power between blacks and whites, Northern Ireland was in a period of *transition* in that Britain was slowly loosening its constitutional ties with Northern Ireland. This meant the balance of power between unionists and nationalists was subtly shifting in the nationalists' favour. The possibility of wholesale transformation of the relationship between Britain and Northern Ireland, and between unionists and nationalists, was a source of anxiety for many Protestants. However, the realisation of that possibility was much less likely, at that point, than was the case in South Africa.

Thus, it is not surprising that more interviewees in the South African congregations expressed uncertainty about the future than was the case in Northern Ireland.[4] Moreover, there was a stronger sense of threat in each of the three South African congregations, as compared with each of their corresponding Northern Ireland congregations.[5] In both cases, this sense of threat was stronger in the urban working-class and rural congregations than in the middle-class congregations. In the former, it was articulated by a majority of interviewees. In both Louis Trichardt and Wespoort, this manifested itself in an acute fear of physical attack. One petrified woman in Wespoort told me 'All the killing is making me worried ... My husband is out at the moment and someone could come in and kill my children'. A man in his forties voiced similar fears, 'I only live day by day. If I think about the future, it doesn't help ... Look at the old people that get murdered on the farms. We are afraid at night'.

The level of anxiety was strongest in Louis Trichardt, where three white people had been murdered by black attackers in the previous two years. Mr De Wet's wife was not the only white woman living on a farm who kept herself locked in the house during the day, for fear of attack. Many farmers said they had taken additional security precautions to guard against the possibility of attack.

Yet, according to a senior army officer, there were no rational grounds for this level of apprehension. In statistical terms, the area was actually the safest in South Africa. Instead, it seemed to be very much a manifestation of a deeper sense of threat posed by the changes which lay ahead. As the officer put it:

They [white farmers] can't accept the fact that things are changing. They've been the *baas* [boss] on the *plaas* [farm] all their lives. They can't accept things are going to change.

One 'liberal' interviewee who lived near the town was candid about the changes that had already taken place:

> If I go to the Post Office and I see fifteen or sixteen black people in front of me, I go 'Oh, Father'. It's not like in the old days when you had all the blacks on one side and just a few whites on the other [in separate queues]. Now you have to wait in the Post Office and in the banks and so on … It's quite difficult to accept that you've got to wait your turn.

The fears expressed by whites in Louis Trichardt were a clear example of the sort of 'settler unease' described by Todd.[6] At a subconscious, if not fully conscious level, the white descendants and beneficiaries of those first settlers knew that their relatively comfortable lifestyle rested on straightforward oppression and exploitation of the 'natives'. Now, the natives' time had come and white unease was growing.

The threat was discursively symbolised by whites both in its institutionalised form, the ANC, and in a more general collective form, as the great black 'uncivilised' mass. In Northern Ireland, some Presbyterians talked of Catholics in the same vein. Often, however, they saw the threat looming in the form of two institutions – the Irish government and the Catholic Church, both of which were portrayed either as being about to stage a takeover or, at least, as being ready to significantly extend their influence in the affairs of Northern Ireland to the detriment of Protestants.

'Dublin [that is, the Irish government] is coming in a lot more,' said one woman in Seaview, shaking her head. 'Perhaps we won't remain part of the UK and, in a united Ireland, we're a minority then, quite a small minority.' 'How would that change things?' I asked her. 'Well, the Catholic Church … there's no divorce and the schools are different', she replied.[7] 'The church and state are tied up in the South and they're not here.'

A man from the same congregation saw the Irish government as being in league with the IRA. 'They [the IRA] are going to keep this up till they get a united Ireland and, no matter what they say, Dublin's behind it,' he said, with a bitter note in his voice. 'All the IRA men's down there and the Dublin government is doing nothing about it.'

The sense of *inevitability* about the likely outcome was very marked in both Northern Ireland and South Africa. While this might have been expected in South Africa, it was rather surprising in Northern Ireland where, at the time the interviews were carried out, the conflict was clearly a long way from being resolved. The minister of Seaview, Revd John Dickinson, summed up the feelings of many in his congregation:

> The whole kind of ethos, the whole context within which Northern Ireland is currently considered by both Westminster and Dublin basically is the inevitability of the reunification of Ireland ... And the Downing Street Declaration is cast in those terms, however much John Major may say that 'now has been enshrined the right of the majority' and all the rest of it. At the end of the day, the majority only have a right on the understanding that eventually they will no longer be a majority ... We're a very small group of people trying to swim against the tide.

However, others not only felt the changes were inevitable, but also accepted them. One woman from Newtownhamilton expressed optimism about the future:

> I think that gradually it's just like what happened in the Free State ... What happened there in the twenties, they had to be integrated and the Protestants lost their identity. I think there will be an all-Ireland and there's no point banging your head against it ... I think the Dublin government will treat the Protestants better than ever the Catholics did ... [i.e., it will show more respect to Protestants than Northern Irish Catholics ever showed].

Her willingness to accept change was unusual in Newtownhamilton. However, it was a view shared by a number of people in Stormont. Their minister, Dr Ron Savage, felt most of his flock could tolerate a united Ireland, if this was the outcome of inter-party talks. 'I think, if you talk it through with most of them, they wouldn't welcome it,' he said, 'but they could see it down the line, and might acquiesce.'

ALIENATION

In both territories, however, this sense of inevitability was often inter-woven with tremendous disillusion and a sense of powerlessness. A police officer in Wespoort said he felt irritated at the lack of influence he had with regard to political developments:

> I do feel frustrated because all the things that are changing – it's not that we *wanted* it to change. It was decided a long time ago and I

think they're bluffing us ... They're not being very open. It's like bush whackers – people who shoot other people in the back ...

Another member of the police force, a forensic scientist and member of the Queenswood congregation, felt his 'no' vote in the referendum on constitutional change had been wasted:

> It would seem the ANC and the government talk and then they do as they like, and no matter what everybody else says, the ANC agenda is enacted. I mean you just have to watch the news to see that ... It would seem the average man in the street cannot do anything about it. You've elected politicians and they do as they see fit.

This particular man felt that the ANC's perceived ability to 'steamroller' through their agenda stemmed partly from the way that the National Party government had behaved in the past:

> The National Party has been in power for very long and – I might meet some great opposition by saying this – but, in days of past, it would seem that the National Party government acts dictatorially in certain ways. Once they've decided on something, no matter what you will cry, they will carry on regardless.

Similar views were expressed by others I spoke to. Observers spoke of a paternalistic culture among Afrikaners. As one person put it: 'The Afrikaner likes to have a "big daddy" who knows best, whether it's politicians or church ministers.'[8] Membership of political parties in the three DRC congregations was certainly high compared to the PCI congregations. Two-fifths of the Queenswood interviewees belonged to a party, while more than half of the Louis Trichardt respondents were party members. However, only a few were active in their organisations. A number of people told me there was a tradition of political party membership and that membership did not necessarily signify an active interest in politics.

There was a somewhat greater interest in issues at a local level in the DRC congregation. A few people were actively involved in groups campaigning on local community issues. Several said they belonged to groups which had set up schemes to try to improve the lives of local people, and a few people in each congregation said they were active members of these groups.

However, three of the four ministers in Queenswood felt there was a large degree of apathy about the broader political situation among their members. Dr Phillippus Loots had no doubt what their main priority was:

> I would say their own standard of living – number one. Secondly, I would say their church affiliation and their personal affiliation with the Lord is also very high. I think they take an interest in what's happening in the political field, but not so actively.

One of his colleagues, Dr Petrus Van Der Merwe, had just spent six weeks travelling round South Africa and said he had encountered widespread apathy. He believed this was engendered by uncertainty over the country's future:

> There is a sort of lackadaisical attitude over the whole of South Africa at the moment, because everyone is uncertain in which way things are turning ... They don't want to get involved at the moment ... It's not only in church matters but you come home and hear about it on the news – there's so many people killed – and you switch it off and go over to sport and you sort of contract into a cocoon ... People don't want to get involved.

These comments were mirrored by Revd David Moore, the Assistant Minister in the Stormont congregation in Belfast:

> I think how people have got on with life here is just that they've turned off the political thing. They've thrown themselves into their families and their jobs, and I think those are the main things which most people are concerned about ... And, probably, family is number one, although career would probably be there too in the sense of providing for your family.

Indeed, if the level of political participation in the DRC congregations was not remarkable, the level of participation in the PCI congregations was almost non-existent. Of the 47 people interviewed in each PCI congregation, only one person in any of the interview samples belonged to a political party. None belonged to any group campaigning on local community issues. Two people in Stormont and one in Newtownhamilton said they belonged to groups which had tried to set up projects to help better the lives of local people. No one in Seaview was involved in such a scheme.

The above statistics bear out the frequently voiced complaint that Protestants seem to lack the motivation to get together and campaign for improved facilities in their districts in the way that Catholics in areas like West Belfast have done. One unemployed woman in Seaview said everyone in her district wanted somewhere where their children could play. 'Everybody complains but nobody gets off their backside and does anything' she said with a wry smile. 'So, why don't you do something about it?' I asked her. 'I'm not a leader in these things' she replied. 'I can talk a lot in the house but I never have the gumption to go out and do these things … I'd go along with it if somebody else would do it … I don't know what it is about Protestants. They seem to be lazier. Catholics will make more of an effort to get facilities.'

While the extent of disillusion with politics was widespread in both the DRC and the PCI congregations, it was greater in Northern Ireland. In the South African congregations, roughly two-thirds of the interviewees in each sample said they agreed with the statement 'I am not interested in getting involved in politics.' However, the proportion agreeing with this comment rose to four-fifths in the Stormont congregation and to around 90 per cent in both the Seaview and Newtownhamilton congregations. Indeed, there seemed to be a positive pride on the part of many of the Northern Ireland interviewees in expressing their disdain for the tarnished world of politics. This stance seemed to be regarded as a rather admirable attitude. Certainly, cynicism with politicians ran deep.

'Politics is a very dirty game,' a congregation member in Stormont told me. 'They're peculiar animals and they're out for their own ends on the pretext of forwarding the community's ends.' A woman in Newtownhamilton was equally cynical. 'I just can't stand politics. I couldn't change it,' she said, shaking her head. 'The politicians just blow a lot of hot air and get paid big money for it. I think they aggravate the situation more than anything.'

However, this person admitted she voted for the very same politicians she criticised: 'You always seem to go out and vote for your side anyway.' Few interviewees seemed to make any link between the act of voting and the end product in terms of the politicians they ended up with. For many Afrikaners and Ulster Presbyterians, there was an important negative motivation for voting; to help ensure that the political dominance of one's ethnic group was not further weakened. Voting was another part of the process of constituting one's ethnic identity.

In order to provide a 'snapshot' of the degree of alienation towards the political process, a Political Alienation Index was constructed using responses on these issues. It was based on responses to each of the following statements:

1. I am not interested in getting involved in politics.
2. I don't feel there is any way my vote can make a difference to the way South Africa/Northern Ireland is run.
3. I don't feel there is any way I can influence the future of Northern Ireland.

Each respondent was allocated 2 points for each 'strongly agree' or 'agree' answer, 1 point for each 'neither agree nor disagree' or 'don't know', and 0 points for each 'disagree' or 'strongly disagree'. As can be seen from Figures 3.1 and 3.2, Queenswood had the largest proportion of members who did not feel particularly alienated from the political process. The most 'alienated' congregations were Seaview and

Figure 3.1 Political Alienation Index: PCI congregations. A = Stormont, B = Seaview, C = Newtownhamilton.

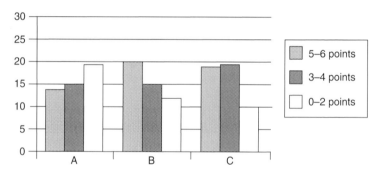

Figure 3.2 Political Alienation Index: DRC congregations. A = Queenswood, B = Wespoort, C = Louis Trichardt.

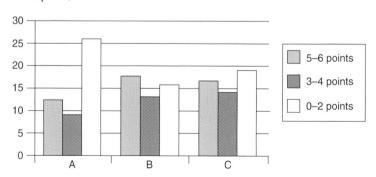

Newtownhamilton. However, in each congregation, many people articulated some sense of alienation as the tables show.

The common thread underlying the negative scepticism expressed about politics could be termed a discourse of alienation; a discourse which said that politics was a waste of time, that politicians could not be trusted, and that ordinary people had no influence anyway. Like the fear of physical attack and the discursive symbolisation of certain 'threats', the discourse of alienation was a resource that interviewees drew on to enable them to make sense of the changes taking place. In South Africa, the readiness to use this discourse may well have been due in part to the paternalistic ethos engendered by the National Party and the DRC. In Northern Ireland, the lack of full democratic accountability of political institutions under Direct Rule must be an important factor in explaining the apathy and alienation expressed by interviewees. In part, this discourse of alienation was also a reflection of the objective lack of political power held by those on low incomes, handicapped by poor levels of education and possessing no links to individuals or organisations with access to the centres of political power. Indeed, detailed analysis of the data suggests that social class was a significant factor; those from a 'manual' background were more likely to have a high score on the Alienation Index than those from a 'non-manual' background.[9] In Northern Ireland, alienation was also less evident among those with relatively high levels of education.

Yet, as we have seen, the discourse of alienation was also visible in both the middle-class congregations. These were congregations with a large proportion of civil servants and professionals who did have access to the centres of political power. Thus, this discourse was not entirely a statement of objective fact. It was also a means of 'opting out', of absolving oneself of any sense of responsibility for the changes taking place. It expressed a feeling of powerlessness but it was also almost a self-fulfilling prophecy. If you tell yourself there is nothing you can do, then, *de facto*, you do nothing and therefore cannot influence events. If you tell yourself that your vote makes no difference, then you can feel free to criticise the very politicians you voted for.

'THEY'RE TAKING OUR JOBS'

Another discourse prevalent among both Afrikaners and Ulster Presbyterians related to measures aimed at ensuring genuine equality of opportunity in the workplace. As far as many interviewees were concerned, in practice, this meant *inequality* of opportunity for them. In Northern Ireland, employers are required by law to monitor the religious make-up of their workforces and to review their recruitment practices to ensure equality of opportunity, and to redress any imbalances. A body known as the Fair Employment Commission (formerly the Fair Employment Agency) co-ordinates this process. Job applicants and employees can take cases to the Fair Employment Tribunal. Victims of discrimination can be awarded compensation.[10] In South Africa, on the other hand, at the time this study was carried out, neither the government nor the ANC had indicated exactly how affirmative action policies would be implemented once the new government was in place. Nevertheless, the subject was a controversial one and was a constant topic of conversation and public debate among whites. In order to try to gauge opinion on the subject in the six congregations, interviewees were asked for their reaction to the following statements:

> *DRC interviewees* If a black and a white person are equally suitable for a vacant post, then the black person should be given the job in order to help correct the present racial imbalance in the pattern of employment.
>
> *PCI interviewees* If a Protestant person and a Roman Catholic person are *equally suitable* for a vacant post, then the Roman Catholic should be given the job to help correct the present religious imbalance in the pattern of employment.[11]

The results are given in Figures 3.3 and 3.4. As can be seen, in each congregation, the numbers of people disagreeing with this statement outweighed those who approved.[12] The greatest opposition to the statement, by far, came from congregation members in Louis Trichardt. Two factors seemed to contribute to their attitude. One was the fact that the town's main shopping area relied for much of its business on the custom of black South Africans from Venda. The main street was divided up with white-owned shops at one end and those owned by blacks at the other, although some (generally better-off) blacks did venture into the 'white' shops. Clearly, those who travelled into Louis Trichardt to do their shopping had higher incomes than many others who lived in Venda. What this meant, however, was that whites in Louis Trichardt saw what many of them viewed as conspicuous consumption on the part of blacks. It was easy to generalise and to

Figure 3.3   Attitudes to affirmative action statement (DRC). A = Queenswood, B = Wespoort, C = Louis Trichardt.

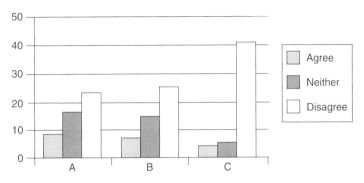

Figure 3.4   Attitudes to affirmative action statement (PCI). A = Stormont, B = Seaview, C = Newtownhamilton.

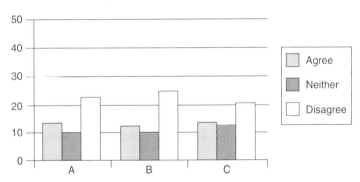

assume that all blacks were relatively well-off. As one white woman put it to me:

> You watch the black people buying their groceries. Black people have two *bags* while white people just have a basket. They [whites] have been bled since 1948 ... Black people are never satisfied. They've been elevated to a very high standard of living but they never stop demanding.

The other factor which influenced attitudes was a deeply ingrained image of the Venda people as uncivilised and barbaric. Where a foreigner such as myself saw a group of people who were fairly westernised in their dress and tastes, many whites in Louis Trichardt perceived Vendas as having changed little from the tribesmen who confronted their settler forefathers.

These underlying assumptions were evident in the views expressed by one relatively liberal couple. Jan Venter was suddenly made redundant from his job as a manager when his company hit financial problems.[13] He applied for no less than three hundred jobs and spent ten fraught months without work. He had only recently secured his present job, as a consultant to a timber group. He told me many jobs he had wanted to apply for had only been open to blacks. 'It was stated "black people only" or alternatively, what they will do is "must be able to speak at least two black languages" and there are very few white people that can do that,' he said. 'And how did that make you feel?' I asked. 'Disappointed,' he replied, with a sigh. 'They come up with the best excuses to appoint black people.'

Mr Venter felt white people in Louis Trichardt were prejudiced in their attitudes towards blacks: 'They've been taught that a black is a black and that he is a dumb, illiterate person. That might have been the case thirty or forty years ago. It might, to a certain extent, still be the case, but I don't think it's holding true too much today.' Yet, a little later in the same interview, Mr Venter contradicted himself. His wife, Helena, was trying to explain why it was much more difficult to relate to blacks in Venda than in two other towns with which they were familiar:[14]

This is a very difficult race to relate to. You know, they are much more barbaric than the others. But, whenever you move to a place like White River or Cape Town, you can relate to them better, you know, normally – you can have a conversation with them. They will understand you, they will accept you …

White River is also a rural area, but there is more races there – they have to mix with each other, they have to mix with whites – but here they feel they don't have to. It's rather part of the country and they don't have to take you in or accept you and this makes it difficult, you know, for us to relate to them, to understand them, to work with them.

Her husband intervened at this point:

Can I put it another way? I believe that, up here, up north, they are a lot more illiterate than anywhere else … and, being illiterate, they are intimidated quickly and easily. They will not accept anything you say if you cannot speak their language. My colleague that's working with me can understand and speak and read the Venda language fluently. He grew up over here. They have a lot of respect for him, just because he can speak their language. If I have to give them instructions to do something for me, they would normally just stand there and look at me dumbstruck, purely because they refuse to listen to what I'm saying because I cannot speak their language.

Mr Venter's inconsistency on the subject of the illiteracy or otherwise of blacks in Venda illustrates the way in which many whites used different, contradictory discourses, to try to make sense of the changes that were taking place. As Mr Venter himself observed, it was a commonly held view among whites in Louis Trichardt that blacks were illiterate. It was also one to which he was able to subscribe in order to explain the poor state of race relations – and, perhaps, to express indirectly his own frustration at a problem caused by his lack of competence in the Venda language. What struck me was the way in which the word 'illiterate', when used by Afrikaners, tended to mean 'unable to read or write in English or Afrikaans'. Vendas were judged harshly by the standards of a culture which had dominated and oppressed them for a long time. However, the judgements of that culture were not going to matter for much longer. My impression was that this was a reality that many whites in Louis Trichardt did not want to face up to.

Mr Venter's experience of joblessness was by no means unique. Unemployment was a problem among whites in both Louis Trichardt and Wespoort. Of course, it must be borne in mind that the average length of unemployment and the scale of the problem paled into insignificance compared with the extent of joblessness among blacks. However, most whites felt it was bound to get worse. It was whites at the bottom of the social scale who were likely to be hit first. One social worker in Louis Trichardt explained their fears:

They know that … they are the first that's going to lose their jobs because they are not well-educated. They don't have proper jobs – and it's cheaper to get a black person in the same job. And it's easier because there's twenty black people who can do the same job. The higher educated people tend to be more 'left' [left-wing] or open [in their attitudes] because it's not a threat to them. The lower educated people – all they have to stand on is their white skin.

It was a similar story in Wespoort, where another social worker put it even more bluntly. 'They [people in Wespoort] are racists' she told me. 'And they have reason to be racists because they are going to lose in the new South Africa.' There were widespread fears in this congregation that whites were already being thrown out of jobs to make way for blacks. This view was shared by one of the two ministers in the congregation, Revd Jan Barnard. 'Many people are being retrenched to allow black people in,' he told me. 'There are 1300 people that I know of that have lost their jobs and they're very negative ... They feel no one wants them.'

This assertion was not corroborated by academic and journalistic experts on this subject. Likewise, in Northern Ireland, the Fair Employment Commission has strongly denied the contention from some unionist politicians that Catholics have gained jobs at the expense of Protestants.[15] Yet, in both the DRC and the PCI congregations, interviewees were often quite adamant that their community was being discriminated against. Revd John Dickinson of Seaview certainly felt many of his congregation were being treated unfairly:

> A lot of people feel they can't get jobs now because they're Protestants and I could quote half a dozen examples of people recently who didn't even get interviews for jobs – one in the Fire Service, one in the Post Office – areas like that – because basically they have to increase their quota of Catholics. So I mean basically in the community that I work in the feeling would be at the moment that fair employment means jobs for Catholics.
>
> Q: And would you share that view?
>
> To a degree, yes, I would ... I'm not suggesting the legislation was designed to do that but the reality of the situation is ... In certain areas where Catholic quotas are low, in particular firms where they have to be got up, I mean basically, although the government deny it, there is positive discrimination being exercised. And if you're a Protestant and you put in an application, you don't get an interview.

COLLECTIVE IDENTITY

The discourse of 'anti-discrimination measures means discrimination against us' was another means of making tangible the sense of threat that hung in the air above both Afrikaners and Protestants. The more nebulous sense of the Other encroaching onto their territory and their rights was symbolised by pointing a finger at blacks or Catholics who were seen as taking the jobs which were rightfully theirs. In South Africa, this fear was heightened by the fact that many blacks were just as capable of carrying out many unskilled jobs as the poorly qualified and educated whites who held them.

However, Afrikaners often stereotyped blacks as incompetent, greedy and lazy. It seemed to be a means of mentally keeping them at bay; as I have already observed, if Afrikaners could no longer dominate in practice, then they would often dominate in the discourse they used to describe the black Other. This tendency was less evident in the discourse employed by Presbyterians when they talked about Catholics. In both cases, interviewees were asked for their reaction to statements which encapsulated stereotypes based on racist or sectarian attitudes. In each of the Northern Ireland congregations, a majority of interviewees disagreed with the following two statements: 'Roman Catholics tend to be lazier than Protestants,' and 'Roman Catholics can't be trusted.' However, in the DRC congregations, a majority agreed that 'Black people could solve many of their own problems if they weren't so irresponsible and carefree about life.'[16] The strongest support for this statement came from interviewees in Wespoort and Louis Trichardt. Nearly half the Wespoort interviewees and a third of the Louis Trichardt interviewees said they strongly agreed with this statement.

The comments made by some people in these congregations did not come as a surprise to me; the West European stereotype of white South Africans is that they are racist, after all. However, the extent to which blatantly racist attitudes were hidden from middle-class Afrikaners was brought home to me by the shocked reaction of a student who acted as my interpreter in the Wespoort congregation. After interpreting an interview with a bitter 70-year old woman who frequently referred to blacks as 'barbarians', the student was aghast and told me she had never heard such language used about black South Africans before. Her middle-class suburb in the wealthier end of Pretoria was a different world, in this respect, and she said the interviews in Wespoort had opened her eyes to the raw reality of racist hatred.

Yet, racism was also very much a feature of the more 'liberal' Queenswood congregation. The precise way in which prejudice manifested itself might have been more subtle, but its existence had important repercussions. Teun A. van Dijk has carried out some excellent work in pointing out the racist assumptions which underlie seemingly liberal statements.[17] Van Dijk points to two strategies used by politicians in Europe and North America which can also be discerned in comments made by both the DRC and PCI interviewees in this study. The first tactic involves denial of one's own racist attitudes through the use of a disclaimer, such as 'I've nothing against blacks, but … ' The second strategy consists of the expression of apparent sympathy for those, such as immigrants, subjected to racist policies while, at the same time, presenting such measures as being in the interests of those at whom they are aimed. In western parliaments, this has tended to mean that immigrants are encouraged to stay away from a particular country because they may face resentment if they enter. Van Dijk observes:

> It is only in such strategic arguments that 'our' country is presented as a disagreeable place to be – for immigrants, that is. At the same time, immigration restrictions may be supported by arguing that they are necessary for 'harmony' in society. That is, it is in our common interest for 'them' to stay away.[18]

As we shall see below and in the following chapters, similar arguments were used by interviewees to justify apartheid policies and segregation along religious or racial lines. These strategies are all structured by a desire to present a positive image of oneself and one's own group. The corollary of the positive presentation of the Self is a negative presentation – either implicit or explicit – of the Other. The following comments by a member of the church council in Queenswood illustrate the use of these strategies:

> If a black man moves in next door, I'd expect him to live the way we do. In other words, he'll have to keep his stand clean, his garden in reasonable order – that also applies to his house – and he'll have to put out the garbage the same way we do. We don't want him to be noisy, so what I'm trying to say is, if he moves in over here, he needs to keep to a certain standard.

> Q: Are you saying that you don't think black people do keep to certain standards?

> That's a really hard one because, look, between white people of the so-called same standard of living, you find bad ones and even worse ones. We have one on the corner here … but what I'm trying to say is that, within limits … I don't think it is impossible to live with black neighbours. I am trying to underscore the fact that I'm saying that there are certain very profound differences …

Q: You also said that you don't believe that apartheid is an oppressive system and should be rejected as sinful. Can you tell me why you hold that view?

… if you apply it in its simple form to whites for instance, you don't find low-class people living among so-called high-class people. In certain suburbs, the guy would be informed quickly 'Look, you don't fit in – get out!' Look, put it this way round – apartheid for the wrong reasons is definitely not right, but for certain other reasons and in my view, mainly [because of] the difference in the cultural backgrounds – simply put – I'd like, if possible, to stay amongst people of my kind, so to speak …

One man who had been actively involved in race relations initiatives in the Queenswood congregation appeared to be less prejudiced. However, like the Venters in Louis Trichardt, Christo Meyer's critique of the paternalism of whites was coloured by his own paternalistic and racist attitudes.[19] Mr Meyer had been very involved in efforts by members of the Queenswood congregation to build a church for members of the 'black' Dutch Reformed Church in Africa (DRCA). He claimed it had been very difficult to encourage local people to be actively involved because they were so used to whites doing everything for them.

The blacks in South Africa have got this attitude of 'the *baas* will give us' – 'you've got to give us because you are white, we are deprived and we got to get'. It is something that is very deep down and you can't really get rid of it easily, so we have got to live with it … 'The government has got to give us land and if the white wants land, he's got to buy it, the black gets it for free'. I think it stems from that attitude of the white has always been the supporter and the one who looked after them.

This man's paternalistic attitude was also evident when I asked him whether he would talk about politics to black South Africans:

No, I wouldn't ever try and talk politics to a black … With those who work with us, when it is outside of the religious context, you do ask them how they feel or what they feel about Mandela or Buthelezi or whoever. But they are the common worker group who rarely have political opinions or they are not well-developed yet. So, no, we don't talk politics with them.

The discursive strategies identified by van Dijk were not so evident in the Northern Ireland congregations. Some blatantly sectarian comments were made. One man in Seaview said, in all seriousness, 'I tar them all with the same brush and then I know I can't be wrong.' Another said he had been let down by Catholic workmates in the past:

> You can never trust them. I'm telling you through experience ... They may be nice to your face but you wouldn't put any trust in any-thing they say – and they don't like Protestant people.

However, in general, interviewees expressed a belief in an essential but unspecified difference between Catholics and Protestants. This was articulated several times when interviewees were asked whether they would live in a predominantly Catholic street. One man in Seaview said:

> I just wouldn't feel comfortable ... I just think it's the way I've been brought up. I wouldn't feel comfortable. It's not because they're Roman Catholic – I wouldn't feel comfortable if they were all Pakistanis or Indians.

A number of people said they would rather be among their 'own people'. One woman began explaining her attitude 'Well, you wouldn't ... I don't mind one or two like, but ...' She cut herself short, evidently feeling she had said enough. 'And why don't you want to have more than that?' I asked. 'They're all right,' she replied 'but I'd rather be in my own place where your own are ... I think it's better not. Maybe if you was in another locality with different types of Roman Catholics who were like Protestants.'

The inability to articulate these differences suggested that there was no clear idea as to what precisely constituted the essential characteris-tics of either Protestants or Catholics. This fragmented sense of col-lective identity was reflected in the responses the PCI interviewees gave to the question, 'If you had to give yourself one label, how would you define yourself?' (see Figure 3.5). As can be seen there were marked differences in the responses given by the three samples. 'British' was the most popular option in both Stormont and Seaview, with 'Northern Irish' the second most popular in Stormont and 'Ulsterman/woman' in Seaview. There seemed to be a feeling that 'Northern Irish' was the new 'politically correct' term; this was most apparent in Stormont. There was also a belief among some that 'Ulsterman/woman' had acquired unsavoury connections, thanks to the use of 'Ulster' in the names of the two main loyalist paramilitary groupings, the Ulster Freedom Fighters (UFF) and the Ulster Volunteer Force (UVF), and also because of the way it was used by

Figure 3.5   How interviewees would label themselves (PCI). A = Stormont,
B = Seaview, C = Newtownhamilton.

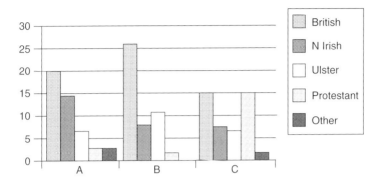

some politicians. Newtownhamilton was the most divided on the
question of identity. As we have already noted, it was the only congregation in which 'Protestant' was a popular label.

   In the DRC congregations, there was a dichotomous sense of
identity, with most respondents choosing either 'Afrikaner' or 'South
African' (see Figure 3.6). There was a parallel here between the label
'South African' and 'Northern Irish'; again, one could discern a sense
that 'South African' was seen as 'politically correct', particularly
among the Queenswood interviewees. At the same time, some of the
interviewees undoubtedly felt 'Afrikaner' had unpleasant political
connotations, owing to the formation of the Afrikaner Volksfront.
Very few interviewees described themselves as 'white', yet further
questioning on the motives behind support for the Volksfront and the
AWB suggested their underlying sense of threatened identity was in

Figure 3.6   How interviewees would label themselves (DRC). A = Queenswood,
B = Wespoort, C = Louis Trichardt.

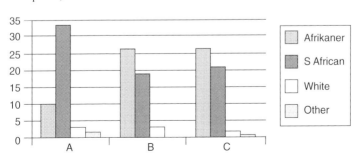

fact 'white' rather than 'Afrikaner'. This issue is explored further in the next chapter.

CONCLUSION

Thus, there was an atmosphere of fear, insecurity and alienation in each of the congregations examined in this study. There were strong parallels in the way that these feelings manifested themselves in South Africa and Northern Ireland: the sense of threat, disinterest in and disillusion with the political system, and a belief that political and social change was inevitable. In Northern Ireland, the Protestant sense of identity as expressed by Presbyterians, seemed to be fragmented. Locality clearly made a difference; until recently, this was a factor that had not been taken into account in studies on this subject with regard to Northern Ireland.[20] However, in both Northern Ireland and South Africa, there was a strong similarity in the way that negative connotations were attached to the labels 'Ulsterman/woman' and 'Afrikaner', while positive connotations were attached to 'Northern Irish' and 'South African'. In South Africa, whites retained a discursive dominance by referring to blacks in a patronising or, at the very least, paternalistic manner. In both territories, however, there was a strong feeling that the ethnic Other was different, although Protestants seemed to find it hard to articulate what exactly the differences were. This process of the constitution of identity in relation to the Other is an issue we shall explore further in the next chapter.

4 Civil Religion: Symbolic Resources and Social Change

As we have already observed, the process of the construction of identity in relation to the Other needs certain powerful symbolic elements to act as motivational building blocks. These symbols are what some sociologists and historians refer to as the symbols of 'civil religion'. We have seen how the Ulster Protestant civil religion became institutionalised in the Orange Order and how Afrikaner nationalists reinvented symbols associated with the Voortrekkers in order to build support for the Afrikaner nationalist movement in the earlier part of this century.

The symbols of civil religion have proved to be most potent during times of rapid social transition. The elite leaders who use these symbols, and the ordinary folk who are inspired by them, are motivated to some extent by material interests. The struggle for identity is interwoven with the struggle for political and economic power. This relationship can be seen very clearly in the way in which civil religion has re-emerged as a cultural and political force among both Ulster Protestants and Afrikaners. However, the struggle is not simply one between the collectivity and its external ethnic Other. There are also contests within the group over the right to use civil religion symbols and to define the meaning attached to them. This has been most evident in South Africa but it can also be seen within the Ulster Protestant community.

AFRIKANER NATIONALISM REDEFINED

In South Africa, prior to 1993, the symbols of Afrikaner civil religion had lost much of their potency. While there was still great pride in the Afrikaans language, active interest in the other aspects of Afrikaner culture appeared to be fading. However, in May 1993, as I arrived in South Africa to embark on my research, a new movement was formed which temporarily revived the motivational power of the Voortrekker symbolism which formed the centrepiece of the Afrikaner civil religion.

It will be recalled that, contrary to what one might have expected, the murder in April 1993 of the general secretary of the South African Communist Party, Chris Hani, far from stalling progress in the constitutional talks, actually added to the momentum. Once the white right wing realised this, its leaders felt they could wait no longer. They urgently needed to build a momentum for their own campaign aimed at halting the talks, or at least ensuring that they did not result in any genuine change in the balance of power between black and white. Right-wing leaders were helped by the fact that they had a willing support-base – white farmers.

Not only were farmers anxious about what was being discussed at the political talks; they had other more immediate grievances and fears. They were on their guard following a series of newspaper reports which had suggested that there was a nationwide campaign of attacks on white farmers by blacks. Their feelings had been inflamed by the leader of the ANC's youth wing, Peter Mokaba, who had led supporters in the chant 'Kill the Boer, Kill the farmer'. He subsequently claimed this was mere rhetoric and not incitement to murder. However, the damage was done. As far as many white farmers were concerned, there was a concerted campaign to get rid of them. Moreover, their pockets and their pride were being hit by legislation which extended basic employment rights to their black farm labourers.

On 7 May, there was the first visible sign of the growing anger within the farming community. Thousands of farmers converged on the Western Transvaal town of Potchefstroom for a mass rally. Many were openly sporting holstered guns on their hips, while a few even carried long hunting knives. They angrily shouted down the agriculture minister, Tobie Meyer, when he attempted to address them. 'Skiet hom!' they yelled, 'Send him home! Get rid of the traitor!'

But then, a small man dressed, like the other farmers, in an open-neck shirt and casual trousers, was called on to speak. General Constand Viljoen was a widely respected figure among whites in South Africa. He was a retired chief of the South African Defence Force who had acquired a reputation as a 'soldier's soldier'. General Viljoen told the crowd the attacks on farmers were part of the ANC's revolutionary strategy and could not be tolerated. He called for the suspension of negotiations in order to quell the violence sweeping the country. His speech was given an ecstatic reception. 'Lead us! Lead us!' the crowd shouted.

General Viljoen did indeed become the symbolic leader of this conservative, racist constituency. Two weeks later, a number of right-wing organisations and other interest groups joined together to form the Afrikaner Volksfront, its proclaimed aim to defend Afrikaner rights and to campaign for an Afrikaner *volkstaat* or homeland.[1] General Viljoen was appointed convenor of the Volksfront's directorate. The Volksfront's strategy and rhetoric were deeply reminiscent of that adopted by the Afrikaner nationalists who had brought the National Party to power in 1948. The Volksfront pledged itself to hold a series of meetings throughout South Africa to consult the volk on what they wanted. It accepted God as the 'Saviour of the Afrikaner' and it urged Afrikaners to go to church and 'pray for the Afrikaner volk in these times of crisis'.[2]

The Volksfront provided an outlet through which conservative whites could vent their frustration and fear. However, unlike many of his colleagues, General Viljoen was careful not to employ any talk of insurrection. 'I'm not for fighting' he told one journalist shortly after the Potchefstroom rally. 'I'm not available for that role – at the moment.'[3] This was in stark contrast to the right-winger who, up to that point, had achieved greatest prominence in South Africa – Eugene TerreBlanche, the notorious leader of the AWB. The AWB's members did talk of armed insurrection. Their insignia was similar to a swastika and some members even wore black uniforms with SS-style cap badges.

The difference in the approach of these two men was epitomised by an incident which shook South Africa just a month after the Volksfront had been formed. On 25 June, armed members of the AWB overran security guards and stormed into the World Trade Centre, near Johannesburg, where politicians were holding their inter-party talks. The intruders tipped soft drinks onto the carpets and urinated on desks. General Viljoen ran among them, trying unsuccessfully to restrain them but they were in no mood to listen. Their loyalty was reserved for Eugene TerreBlanche who marched triumphantly into the building's foyer to address them. Viljoen was clearly uncomfortable about the incident but, no doubt sensing he was in danger of losing his supporters, he refused to condemn the AWB's antics.

However, the Volksfront and the AWB were not the only movements harking back to the comforting notion of the volk. The

Federasie van Afrikaanse Kultuurvereninginge or Federation of Afrikaans Cultural Associations (FAK) was also attempting to mobilise support among Afrikaners. This umbrella body represented no less than 3000 groups involved in practising and promoting different aspects of Afrikaans culture, including language, music, folk dancing and drama. Observers often referred to it as the 'public face of the Broederbond', although this link was denied by its chief executive officer, Henno Cronje.[4]

In July 1993, the FAK staged a conference on the problem of poverty among Afrikaners. It claimed the problem was worse than it had been during the 1930s. At that time, the nationalist movement had held a *Volkskongres* to draw up an economic policy which could help bind together the Afrikaner cause. Originally, the FAK's conference was given the same title, but Mr Cronje said the organisers decided to change it to the 'FAK Congress on Poverty' because, whilst it was aimed primarily at Afrikaners, it was open to anyone. 'Our primary interest is in helping our own people,' Mr Cronje told me 'but we also feel the responsibility to help other communities. But we should start with our own people and we don't apologise for that.'

However, Mr Cronje's initiative had relatively little impact. While the original *Volkskongres* launched an ambitious scheme to channel Afrikaner savings into investment, the 1993 conference merely resulted in plans for a few small projects. The conference received scant attention from the media. Moreover, many of the DRC members I interviewed did not know what the FAK was. In terms of a public profile, the Volksfront and the AWB completely eclipsed this remnant of the golden days of Afrikaner nationalism.

Even if the FAK was not directly linked to the Broederbond, many of its members belonged to both. The FAK's chairperson was the late Professor Johan Heyns, who was then Vice-Moderator of the DRC and a leading member of the Bond. The ambiguity over the precise purpose of the conference was mirrored in the quest for relevance and a new identity within the Bond. During 1993, the organisation appeared to undergo an internal crisis which culminated in a decision to open up its membership and to become somewhat less secretive. Neither the FAK nor the Bond appeared to have any meaningful political role any longer, however. The 'poor whites' whom the FAK's initiative was designed to help were not interested in an organisation which trod so softly. They were far more attracted by the fighting talk of the AWB and the Volksfront.

While the FAK insisted that its initiative was a cultural and economic rather than a political one, it was clearly an unsuccessful attempt to try to stem the flow of Afrikaner support for the right-wing groups. Since 1948, the cultural organisations which the FAK represented had developed the various elements of Afrikaner culture. The history of the Afrikaner volk formed an important part of this heritage. However, this civil religion had become a collection of rather empty signifiers. A number of DRC ministers and others told me there was little genuine interest in Afrikaner culture outside well-educated circles. This was borne out by the low level of enthusiasm and involvement in such activities in the fieldwork congregations. Of the three congregations, the members of Queenswood appeared to have the greatest degree of interest; one in five of the interviewees in Queenswood was involved in at least one cultural group. However, even there, one of the ministers told me that the Afrikaner equivalent of the scouting movement, itself called the Voortrekkers, was having a problem recruiting new members and that interest in *volkspele*, Afrikaans folk-dancing, had almost died out.

Moreover, there was no great enthusiasm for the annual Day of the Vow commemorations. Only a minority of interviewees in the three DRC congregations said they regularly attended special events or services on that day. Even in Louis Trichardt, which had the highest level of active participation, the news editor of a local newspaper told me there was no longer any meaningful sense of Afrikaner culture in the area:

> There's a lot of talk [about cultural identity] ... There is a cultural identity, yes, but it's more a western-type identity rather than an Afrikaner-type identity. The difference between the Venda culture and the culture they call the Afrikaner culture is more the difference between the Venda and the American or European culture.[5]

However, Louis Trichardt was the congregation in which the strongest level of support was expressed for the Afrikaner Volksfront and the AWB. Just over half the interviewees said they supported some or all of the aims of the Volksfront. Shortly after the Volksfront was formed, it held a public meeting in Louis Trichardt which was attended by several hundred people. There appeared to be a high degree of awareness of the Volksfront and what it stood for in the town. The AWB was almost as popular; just under half the interview sample said they agreed with some or all of its objectives, and a quarter of the interviewees had attended one of its meetings.

Pieter De Wet, the farmer who shot monkeys to scare his employees, had joined both organisations. He said he believed Afrikaners must stand up for their own rights:

> Sometimes everyone seems like jellyfish – everybody's waiting for somebody else to do something. There were thousands of people at the Volksfront meeting in Louis Trichardt ... I had no faith in the future but after that meeting, I thought 'There are people standing up and prepared to speak for us.'

However, like so many Afrikaners and Ulster Protestants, Mr De Wet's comments betrayed a desire for others to bear the burden of responsibility for the political process. In common with a quarter of the interviewees in his congregation, he supported the idea of an Afrikaner *volkstaat*. I asked him if he would move all the black people who happened to live in the chosen area to make way for it. 'It's a difficult thing', he replied. 'You can't say "Here's a border" ... There are people that are busy with it [that is, drawing up plans for it]. I think there would be a bigger chance for them to think of something than me.'

The *volkstaat* concept was also supported by a quarter of the interviewees in Wespoort. While the AWB was active in Wespoort, the Volksfront appeared to have made no attempt to enlist support there. One in ten of those interviewed in the congregation had attended an AWB gathering, while just over a third expressed support for some or all of the aims of the Volksfront and/or the AWB. One local DRC social worker said the label 'Afrikaner' meant a great deal to those who had relatively little in material terms:

> To be identified as an Afrikaner – they have a future ... Individually they don't have the self-esteem to do something. In a group, they find power to do something, but not on their own ...
> Q: But they could see themselves as whites or South Africans, couldn't they?
> It sounds better. It's just that they are Afrikaners and they don't have anything else, so they live for being an Afrikaner and all these years it helped them and suddenly, it's nothing and they're sort of losing everything – their identity. That's a crisis for them. I think that's why they are so fanatic in their believing and fighting for the Afrikaner.

The label 'Afrikaner' had undoubtedly fallen by the wayside to some extent in recent years in South Africa, only to be picked up and dusted down by groups like the Volksfront and the AWB. One Wespoort interviewee explained why he would now call himself 'Afrikaner' rather than 'South African'. 'The problem is that South African symbols like the springbok and the flag have been taken away,' he told me. 'I can't relate to the idea of being a South African because there's nothing to relate to any more ... All that's left is being an Afrikaner.' 'You feel there are still Afrikaner symbols?' I asked him. 'Yes,' he replied, with pride. 'And you must leave those symbols alone. You mustn't interfere with them.'

The overall impression one gained was that the 'Afrikaner' label formed a badge of identity. The sense of that identity was strengthened by the political rhetoric of groups like the Volksfront and the AWB. However, the rhetoric of such groups seemed, to a large extent, to rely on conjuring up from the past a mythical image of the Voortrekker Boer. That image hardly related to the real situation of most Afrikaners. Indeed, closer questioning of those who voiced support for both groups suggested that, while many passionately identified with Afrikaner symbols and rhetoric, their core sense of identity centred on the fact they were whites losing power to the blacks they had dominated for so long. In other words, their underlying sense of identity was constituted in relation to the black Other by whom they felt threatened.

This core identity was articulated through the same discourse I referred to in the previous chapter; it was one which enabled them to express a desire to dominate in discourse where they could no longer continue to dominate in practice. Much of this discourse centred around the issue of 'standards' – 'good', 'decent', white standards of behaviour, education and culture which were now perceived as being threatened by the likelihood of black majority rule. This extract, from an interview with a parent in Wespoort, was fairly typical:

> For instance, in school, the coloureds are reading out of the same Bible [as whites] but the Indians read out of the Koran. What's going to happen when they are reading something out of the Bible? ... It's going to intimidate [sic] my daughter's way of life ... we let her grow up in a certain way and they'll be wanting to change it ... We've got living standards and they can't live up to our expectations ... The cultures are too wide apart.

As we saw in the previous chapter, this concern about standards was also expressed by interviewees in Queenswood. In that congregation, there was relatively little interest in and much disdain for the AWB and the Volksfront. No one had attended a meeting of either organisation and only a few people said they supported some or all of the aims of the AWB. A third of the sample said they supported some of the aims of the Volksfront, but only one person said they wholeheartedly backed its principles. This was not surprising, given that neither organisation appeared to have tried to gain support in the district. Two-thirds of the Queenswood interviewees said they would vote for the National Party, while only one in six said they would vote for either the right-wing Conservative Party or the type of right-wing groups which the Volksfront had taken under its wing. In the other two congregations, on the other hand, political allegiance was much more evenly divided between the National Party and right-wing groups.

Summary

Although many of the members of the Queenswood congregation did not identify with the Volksfront and the AWB, the use of civil religion symbols and mythology by these groups clearly inspired many Afrikaners in Wespoort and Louis Trichardt. The way in which these organisations employed civil religion struck a chord, in particular, with those whose low level of qualifications rendered them vulnerable in a situation where blacks could compete on an equal footing. It also appealed to white farmers whose livelihood often depended on the exploitation of cheap black labour. Thus, as in the 1930s, the Voortrekker symbolism and the discourse which was woven around it by right-wing groups helped to provide meaning to those whose material interests were threatened by change. However, the core sense of identity of many of those who supported the Volksfront and the AWB seemed to centre on perceiving themselves to be whites threatened by blacks. The identification with Afrikanerdom seemed to be more symbolic and rhetorical. An important aspect of this 'core' discourse lay in portraying themselves as superior to the Other, in order to dominate through discourse where they could no longer dominate in practice.

THE ORANGE ORDER

In Northern Ireland, the contest for the ability to authoritatively define and use the symbols of civil religion was played out in a rather different way. This is partly explained by the somewhat different structure of civil religion in Northern Ireland. In South Africa, the symbols and myths of Afrikaner civil religion became part of an Afrikaner culture which was assembled in the run-up to 1948. During this period, all the elements that one normally associates with an ethnic culture were established and developed. Thus, Afrikaners could boast their own language, poetry, music, folk dances, art, drama and sports, alongside a shared history and heritage. In comparison, the elements of Ulster Protestant culture appear a little thin. There was no language and no sports or folk dances which Protestants could call their own. There was also little in the way of poetry, drama or art. Those who were keen to develop a 'Protestant culture' tended to place great emphasis on a link with Scotland and its highly developed indigenous culture.

However, what Protestants did have was the Orange Order, an organisation whose activities centred around the use of ritual, traditional dress and music. To the extent that Protestants could boast of having a culture, this was its key element. There were many similarities between the Order and the Broederbond; both created an informal social network which critics saw as having the ability to wield influence in various ways. However, while the Bond carried out its business behind closed doors, the Order was a more open body which brandished its symbols and rituals with a flourish.

Thus, civil religion had developed into one, fairly monolithic, institutionalised form in Northern Ireland, whereas it was employed by a number of different groups and interests in South Africa. This meant that, in Northern Ireland, the Orange Order had a virtual monopoly on the authoritative use of civil religion symbols. There were challengers, though. Chief among these were the loyalist paramilitary groups, the Ulster Freedom Fighters (UFF) and the Ulster Volunteer Force (UVF) which rose to prominence during the Troubles. Their symbolic influence could be found in wall murals which dominated many Protestant estates.[6]

However, since the loyalist ceasefires in October 1994, attention has switched to the two political parties regarded as the 'political wings' of the paramilitary groups, the Progressive Unionist Party (PUP) and the Ulster Democratic Party (UDP). Unlike the Volksfront and the AWB in South Africa, these two parties have not employed civil religion symbols to help them win support. This does not mean that the loyalist paramilitary symbols have lost their relevance, however. For these symbols also appear on the uniforms, drums and flags used by a growing and largely autonomous offshoot of the Orange Order, the plethora of 'blood and thunder' or 'kick the Pope' marching bands which have emerged in recent years.

The sociologist Desmond Bell carried out a fascinating study of these bands and the culture surrounding them in the Protestant community in Derry.[7] He drew a distinction between the newer 'blood and thunder bands' and the more traditional bands. According to Bell, the more traditional bands take tremendous pride in their musical accomplishment. They have 'musical directors' and use arrangements which involve harmony and counterpart. 'Blood and thunder' bands, on the other hand, generally use only single-key flutes which members play in unison.[8] However, what marks out these newer bands is their aggression and their contempt for Catholics. It is the 'blood and thunder' bands which have provided a focus for many Protestant young people in working-class areas. In addition to giving these young people a sense of identity, the band practices and parades create a ready-made social life.

Most bands have no formal link with the Orange Order, although they do provide the musical accompaniment and much of the interest for Orange parades. The Orange Order has attempted, with only limited success, to curb the use that these bands have made of loyalist paramilitary regalia. What is most interesting about these bands, however, is the extent to which they have grown in popularity at a time when interest among young people in the Orange Order is declining.[9] According to Neil Jarman and Dominic Bryan, this popularity is symptomatic of a lack of respect among many loyalists for the leadership of the Orange Order, and the weakening grip of that hierarchy on its own members and supporters. What the 'blood and thunder' bands have done is to redefine the ritual and symbolism of Orange Order civil religion into a phenomenon which is far more up-front in its contempt for the Catholic Other.

Civil Religion in the Congregations

These 'blood and thunder' bands did not attract recruits from those interviewed in the three fieldwork congregations. However, elements of this contest within the broad Orange movement over the meaning attached to the ritual and symbols of the Twelfth were evident in comments made by the interviewees. Newtownhamilton was the only one of the three congregations in which a significant proportion (one third) of the interviewees were involved with the Orange Order or a related organisation. Both the female branch of the Order, the Loyal Association of Orangewomen, and the youth version, the Junior

Orange Institution, had local groups. Some local Protestants also belonged to the Royal Black Institution, which is smaller than the Orange Order but is run along very similar lines. A few interviewees were involved with a band associated with an Orange lodge, but not one they styled as 'loyalist'. Three quarters of the interviewees in Newtownhamilton said they regularly attended an Orange Order parade on the Twelfth of July. All of them had done so for more than five years. There was clearly a strong sense of continuity and tradition associated with the Twelfth, very much in line with the meaning preferred by the Orange Order hierarchy.

'It's a day when you meet a lot of people who you don't see for a year,' one Orangeman told me. 'There's a sense of tradition there that your father and your grandfather and your great-grandfather did this. There's a sense of history about it ... I don't need to put on a collarette and march about the roads to celebrate the fact I'm a Protestant. Some people think heritage means your right to walk along a street. For me, it goes back through the years. It's a family thing – when I was young I was taken along to the marches.' I asked him how important the Orange Order and the Twelfth were in terms of his sense of identity. 'It's not really important to show myself off,' he replied. 'I'm happy enough knowing myself what I am. But I do enjoy the day itself – I think a lot of people are there for the enjoyment of the day and meeting up with their friends.'

However, others defined the meaning of the Twelfth in a way which showed a strong sense of threat posed by the Catholic Other. 'It's something that we haven't worked too hard at compared to the Roman Catholics – to build up our heritage,' one woman told me. 'And I suppose that [the Twelfth] is one straw we can clasp onto ... I think Catholics all know Irish history much better than Protestants [know about their traditions and history] ... But at least the Twelfth gives you an indication [that is, a bit of a flavour] of that ...'

One woman who was involved in three organisations related to the Orange Order made a similar comment. 'The Orange Order would be my definition of a culture for Northern Ireland' she said. 'That would be what I would class as the Northern Irish culture as opposed to other cultures – the Irish culture.' I asked her how important she felt the Twelfth was to that sense of culture. 'I think it's very important. More than anything, just to uphold the Protestant faith.' was her reply. Another woman used a turn of phrase which summed up this motivation in a candid way: 'Just to keep up your end and be counted as a Protestant on the Twelfth of July.'

This 'siege mentality' and emphasis on the importance of standing up for Protestants was evident in the reason given by one teenage boy from Newtownhamilton for the fact that he and a number of his contemporaries had joined the Junior Orange Institution. 'They're worried that we're going to overruled [sic] by the Roman Catholics,' he told me. I asked him why he felt joining the Junior Orange Institution would make a difference. 'You're making the Orange Association [sic], by having more members, become more powerful, and you're letting them [Catholics] know our concern about the way things are going', he replied.

One of the congregation's elders said the Junior Orange Institution appeared to have staged a local recruiting drive and that there had been an increase in the number of young people joining the organisation. The former master of the local Orange lodge confirmed that there had been a slight increase, although he denied that there had been any concerted effort to attract younger members. He believed young people were attracted by the sporting activities offered by the Institution.

However, a young woman in her early twenties who had been in a flute band felt the reasons for joining such groups were not quite as innocent as that. While she did not think there was a real political motive behind the involvement of most young people, she felt it was a means of asserting their identity. 'I think they see themselves as real tough loyalists, as though being in a band is going to change Northern Ireland', she said. She told me this was not an attitude particularly encouraged by the band leaders. She pointed the finger at parents, asserting that, in some cases, either parents encouraged their children to think in this way or their parents' attitudes rubbed off onto them. This hardening of attitudes was then reinforced through peer group pressure.

At the same time, others were more sceptical as to the reasons for the pull of the Twelfth and the Orange Order. I asked another woman, whose husband was in the Order, what she felt was the attraction of the Order for the men. 'A night out from the house!' she replied, laughing. 'They feel they've got the Orange Order and they feel they have to support it and it is their heritage.' 'But do you think they feel passionately about what it stands for or is it more just that they've always gone along and it's tradition?' I asked:

> The woman thought for a moment. 'I don't think they feel passionate.' she replied. 'Maybe around the Twelfth but the other 364 days

of the year, no. Their blood seems to get quite high around the Twelfth and then it gets forgotten … I feel my husband is inveigled to go along to a certain extent. They ring him up and he goes along out of duty … You're kind of expected to go when you belong.

In the Seaview congregation, there was less active participation among the interviewees in either the Twelfth or the organisations associated with it. One in ten of the interviewees was involved in either the Orange Order, the Royal Black Institution or the Association of Loyal Orangewomen. None belonged to the Junior Orange Institution or to a band, although there was a local band which I was told was somewhere between the 'blood and thunder' bands which Bell observed in Derry and the more traditional bands. The Seaview minister, John Dickinson, told me a number of church members did belong to flute bands. Two fifths of the Seaview interviewees said they regularly attended a Twelfth parade. The reasons given for participating in the Twelfth echoed those made by people in Newtownhamilton.

'It's just tradition' one man said. 'I think it's important to keep it going. It lets everyone know, like, that there's still a lot of Protestant things about.' A woman who had always gone along to watch the Twelfth parade said 'You have to make an effort for everything in your life. If you didn't, things would change … You do what you've done when you're young.' One man, who was in both the Orange Order and the Royal Black Institution, had no sympathy for Catholics who felt offended by the parades: 'If Catholics are put off by it, that's their hard luck. I'm doing it to prove I feel good about myself.'

A third of the interviewees in Seaview said they had once gone along to the Twelfth parade on a regular basis but no longer made the effort. In some cases, this was due to age or ill health, but others felt the nature of the celebrations had changed. One man said 'I don't think it's worth the hassle. It's not as good as it used to be. There seem to be less and less people going.' He felt it had been much better in the old days when there had been a wider variety of bands. 'It's all flute bands these days' he said, shaking his head. I asked him why he enjoyed watching a decent Orange parade. 'I feel quite … uptight' he said, searching for the right word. 'Not from a malicious point of view. Just a bit high, you know.'

The belief that the character of the Twelfth had changed was also voiced by interviewees in Stormont. Just one interviewee belonged to an 'Orange' organisation and only a few said they regularly took part in Twelfth celebrations. As in Seaview, however, many people had stopped going. One woman explained why she no longer went along:

> It's gone political and it shouldn't be a political organisation. It's used as a platform for politicians now. When we were young, it [the Twelfth] was a day to see the bands and the Orangemen walking.

Indeed, most people in Stormont said they did not regard the Twelfth as a particularly important day and did not attach any special meaning to it. Only a quarter of the interviewees in the other two congregations shared this indifference. A small minority of respondents in these two congregations felt that the religious significance of the day was paramount. However, most people in Seaview and Newtownhamilton viewed the Twelfth primarily as 'an opportunity to celebrate one's identity and heritage as a Protestant'.[10]

Summary

Jarman and Bryan are unable to quantify the growth in the 'blood and thunder' type band. In some ways, the precise number is of limited interest. What is significant about these bands is their loud, vibrant nature which means that they tend to stand out in the parades they take part in. They have become visually prominent and, therefore, important in symbolic terms in the offence they can cause for Catholics and the aggressive, anti-Catholic stance which they signify to their followers in the Protestant community. They were also one source of antipathy for those in Stormont and Seaview who did not approve of the character of contemporary Orange parades.

Clearly, for some young people in Newtownhamilton, the appeal of the Junior Orange Institution and musical bands was not dissimilar to the pull of the 'blood and thunder' bands among teenagers witnessed by Bell in Derry. What was also evident, however, was the waning interest in the Orange Order and the Twelfth celebrations in both Belfast congregations. The Protestant civil religion, in the institutionalised form of the Orange Order, was alive in a much more meaningful way in Newtownhamilton. It is clear that in this rural congregation, there was a much greater sense of continuity than in the urban congregations and, therefore, the Order retained greater significance.

One might have expected to find those without jobs in Seaview obtaining a sense of collective identity and empowerment from the Orange Order or musical bands, much in the manner that many of the supporters of the Volksfront and AWB in Wespoort appeared to do.

Very few of the interviewees in that congregation had actually joined either a band or any of the 'loyal' orders. However, according to Revd Dickinson, many of the local members of the Orange Order did not have church connections. 'The Orange Order satisfies more of a quasi-political motivation rather than a religious motivation', he told me. 'For a lot of the people who go to it, it *is* a religion in itself.'

CIVIL RELIGION AND POLITICS: DRUMCREE

The meaning attached to the Twelfth underwent a transformation between 1995 and 1998. In 1995, the mid-Ulster town of Portadown became the focus of media attention when 300 nationalist residents staged a protest against a planned Orange parade held annually on the Sunday before the Twelfth of July. The parade was to go along the Garvaghy Road which runs alongside a nationalist estate. There had been bitter opposition to this particular parade from residents in the past. Previous residents' protests had been organised by a different group, however. On this occasion, the RUC told the Orangemen it could not guarantee their safety.

The Orangemen had been attending a church service at Drumcree Church, which is part of the second largest Protestant denomination in Northern Ireland, the Church of Ireland. The men decided to remain at the church. It was soon evident that the police were not planning to move the demonstrators or force the parade through, so the Orangemen decided they would just continue waiting. As the day wore on, their ranks swelled as supporters from all over Northern Ireland joined them. The local Ulster Unionist MP, David Trimble, had been at the service. He announced 'I am here supporting the right of Portadown District [the local Orange lodge] to march their traditional route, the route they have taken for the last 188 years.'[11] The DUP leader, Ian Paisley, also weighed in. He arrived on Sunday evening and claimed he had a mandate to negotiate with the police because he was a Northern Ireland representative in the European Parliament.

As talks continued between the RUC, the residents and the Orangemen the following day, thousands of Orangemen and their supporters gathered for a rally in Portadown. Throughout Northern Ireland, people watched with bated breath, fearing mass violence. Eventually an agreement of sorts was reached by which members of the local Orange lodge were allowed to walk the route on Tuesday morning. However, loyalists staged a show of strength elsewhere. While the rally was taking place in Portadown, Orangemen blocked major roads around the port of Larne. Police failed to remove the blockade and the Orangemen only stopped their protest once agreement had been reached over the Drumcree parade.[12]

The events surrounding what became known as the 'siege of Drumcree' were eclipsed, however, by the much more violent scenario which unfolded the following year. This time, the RUC announced it was not going to allow the Orangemen to march back along Garvaghy Road after their church service. Once more, thousands of Orangemen and their supporters gathered outside Drumcree church. Some of them pelted police lines with rocks and fireworks. Again, David Trimble, now leader of the Ulster Unionist Party, was present. He tried to negotiate with the police. Next on the scene was the head of the Orange Order and Ulster Unionist MP, Martin Smyth. Orangemen were heard to comment on the fact he had not appeared at Drumcree the previous year. However, the loudest cheer of the day was reserved for the DUP leader, Ian Paisley. He blamed both the British and Irish governments for the stand-off. 'The little children who are here today – we do not want them under the tricolour or under Dublin,' he bellowed. 'It's not going to be easy. I do not promise an easy victory this time. It was easy last year. Now we've all the power of the British government against us, aided and abetted by the skunks from Dublin. We are fighting for the promise of the life to come and that's worth fighting for and that's worth dying for.'[13]

As he spoke, loyalists swung into action across Northern Ireland, staging blockades which disrupted traffic in many places. There was fierce rioting in many areas. The tense stand-off lasted for four days. Feverish attempts were made to negotiate a compromise agreeable to both the residents and the Orangemen. However, the mediation efforts failed. To the dismay and anger of nationalists throughout Northern Ireland, the RUC finally announced that the Orangemen would be permitted to parade down Garvaghy Road.

As far as nationalists were concerned, the British government and the RUC had completely capitulated to loyalist thugs. The Irish premier, John Bruton, was forthright in his condemnation of the RUC's decision, for which he clearly felt the British government must take ultimate responsibility. 'I believe that once a government makes a decision in a democracy under the rule of law that it is going to hold a particular line, it must hold that line.' he declared. 'If governments are seen to yield to that sort of pressure, then governments will not be taken very seriously in the future.'[14]

The government's decisions on Drumcree and on another controversial parade in south Belfast raised tension and brought to the fore old wounds. During the following two weeks, there was what the *Irish News* described as a 'litany of violence and intimidation' across Northern Ireland.[15] Vandals and arsonists targeted Orange halls, Protestant gospel halls, and both Protestant and Catholic churches and schools. The public housing authority, the Northern Ireland Housing Executive, reported that there had been more than two hundred incidents of intimidation involving its tenants, with many families burnt out of their homes.

For the British government, then under the Conservatives, the handling of the parades issue had been a disaster. However, the Conservative majority in Parliament was a slim one and the government was relying on the support of unionist MPs to attract sufficient support in Parliament. All this changed when Labour came to power in May 1997. With a huge parliamentary majority, they had no need to kowtow to the unionists. The resulting shift in the balance of power between unionists and nationalists was swift and tangible. In addition to putting great pressure on the unionists to come to the talks table, the new government had no fear of parliamentary revolt from unionists in any decisions it took during the marching season. However, it did have to contend with the possibility of widespread violence and the ability of its security forces to contain that violence.

The new Northern Ireland Secretary, Mo Mowlam, certainly made every effort to achieve compromises on the 1997 Drumcree parade. She personally talked to both sides and, at times, appeared on the verge of achieving agreement. Yet, it was not to be. It was left to the RUC to make a decision. At the last minute, the Chief Constable announced that the parade would be allowed to go ahead. Nationalists were furious; they had expected the government and the RUC to call the loyalists' bluff. Rioting erupted in Portadown and several other towns. However, on this occasion, the Orange Order did make vital concessions on other parades through nationalist areas. The threat of an escalation of violence had hung like a black cloud over Northern Ireland following the Drumcree decision. The Orange Order's subsequent concessions ensured that that threat evaporated.

The decision also meant that the Orange Order won praise from elite members of the Protestant community for its 'responsible' stance. Lord Alderdice, then leader of the Alliance Party, said 'I think it has to be said that these decisions required real courage and maturity on the part of Orange leaders.' The Presbyterian Moderator, Samuel Hutchinson, said 'I warmly welcome this decision to waive their right to parade in certain areas.'[16]

However, the following year, 1998, the Order was being condemned as extremely irresponsible by leading members of the Protestant community. This time, Drumcree was played out against the backdrop of successful political negotiations which had resulted in the Northern Ireland Agreement. This historic document set out the framework for a new Northern Ireland Assembly which would have executive responsibility for most areas of government. There was considerable unionist unease over the Agreement. Many were deeply unhappy at the prospect of unionist leaders sitting round a table with Sinn Fein in government, and at the powers accorded to an inter-governmental North–South body. While a majority of voters in Northern Ireland gave their backing to the Agreement in a referendum in May, the results of the first Assembly election in June suggested that the number of unionists who opposed the Agreement was greater than the number who supported it.[17] During the election campaign, the UUP's party leader, David Trimble, remained firmly behind the Agreement. Although there was some speculation that his deputy, John Taylor, might take the post, Trimble was set to take on the pivotal role of First Minister of the new Assembly; effectively, he would be the leader of the new government. Following the election, Trimble did indeed take the job and was immediately faced with the challenge of dealing with the annual Drumcree controversy.

On this occasion, the decision as to whether the parade should be allowed to proceed down the Garvaghy Road lay in the hands of the British-government-appointed Parades Commission. The British government insisted the Commission was independent, but it is hard to believe that the Commission did not listen very carefully to the views of government ministers before it pronounced on Drumcree. Its decision was a reversal of that of the previous year – the parade would not be allowed to go down the Garvaghy Road. This time it was clear that the government intended to stand firmly by the ruling. As in 1996, a huge crowd of protesters gathered by Drumcree Church while loyalists staged road-blocks and petrol-bombed Catholic homes in many parts of Northern Ireland. As before, Paisley quickly arrived on the scene to provide his highly visible and vocal support. However, this time, David Trimble stayed away.

When the decision to ban the parade was taken by the Parades Commission, Trimble had condemned it as a 'massive assault on the civil rights of an important sector of the community in Northern Ireland'.[18] However, once the Orangemen had begun their protest, the First Minister concentrated on efforts to reach a compromise that might suit both the marchers and nationalist residents. Publicly, he retained a united front with his SDLP deputy minister, Seamus Mallon. Both said a solution must be found. Yet, with a refusal by the Orangemen to talk to the residents and no public sign of any mood for compromise on the part of the residents, there appeared to be no room for manoeuvre.

Then, in the early hours of Sunday 12 July, the people of Northern Ireland woke to hear that three boys had been killed in a petrol-bombing which police said was undoubtedly sectarian in its motive. Richard, Mark and Jason Quinn had a Catholic mother and it seemed clear that loyalists were the culprits, although some Orangemen tried to suggest otherwise. Reaction from the Protestant community was swift. Crucial was the reaction of church leaders which is examined in greater detail in the next chapter. A key role was played by Revd William Bingham, a Presbyterian clergyman and the Orange Order's Deputy Grand Chaplain. He invited television cameras into his church service that morning to tell the world that the Orangemen should abandon their protest. His call was followed by a similar joint plea from David Trimble and Seamus Mallon. It fell on deaf ears and the protest continued. However, the number of Orangemen and support-ers at Drumcree rapidly dwindled and loyalist violence elsewhere quickly subsided.

The transformation in the stance of David Trimble from champion of the Drumcree Orangemen to dispassionate government leader and arbitrator is remarkable but hardly unusual in politics. In 1995, Trimble needed to convince hardliners in his party that he would be a tough defender of the unionist cause if he was to win the party's lead-ership contest; his appearance at Drumcree that year clearly helped him achieve that aim. In 1998, he had been bestowed with the leading role in the new Assembly; if he did not distance himself from the actions of the Drumcree Orangemen, the fledgling government insti-tution might have fallen apart even before it got off the ground. In effect, one can argue that Drumcree '98 enabled Trimble to establish his credentials as a politician capable of leading a cross-community government.

CONCLUSION

In some ways, it can be argued that the Orange Order's parades enabled Protestants to play out symbolically the dominance they no longer actually possessed in practice; just as one can continue to dominate in discourse when one can no longer do so in practice, so one can continue to live out a fantasy of dominance through symbolic ritual. Indeed, Gellner has suggested that constitutional monarchy works as 'ritual theatre' in this way because it 'contributes to social stability by not endowing temporary and technical centres of power with any sacred aura, and not imperilling them by linking their legitimacy to doctrines which may be proved false tomorrow. This disconnectedness seems to work rather well.'[19] Gellner argues that this 'ritual theatre' re-enacts the previous power structure, prior to the establishment of secular authority.

On the face of it, it would seem one could apply this analysis to the Orange Order parades. However, what Drumcree illustrated was the way in which the symbolic and the 'real' interweave. The response to Drumcree and other controversial parades by the British government, the RUC and the Parades Commission became a gauge of the *real* balance of power between unionists and nationalists, as perceived by both sides. While Orangemen had been able to parade unhindered, despite nationalist protests, unionists could take comfort in a symbolic balance of power that had not changed and thus had an aura of 'reality'. Once the government withdrew its recognition of this unqualified right to march, regardless of nationalist feeling, the shift in the balance of power between unionists and nationalists was exposed.

Thus, in the case of Northern Ireland, there was no sharp demarcation between the ritual (or civil religious) and the political spheres; the state's decisions on civil religion ritual had real consequences and were defined by nationalists and unionists as a measure of the 'real' balance of power between each community. As that balance of power shifted, so did the nature of the relationship between civil religion and unionist politicians. The latter were able to come to the aid of the Orange Order and what it saw as its right to march in certain areas. However, in so doing, those politicians hoped to maintain or increase their political support; civil religion was a resource on which they could draw. Yet, while David Trimble had used it to help him gain his party's leadership in 1995, civil religion was used by him in quite another way three years later. Now, it became a means by which he could demonstrate his fitness for government leadership by distancing himself from the actions of the Orange Order. This is not to suggest that he was entirely cynical in his motives. Rather, the deaths of the three Quinn boys undoubtedly led many Protestants to reassess their view of the Order. By calling on the Orangemen to abandon their protest in the wake of those murders, Trimble was drawing a firm line between himself and the Orange protesters he had once supported so enthusiastically. In this sense, civil religion still provided a symbolic resource but this time Trimble was employing it to define what he was not, rather than what he was.

The convergence between the 'real' and the 'symbolic' could also be seen in South Africa as social and political change took place. Once Nelson Mandela came to power, he was careful to give the appearance of seriously considering the right-wing Afrikaner demand for a *volkstaat*, a symbolic dream which eventually faded away as Mandela surely knew that it would. He took care to bring Constand Viljoen, the leader of the Afrikaner Volksfront, into his government. His government also kept the Day of the Vow as a public holiday but renamed it the 'Day of Reconciliation', an example of giving a new inclusive meaning to an occasion which had symbolised white dominance.

In the tense period which this study covers, one can see certain common themes emerging in the way in which civil religion symbols were utilised in both Northern Ireland and South Africa. They clearly provided a sense of continuity and a sense of collective self-esteem for many Afrikaners and Ulster Protestants. At the same time, there were contests for *definitional authority* over the meaning attached to these symbols. In South Africa, the FAK failed in its attempt to activate support by drawing on civil religion rhetoric to rerun the mobilisation of Afrikaner nationalism which had taken place in the 1930s. Afrikaners were far more attracted to the tough language of the Volksfront and the AWB. In Northern Ireland, the Orange Order's definitional authority over civil religion was challenged by 'kick the Pope' bands and loyalist paramilitaries. However, while some Afrikaners and Ulster Protestants were motivated by the fiery language and behaviour of the 'militant' groupings, others were alienated by it and viewed such groups as the Other within their own ethnic collectivity.

There is one important difference between Afrikaner and Ulster Protestant civil religion. This lies in the degree of institutionalisation of the symbols and ritual. The Orange Order has a 200-year history and claims to have some 100000 members, although the actual number is thought to have fallen to nearer 40000.[20] Nevertheless, it remains much more embedded into Ulster Protestant culture as an institution than is any aspect of Afrikaner civil religion among Afrikaners. This helps to explain why there was no confrontation between Afrikaner civil religion and the state in South Africa which quite parallels the scale of events at Drumcree during the mid-1990s. The embedded nature of the institutionalisation of civil religion in Northern Ireland also made it more difficult for the Presbyterian Church to loosen its symbolic links with the Order, a dilemma which is explored in the next chapter.

5 The Church as *Volkskerk*: A Church of 'The People' or a Church for All?

The previous chapter has illustrated the ability of the symbols, rituals and institutions of civil religion to move people in a way not dissimilar from 'religion' in the more conventional sense. Denominational religion and civil religion are not disconnected; links between the two are often to the benefit of both. However, this relationship can sometimes pose a dilemma for church leaders. This chapter examines the nature of this relationship with regard to both the DRC and the PCI.

THE PCI AND THE ORANGE ORDER

If Drumcree posed an enormous dilemma for the British government, it also provided some awkward questions for the main Protestant churches. For the Orangemen were attempting to parade along the Garvaghy Road on their way back from a service at a Church of Ireland church. This quiet, country church suddenly formed the backdrop for a series of bitter confrontations that went right to the heart of the Northern Ireland conflict. The irony of this was not picked up initially by the media, but it was highlighted by a prominent Church of Ireland clergyman who accused his denomination of ducking very serious questions. Canon William Arlow, who had been a prime mover in negotiating an IRA ceasefire in the 1970s and was a former Secretary of the Irish Council of Churches, pulled no punches in a scathing article in the *Irish Times* in the aftermath of the confrontation at Drumcree in 1996:

> I could not believe what I was seeing. I always thought a church was a symbol of reconciliation, but here it was undoubtedly a symbol of insurrection. The church ... is now a familiar sight on our television screens. There, angry Orangemen confronted the police and mob rule won the day ...

It would not have happened if the Church of Ireland had learned the lesson of Drumcree 1995 and made it clear to the Orangemen that they would not be welcome at the church unless an undertaking were given that their parade to and from it would be kept within the law.

Such a courageous stand was not made and Drumcree church, with its barbed wire fence and mobs in conflict with the police, became a centre for insurrection ...

What happened at Drumcree raises important questions for the Church of Ireland, and, not least, for its role in promoting reconciliation between a divided community in Northern Ireland. Drumcree cannot be described as a symbol of reconciliation and so it calls into question the credibility of that role. Drumcree has now come to be perceived as a symbol of the Church of Ireland, at least the part of it which is in Northern Ireland.

It is a symbol of a church which seems to be an adjunct of a particular political party that is too preoccupied with reflecting the political views of the majority of its members [i.e., the Ulster Unionist Party], that is clearly identified with an organisation regarded by many Protestants and most Roman Catholics as sectarian and divisive [i.e., the Orange Order] and that it bends over backwards to be supportive of those who willingly use force to achieve their political goal.[1]

During the annual marching season, the Orange Order holds services at many Church of Ireland and Presbyterian churches. These generally take place on Sunday afternoons and involve a parade from the local Orange hall to the appropriate church prior to the service. Normally, they do not attract a great deal of attention, partly because there are only one or two bands present and the parade is not as colourful as a Twelfth demonstration. Nevertheless, there is a symbolic significance attached to these parades which is highlighted by Drumcree.

The involvement of the church is a matter of pride and of great importance for the Orange Order, as a leading article in the July 1997 edition of the Orange Order's own newspaper makes clear:

The Orangemen are attending a service of divine worship in Drumcree Parish Church – a service which goes back 190 years. That must not be forgotten, and it cannot be ignored that this is a religious service in a place of worship.

Orangemen show great respect and diligence in their attendance at divine worship, and they certainly do not walk the roads of Ulster on the Sabbath to cause offence or provide provocation for anyone. Amid all the welter and huge amount of publicity centred around the Drumcree parade, this fact is often overlooked.[2]

In order to counter the bad publicity about the unruly behaviour of many of its supporters at Drumcree and elsewhere, the involvement of the church was a crucial means by which the Orange Order could attempt to construct a dignified image, one which was morally superior to what, in Orange eyes, were those troublesome nationalists who chose to protest against its parades. The visual representation of this link with the Protestant churches forms a prominent part of Orange parades. One study carried out between 1990 and 1996 found that 16 per cent of banners carried in such parades portrayed a church.[3]

To be fair to the Order, the religious self-image is one which many Orangemen genuinely believe in. The Order lays great stress on the fact that it is an avowedly religious organisation representing the 'Protestant Reformed' faith in a broad sense. However, the moral dilemma posed by Canon Arlow cannot be ignored. By allowing its churches to be used by the Order, both the PCI and the Church of Ireland were enhancing the credibility of the Order. They were investing it with a version of 'religious capital'; in other words, a status which stemmed from being given a 'stamp of approval' by the churches.[4]

The extent of this link can be seen by examining the results from a postal survey of PCI clergy and active laity which was conducted as part of the study on which this book is based.[5] Three-quarters of the ministers said their churches were used for Orange Order services. A third said their churches provided the venue for such services at least once a year. 72 per cent of the ministers said they also preached at these services, although most said they only did so on an occasional basis. Both these practices were more common in rural than in urban congregations.[6]

The decision as to whether a particular church is used for Orange Order services is taken by its kirk session, the ruling body of the congregation. Ministers decide themselves whether they wish to preach at such services. Some of those who do are equivocal about their role. One rural minister told me he felt it sent out the wrong message to Catholics. However, he still preached at such services if he was asked and if they were held in his own church:

It gives me an opportunity to address some issues that I think Orangemen need to hear – not condemning the Orange Institution

[Orange Order] as an institution as anti-Catholic, but encouraging individual Orangemen to look at their spiritual roots. A lot of men belong to the Orange Institution for no spiritual reason whatsoever, and yet the Orange Institution would tell you that it had a spiritual reason for existing.

This particular clergyman was deeply troubled by the fact that his congregation could not afford its own church hall and so had to make use of the local Orange hall for certain church functions:

> The Orange hall is seen by some in much the same light as the Orange organisation as a whole. Therefore, if I am associated with the Orange hall, even to the extent of using it as a venue for some of my meetings, then it's sending out messages to folk that I don't want sent out.

Indeed, data from the postal survey revealed that almost one in ten ministers presided over congregations which made similar arrangements. Nearly all the relevant clergymen were from rural congregations.

Of the ministers in the three PCI fieldwork congregations, only John Dickinson of Seaview was a member of the Orange Order and preached at its services. Although he said he did not play an active role in the Order, he was also one of approximately 35 Presbyterian clergymen who were entitled to attend meetings of the Order's 300-strong Grand Lodge of Ireland, the organisation's highest body.[7] Revd Dickinson said he joined the Order when he was ministering to a rural congregation in Killyleagh in County Down. He still went back to this congregation to preach at Orange Order services. He said he had originally joined the Order so that he could be more fully involved in the life of the community:

> Just through getting to befriend people, to become parish minister and get involved in family life and the life of the community, it seemed the logical thing to do ....
>
> Q: Some people would say ministers shouldn't preach at Orange Order services, that it's getting too much into the political realm. What would you say to that?
>
> I'd say there's a certain justification for that argument. Obviously, by being an Orangeman, to some extent, it may mean there are people to whom your ministry will cease to be of any value ... But there's another set of factors which says that, to a certain group of people, you can be a more effective minister. And, in the communi-

ties in which I've been called to work – first of all, in Killyleagh, and now in Seaview, membership of the Orange Order to me is probably a positive advantage.

Q: What about the fact that many Catholics regard it as offensive?

I understand that too and I understand why they feel it to be offensive. And, therefore, Roman Catholics are probably the one group of people who'd make it very difficult for me to be an effective minister to, and I have to accept that to a degree …

Q: But you feel that's their problem rather than yours?

No, it's partly my problem and it is a dilemma of mine with which I constantly wrestle. But it's a feature of the cultural life of my community and I don't see that you should need to deny it to be a Christian. I mean, at the end of the day, I've got to say to my Roman Catholic fellow countrymen, 'Don't judge me on the basis of being an Orangeman, judge me on the basis on which I live with you as a person.'

Revd Maurice Wade of Newtownhamilton had been a member of the Orange Order but had left. He explained why:

I left when I became a Christian [i.e., was 'born again'] because I don't think it's the Orange Order's job to defend the faith. I believe that's the church's work … And, secondly, I felt that, in a Christian life, that membership of the Orange Order would be a hindrance rather than a help, because it's baggage that you don't need. As you gather, most Roman Catholic folk would see all Protestants as Orangemen – that was a decisive point for me.

Revd Wade also told me why he had turned down requests to preach at the biannual Orange Order services at his church. 'Because I'm not a member of the Order and because I'm not overly sympathetic towards it,' he said. 'And I feel that that would be seen as identification or giving some sort of help or encouragement … I'm not asked now because it's known that I wouldn't and I don't go to it.'

I asked him whether he was happy about his church being used for such services. He thought for a moment before answering. 'I'm not personally overly happy, if I'm honest. I have to be honest and say I've never raised the issue at kirk session,' he said. I asked him why he had not. 'Well, when a minister comes into a church, you've got to try to decide which issues are the most important to deal with and which are less important,' he replied. 'I'm perhaps side-stepping the issue by saying that, to this point, I don't feel it's one I should personally pursue.'

Revd Wade also pointed out that the minister does not have a veto on the purpose for which church buildings are used. However, while Revd Wade had put pragmatism before principle on this particular issue, he had alluded to the Orange Order in a recent sermon. In it, he said that it was the church and not the paramilitaries or the Order which was the 'custodian and defender of the faith'. I asked him what reaction he had had at the time. He smiled before answering. 'Nobody actually came and spoke to me on that particular issue,' he said. 'But sometimes you get a feeling that maybe certain people aren't happy with it, although they may not actually say.'

Neither of the Stormont ministers was a member of the Orange Order. The Order had never asked to hold services at the church, so the issue had not arisen. Stormont was the only one of the three congregations in which a large proportion of interviewees felt that ministers should not belong to the Orange Order. While only a few interviewees in Newtownhamilton and Seaview took this view, almost two-fifths of the Stormont sample said ministers should not be members.

A minister who was a former Moderator and a senior figure in the Orange Order, the late Dr Robert Dickinson (who was, in fact, the father of John Dickinson), clearly believed that Orangemen could use their influence within the Protestant churches to oppose efforts at ecumenism. He wrote the following plea in an article in the *Orange Standard* in March 1990:

> It would seem right and proper ... that in a time when rampant ecumenism is making ever more subtle and sinister efforts to foster the unity of Protestant churches with Romanism under the primacy of the Pope, those members of our Institution [the Orange Order] should use their best endeavours to expose and defeat such efforts at the local level in their own churches and denominations. The onslaught of Rome was never more virulent than in these days. For evil to prosper it is necessary only for good men to do nothing.[8]

If his words have been heeded anywhere by Orangemen, they are more likely to have acted on them in rural congregations. The lay members who took part in the postal survey conducted for this study all held the post of Clerk of Session, the most influential lay role within a kirk session. 17 (27 per cent) of the PCI session clerks who responded to the postal survey said they belonged to the Orange Order. All but one of them were from rural congregations. 15 said they would not be happy to attend joint services with Catholics. They were also more negative than the sample as a whole over the question of church involvement in cross-community efforts.

One former PCI minister has spoken publicly about the opposition he faced to his friendship with a local priest. Revd David Armstrong eventually left the County Derry town of Limavady, unable to withstand the pressure being put on him. He points the finger at local members of the Orange Order and contends that many clergymen give in to a 'softly softly' approach used by Orangemen to stop ecumenical and cross-community efforts from taking place:

> You see they're not people who come as blunt, wicked, evil people. They come with sweet reasonableness. They come as people who work very hard for their church ... So, the temptation for any clergyman, therefore, is even greater to listen to them and not to disappoint them.[9]

During the course of my research, I spoke at some length to several rural ministers. One alleged that local Orangemen had whipped up opposition to a scheme for cross-community contact in his area, and had persuaded another Presbyterian minister to take their side by putting him under the sort of pressure described by David Armstrong. However, none of the other clergymen I spoke to felt under any sort of pressure from church elders who also belonged to the Orange Order. As we shall see in the next chapter, this may well have been because, in practice, it would seem that ministers often have more autonomy than the organisational structure of the Church would suggest.

There are signs that both the Church of Ireland and the Presbyterian Church are beginning to loosen the link between their denominations and the Orange Order. On Sunday 6 July 1997, the Church of Ireland Primate, Archbishop Dr Robin Eames, sent a message which was read out to Orangemen during their annual service at Drumcree Parish Church. It urged the men

> to act with dignity, restraint and honour when they leave the parish church. On no account should they respond to any situation in ways which will increase the apprehensions of the Province, increase the problems of the police or attempt to make use of church property in ways which will question the integrity of the Church.

Two days earlier, the Presbyterian Moderator, Dr Sam Hutchinson, had issued a statement on the situation. It was addressed to both sides in the controversy, entreating the Orangemen to consider waiving their right to march while at the same time asking local residents to consider waiving their right to protest. 'I would see such a gesture as a temporary respite and also as a responsible and positive step towards beginning a new dimension of bridge building', he said.[10]

In 1996, a special subcommittee of the PCI's Church and Government Committee had produced a report on parades. While it did not address the issue of the link between the Church and the Orange Order, it did urge both those who wanted to parade and those who were opposed to certain parades to listen to each other and to treat each other with respect.[11] The following year, this Committee gave a broad welcome to a special report commissioned by the government on the issue of parading. The Committee supported, with some reservations, the recommendation of the Independent Review of Parades and Marches that a new body be set up to adjudicate on controversial parades.[12] Thus, the Church was anxious to show that it had views on the issue of parading which were independent of the Orange Order. Nevertheless, at the time of writing, it has not turned the spotlight on its own symbolic but significant connection with the Order.

The tragic deaths of the three Quinn brothers amid loyalist protests over the ban on the Orangemen's parade down Garvaghy Road in 1998 may bring a more fundamental reassessment within both the Presbyterian Church and the Church of Ireland. Dr Eames urged the protesters at Drumcree to return home. 'The Church of Ireland is not going to condone the violence, it's not going to condone the confrontation. And as far as I am concerned, I totally distance the Church of Ireland from what's going on.'[13] That year's Presbyterian Moderator, Dr John Dixon, urged 'those who are in disagreement to step back, think clearly and courageously and compassionately to resolve the impasse that threatens to engulf us all'.[14]

However, the Presbyterian cleric who received greatest public attention in the wake of the Quinn murders was Revd William Bingham, a Deputy Grand Chaplain of the Orange Order and County Grand Chaplain of Armagh. He invited television cameras into his Sunday morning service just hours after the deaths, so the world could hear what he had to tell his congregation. He said he was not ashamed to say that he had wept when he heard of the murders. 'I believe wholeheartedly in the principles of Orangeism', he continued. 'I believe in the civil and religious liberties of everyone. I believe in the right of Orangemen to walk. But I have to say this. That after last night's atrocious act, a fifteen-minute walk down Garvaghy Road by the Orange Order would be a very hollow victory.'[15] Like Archbishop Eames, he called on the Order to abandon its protest. Two days later, a group of senior Orange Order chaplains issued a statement backing Revd Bingham's call.[16] Indeed, three chaplains reportedly resigned from the Order and others were said to be considering their positions.[17]

At the same time, the Church of Ireland came under pressure from within its ranks to distance itself from the Order in a much more decisive way. Speaking shortly after the deaths of the Quinn brothers, the Church of Ireland Dean of Christ Church Cathedral, Dublin, the Very Revd John Paterson, said that the churches had 'a lot to answer for the situation in which we find ourselves. The Church of Ireland says it has no links with the Orange Order. That's only a sort of half-truth we should be ashamed to make'.[18] A fortnight later, a group of Church of Ireland clergy and laity wrote an open letter to Dr Eames in which they asked that bishops should be given the authority to postpone, cancel, or change the venue of a service where there was the likelihood of civil disturbances during parades.[19]

THE DRC AND CIVIL RELIGION

In South Africa, a similar symbolically significant relationship between church and civil religion could be seen in the extent of participation by DRC clergymen in the Day of the Vow celebrations, which commemorated a white victory over Zulus and was an event resented by many blacks. Just over three-quarters of the ministers who took part in the postal survey said they preached at such events. However, as we have noted, the evidence from the fieldwork interviews suggested that interest in this commemoration was declining. Just as some of the PCI interviewees saw the Orange Order as having acquired 'political' overtones, so some of the DRC members claimed that Day of the Vow commemorations were often becoming events organised or used by right-wing politicians to gain support for their brand of politics.

In South Africa, there had been a close and extremely controversial relationship between the DRC and the secretive Broederbond. One writer worked hard to uncover the nature and extent of this relationship. In a book which was highly critical of this link, J. H. P. Serfontein alleged that, in the mid-1970s, nearly half of all DRC ministers belonged to the Bond, and that Bond members occupied almost all the most important posts in the Church:

> The church is totally and absolutely controlled by it [the Bond], in ideology, in practice and in decision-making – regardless of what happens in other spheres of society.[20]

He also claimed that the Bond had an insidious influence at local level:

> The senior elders in most church councils are Broeders. A few key men are sufficient to control a whole council and make life unbearable should their minister stray from the Broeder vision of Afrikanerdom.[21]

While the DRC has never accepted that the Bond wielded the kind of influence suggested by Serfontein, it did partially address the issue in 1986 when the General Synod called on the Bond to become a more open organisation. Subsequently, a number of ministers did choose to resign from the Bond.[22] A prominent DRC clergyman and member of the Bond's Executive, Professor Flip van der Watt, confirmed to me that about 60 per cent of DRC ministers had been Bond members in the early 1980s. He estimated that the proportion had fallen to between 30 per cent and 40 per cent by 1993. He admitted that about half the members of the Moderamen (Executives) of the General and Regional Synods were still Bond members, and that nearly all of them would have been at one time. However, he was adamant that the Bond had never exercised any decisive influence over the DRC: 'In the 26 years I've been a member of the Broederbond,' he told me 'there's never been any decision by the Bond to tell the Church "You have to do this".'

Not everyone I spoke to in the Church shared this view. However, they did generally agree that the Bond's influence had greatly waned. Professor Pieter Meiring, the Church's Director of Ecumenical Affairs and Information in 1993, told me he had never joined the Bond as a matter of principle. At one time, he had felt a little 'out in the cold' but not these days:

> The Broederbond used to have a large amount of influence in the Church. Many ministers belonged to it ... I think the Broederbond, with its meetings and discussions, did influence many things in the Church. In the election of senior officials in the Church, it was impossible not to ask whether the Broederbond had had a hand ... I

think it still has some influence. The discussions they have and the documents they draw up have influence in the church. But I don't think the influence of the Broederbond is that large at the moment. If they come out into the open or decide to disband, I don't think it will have a very large influence in the Church.

Indeed, in late 1993, the Bond did take some steps to try to become a more 'open' organisation and to shake off its reputation as one of the chief pillars of apartheid. The dilemma posed by the past associations of the DRC, the Bond and apartheid were epitomised in the highly symbolic resignation from the Bond of the Moderator of the DRC, Professor Pieter Potgieter. He revealed that he had recently left the Bond when he was interviewed as a candidate for the newly consti-tuted Board of the South African Broadcasting Company (SABC) in May 1993. The SABC had formerly been seen as another pillar of apartheid and had established a new Board to implement radical changes in line with the political changes on the horizon. It would have been highly embarrassing to have had a prominent member of the Bond on the new executive.

The news was welcomed by the 'black' and 'coloured' sister Dutch Reformed Churches which had criticised the close relationship between the DRC and the Bond. Professor Potgeiter was adamant that he had not resigned because of his candidature for the SABC Board and that criticism from the DRC's sister churches had only been one factor in his decision.[23] Nevertheless, it was a timely move which seemed designed to send out a signal both to members of his own Church and to the Church's critics.

However, the DRC's then Vice-Moderator, the late Professor Johan Heyns, retained his membership of the Bond. He was inter-viewed about his membership by the DRC's newspaper, *Die Kerkbode*, which had carried several letters from members who opposed minis-ters belonging to the Bond. Like Professor Potgieter, Professor Heyns denied that the Bond had any influence on decisions taken within the Church. He said it was a 'cultural' rather than 'political' organisation which 'wishes to serve the cultural life of the Afrikaner nation.'[24]

This echoes the emphasis which the Orange Order prefers to place on its activities; publications which attempt to explain the Order to non-members stress its cultural and religious aspects rather than its political features.[25] However, the events at Drumcree and the many stories of the Bond's previous influence in South Africa demonstrate that one cannot separate these spheres. The 'religious' and the 'cultural' *are* political because politics is about the way we organise society and that includes its religious and cultural life.

SPEAKING OUT

The fact that the religious, the cultural and the political cannot be separated is starkly illustrated by another problem both churches have wrestled with – the question of whether a denomination should put the political and ethnic interests of its own members before those of other groups. As we have seen, the DRC was at one time quite proud to be a *volkskerk* for its own people. It is evident that the Presbyterian Church adopted a similar role in Northern Ireland in the earlier part of the century over the issues of Home Rule and education. More recently, however, both churches have made it clear that they do not believe they should have a *volkskerk* role.

In the early 1990s, both churches came under pressure to adopt this type of role from organisations which used the symbols of civil religion. In South Africa, General Constand Viljoen met senior members of the DRC in June 1993, to urge them to help make the government understand 'the Afrikaner's case is not unjust' and that 'time should be given for the Afrikaner to argue in favour of his self-determination in a suitable manner.'[26] A week after this meeting, the AWB captured worldwide publicity with its invasion of the World Trade Centre. The action was condemned by an editorial in *Die Kerkbode*. However, the editorial did express some sympathy with the aims of the right-wingers, in telling its readers that

> there is a close connection between the Afrikaner nation and this Church. The right to love one's own nation and one's own cultural values is recognised [by the Church]. *Die Kerkbode* wants to state clearly that it has sympathy and understanding for the freedom ideal of the Afrikaner, an ideal which has come a long way …
>
> … it would be very unwise of Kempton Park's negotiators [i.e. the political negotiators at the World Trade Centre] not to pay attention to the demands of certain nations and groups in the country to govern themselves (or largely govern themselves). And, we want to add, it would be very unwise of those nations to put forward non-negotiable demands which do not take the past century's history into account and do not understand that 'negotiate' has become the byword, not 'demand'.[27]

However, *Die Kerkbode* was more strident on another issue on which the Volksfront was campaigning. There was much speculation during the World Trade Centre talks that Afrikaans would no longer be the official language under the new government. Afrikaans was hated by many black South Africans, who associated it with the many years of oppression they had suffered under apartheid. Another editorial in *Die Kerkbode* noted with alarm that one recent debate during the constitutional talks had been conducted entirely in English:

> English is in front and Afrikaans apologetically takes a place at the back … and whoever speaks Afrikaans in public places in our big cities gets a condescending glance. Just try flying with SAA [South African Airways] or any of our other airlines – the passenger has to prove that he is Afrikaans, or else the flight personnel simply assume that he is English …
>
> For the Dutch Reformed Church, the preservation of the language which most of its members speak is, therefore, an important issue. And the church should also raise its voice if this language is threatened or neglected.
>
> While we accept that there should be other official languages alongside Afrikaans and English in South Africa, and we do not want to promote Afrikaans at the expense of other languages, we say that a language spoken and understood by more people than English is, should not give up its place for the benefit of English. And, whoever thinks that Afrikaans should be punished as the language of the oppressor, should think deeply about why it should be replaced by the language of the former colonial oppressor.[28]

In highlighting this issue, *Die Kerkbode* had hit on something which went right to the heart of the Afrikaner sense of identity. Many interviewees in the fieldwork congregations expressed their fears about the imminent demise of their language. Some spoke bitterly about the colonial attitudes of the British towards the Boers in the earlier part of the century, a collective memory which clearly still resonated deeply with Afrikaners. There was a strange mixture of shame and pride surrounding the language. I noticed that Afrikaans-speakers nearly always switched to English in the presence of an English-speaker such as myself and that many clearly enjoyed demonstrating their articulacy in that language. However, there did seem to be an underlying assumption that English was more sophisticated, an attitude adhered to by most English-speakers. Many English-speaking whites in Johannesburg looked down with disdain on their Afrikaner neighbours in Pretoria as relics of a bygone age. It certainly seemed that, in some middle-class circles where English- and Afrikaans-speakers mixed, the latter were trying to fit in with the values of 'the former colonial oppressor'.

Die Kerkbode also reminded its readers that the Church had played a major part in encouraging the use of Afrikaans through the publication of an Afrikaans bible in 1933. The language question was one of a number of issues which Church leaders raised with F. W. De Klerk when he met them a few weeks later. They also spoke to him about the desire among some Afrikaners for self-determination. However, there were no front page headlines such as 'DRC castigates government'. Moreover, the meeting formed part of a series that the Church was carrying out at the time with a range of political leaders. Earlier that year, in April 1993, Church leaders had met Nelson Mandela. Mandela had requested the meeting which was arranged by Beyers Naudé, the clergyman who had been demonised by the DRC in the 1970s.

At that meeting, which lasted almost three hours, the DRC representatives raised two other issues with Mandela. One was Peter Mokaba's 'Kill the Boer, Kill the farmer' cry. Mandela assured them that this did not represent the policy of the ANC. The other was the link between the ANC and the South African Communist Party, an organisation loathed by many in the Church who had been raised on a fiercely anti-communist ideology. Mandela explained that many blacks did not see an incompatibility between Christianity and communism and that they could not understand how whites could reconcile Christianity and apartheid.

These meetings suited the style of the DRC leadership which had always preferred to lobby discreetly, rather than seeking publicity on particular issues. Results from a postal survey of ministers and active laity in the Northern Transvaal region suggested that there was little appetite for a more trenchant role on the part of the DRC; only 11 per cent of the ministers and 36 per cent of the lay members surveyed agreed with the statement: 'The Dutch Reformed Church should give priority to speaking out in defence of (that is, to help protect) Afrikaner interests.'[29] Among the fieldwork congregations, the only congregation which showed a marked enthusiasm for this statement was Wespoort, where 58 per cent of those interviewed favoured such a role.

However, there was much greater support for this type of stance among laity within the PCI. Both postal survey and fieldwork respondents were asked for their reaction to the following statement:

> The Presbyterian Church should give priority to speaking out in defence of Protestant interests (e.g. in terms of Protestant political rights and in terms of the right to fair treatment for Protestants with respect to jobs and housing).

Three-fifths of the active laity who took part in the survey agreed with this statement, as did two-thirds of both the Newtownhamilton and Seaview interview samples. There was less enthusiasm in Stormont, where just over half those interviewed agreed with the statement, and among the clergy, of whom only a quarter supported the proposition.

Like the leaders of the DRC, the PCI's leaders also held meetings with the government at which they could lobby ministers on particular concerns. Prior to the IRA's first ceasefire, the PCI had rarely adopted a high profile in the media. It was certainly the case that the media in Northern Ireland sought the views of senior churchmen far more frequently than did the media in South Africa. However, for many years, the Northern Ireland media tended to go first to the Church of Ireland Primate, Dr Robin Eames, if they wanted a Protestant church spokesperson. Dr Eames was generally very willing to talk to the press. There was no similar figurehead in the PCI because a new Moderator was chosen every year. No sooner had one Moderator established themselves with the media and the public, than the election of the next one was underway.

Nevertheless, the PCI did begin to adopt a higher profile after the announcement of the first IRA ceasefire in 1994. There was a distinct difference in the tones of the statements put out by the Church of Ireland and the PCI after this dramatic move by the IRA. While Dr Eames said 'One of the most important assurances [from the British government] is that no secret deals have been done', the Presbyterian Moderator, Dr David McGaughey, said he had been assured by the Northern Ireland Secretary, Sir Patrick Mayhew, that there would be 'no sell-out' of unionists.[30]

In a sermon at St Paul's Cathedral in London, following the loyalist ceasefire, Dr Eames talked of the 'challenge' of peace and of a Northern Ireland community 'daring to hope'.[31] Like other pronouncements in the wake of the two ceasefires, his tone was cautious but positive. By contrast, the Presbyterian Church sounded cautious and suspicious. Part of a statement from the PCI's Church and Government Committee, reacting to the IRA ceasefire, read as follows:

> Assurances have been given by both the British and Irish Governments that there will be no change in the constitutional position of Northern Ireland without the consent of a majority of its people. Nevertheless, since the Anglo Irish Agreement gave the Irish Republic a role in the affairs of Northern Ireland, Irish and Irish American pronouncements on Northern Ireland affairs have been increasing in number and significance, which is deeply resented by many who live in the Province, and who never approved the 1985 Agreement.[32]

This apparent difference in emphasis between the two churches was put to Dr McGaughey in an interview with the author which coincidentally took place on 13 October 1994, the day of the loyalist ceasefire. Dr McGaughey said he was not sure there really was any great difference in tone between the PCI and the Church of Ireland, but he readily acknowledged that his own church was extremely cautious and might well come across as suspicious of any guarantees which were given:

> I think the Presbyterian people since 1985 have indeed had suspicions concerning the government. I think the fact we weren't consulted in 1985 when the Anglo-Irish Agreement was brought into being – I think that has had repercussions and there are many, many Presbyterians who are still suspicious of the government …
> … We are suggesting that yes, we advance and we make progress, but we do so slowly and we don't give our people any assurances that, at the end of the day, we can't of ourselves stand over.

Dr McGaughey said he believed the Church had a duty to represent the political views of its people:

> At times, I think, in the past, politically, we haven't been well represented. We've had MPs, we've had others who haven't articulated the position of the Protestant community as well as they might have done. I think the people – the reports that you've had [in this study] – are indicating that view that they want people to speak on their behalf – people who have no axe to grind with regards to money and position. But people who know them and who have lived with

them. People who know the pressures under which they are living. I think that's one of the things we can do as ministers ...

Q: So do you see the Church as filling a vacuum?

I think the Church are doing that, they are filling a vacuum. I think many people would believe that the media over the years has not been as fair as it should have been and they would feel that the Protestant/loyalist viewpoint has not been put forward on the media as it might have been. And so they rely on churchmen.

In May 1995, the PCI's own response to the Joint Framework Documents, designed to further the 'peace process', described the proposals as 'too "green"'; in other words, biased in favour of nationalists as opposed to unionists.[33] In a second interview with Dr McGaughey, carried out just after he had left office in June 1995, I asked him whether such a comment was going to help achieve the degree of harmony needed to sustain peace:

Well, I think myself that one has to be truthful and if I believe that a document which is political in nature is too green then I should be in a position to say that. I don't think that affects my proclamation of the grace and the love of God. At least, I can't see that it does. Otherwise, I become a minister or a preacher who is restricted in what I proclaim because of how it may affect a situation and that's dangerous ... that certainly isn't biblical.

Q: Why do you think that's dangerous?

Well, I think then you become the voice of the Northern Ireland Office. Indeed, that is one of the fears that many within the Church would have at the moment – that the Church should become the voice of the Northern Ireland Office which wants us to push the Framework Documents and wants us to say to our people 'These are fine documents. There's nothing to fear within them.' But, when we read the documents for ourselves, we discover that there are things to be feared and therefore we must never become the voice of the Northern Ireland Office ...

I asked Dr McGaughey whether the Northern Ireland Office had, at any point, approached either him or the Church, and asked or, at least, suggested that the Church should put across the Framework Documents in a positive light. His response was diplomatic. 'I think what they would have liked us to be is "persuaders". That's their phrase not mine,' he replied. 'So "yes"?' I persisted. Dr McGaughey merely smiled but said nothing.

In his address as outgoing Moderator, Dr McGaughey expressed concern over the speed with which 'paramilitaries and their associates' were being permitted to take part in the political process. His stance received warm praise from the unionist *News Letter*, which declared in an editorial, 'In his assessment of political developments arising from the peace process, Dr McGaughey really has his finger on the pulse of what ordinary people in Northern Ireland are thinking.'[34]

The desire for the Church to articulate the views of 'ordinary people' was evident in comments made by a number of interviewees, including one woman from the Stormont congregation:

> I think it's very difficult for the ordinary people like myself to have their voice heard [in terms of discrimination against Protestants]. I don't say so much the unionist cause as the Protestant cause. If they think there's something not being done ... houses knocked down and not replaced in certain areas, for instance ... I really think the Presbyterian Church should be looking after the interests of the Protestant people. The ministers are able to speak out.

Other interviewees pointed at the Catholic Church, such as this man in Seaview:

> I think it's a very relevant thing in reference to the Roman Catholic Church. Their church hierarchy is always speaking out for the Roman Catholic faith and all these discriminations [i.e. allegations of discrimination] and Fair Employment Commissions have developed around the church hierarchy. And I think we need exactly the same protection from our church.

This was a view shared by the Orange Order. In an article bluntly entitled 'Prod. clerics should stand up for their flocks', the Order's newspaper, the *Orange Standard*, welcomed a speech by the Church of Ireland Bishop of Down and Dromore, Dr Gordon McMullan, in which he said Protestant ministers could do more to tackle unemployment. The *Standard* commented:

> Dr McMullan's welcome speech underlines the widely held view among many Protestants that their Churches have not been as vigorous or active as the Roman Catholic Church in campaigning effectively for jobs, housing and other amenities.

In the 1960s and 1970s when great housing redevelopment schemes were taking place in Belfast, the Roman Catholic was alert to the need to have the maximum number of new houses put back into districts to ensure that there was no loss of population.

Protestant ministers, in contrast, often appeared unaware of the need to promote this sort of campaign, and as a consequence Protestant districts were often denuded of population, resulting in the closure of many Churches and schools, and greatly reduced numbers in the housing put back to replace those demolished.[35]

These comments highlight the extent to which clergymen are expected to act on behalf of the interests of people in their own district. In Northern Ireland, where the population is largely segregated along religious lines, campaigning for facilities for a particular area often means campaigning for the interests of either Protestants or Catholics.

The article is also underpinned by the clear perception that Protestants are losing out to Catholics. As we have seen, this was a view shared by many in the fieldwork congregations with regard to jobs. Where people feel they are being discriminated against, it is easy to turn to politicians and clergymen as scapegoats. The then Grand Master of the Orange Order, Revd Martin Smyth, hit out at both in a special message to mark the Order's Tercentenary. In it, he accused politicians of having betrayed Protestants and added 'The warbling of church leaders when we looked for sure trumpet sorely tried us.'[36]

CONCLUSION

Although the PCI achieved a higher media and public profile during the period studied, it had not become any more than a tentative protagonist for the interests of its own people. The leaders of both the DRC and the PCI seemed well aware that they had little choice but to face reality and encourage their people to accept change, rather than turn their backs on it. However, it is clear that, in times of rapid change, an ethnic group likes to feel it has a strong figure speaking up on its behalf. While Ian Paisley might have performed that function for DUP supporters, he was reviled by many of the interviewees in the PCI fieldwork congregations. Since David Trimble became leader of the Ulster Unionist Party in September 1995, he has taken on this role to some extent, talking tough to his supporters but, unlike Paisley, actually being willing to compromise in order to get on with political progress. To this extent, there is a strong parallel with Constand Viljoen, who performed a very similar role in South Africa. Viljoen's presence on the political scene in South Africa at the time interviews there were carried out may be one reason there was far less of a demand for the DRC to adopt a 'spokesperson' role than was the case in the PCI.

There is a distinction to be made between civil religion, which such political leaders draw on as a form of 'cultural capital', and denominational religion, which has always occupied the religious and cultural mainstream. Civil religion can be used to challenge the state and even, indirectly, to threaten its very existence as happened in South Africa. While Viljoen never advocated violence, there was much speculation in the media that the Volksfront had contingency plans to use a network of part-time white soldiers in South Africa to stage a coup. In Northern Ireland, threats from supporters of the Orange Order, who vowed to bring widespread disruption to essential services, helped to ensure that Orangemen were able to march down Garvaghy Road prior to 1998.

It was unthinkable that either the DRC or the PCI would engage in such activity. If they had, their credibility would have been destroyed. In order to continue to occupy the religious and cultural mainstream, they had to remain supportive of the state. That was one important factor in ensuring that, if not always wholehearted supporters of every political change, they could not oppose it once the state had decided to push ahead with reforms.

Acting as a 'spokesperson' for the ethnopolitical interests of its members is one aspect of the *volkskerk* role of the church. As we have seen, another vital way in which the two Churches acted as *volkskerks* was through their symbolic links with the institutions of civil religion. This was of particular significance in Northern Ireland where the Orange Order was able to enhance its credibility and moral authority through its connection with the major Protestant churches. This relationship posed a dilemma for these churches when widespread violent confrontations broke out over the Orange parade at Drumcree. While there have been signs that the PCI wishes to publicly distance itself from the Order, it has not thus far addressed the issue of a relationship which, in many ways, has been of benefit to both the Order and the PCI.

6 Church and Politics: The Interrelationship between the Religious and the Political Spheres

The question of whether the church should act as a 'spokesperson' for its people raises the wider issue of the relationship between denominational religion and politics. In pronouncing on political questions, the hierarchies of each Church had to negotiate between profoundly differing viewpoints within their institutions; while some urged change, others stuck resolutely to the belief that the *status quo* was the best option. The tortuous process of trying to mediate between these discourses of continuity and change can be seen in the ambiguous nature of many statements issued on political questions by both Churches. At the same time, many members drew on a discourse of *separation* between church and politics which seemed to mirror the discourse of alienation as a means of allowing individuals to avoid taking responsibility for what was happening in the political sphere. This discourse of separation merely masked what was an interdependent relationship between religion and politics, one which illustrated the impossibility of drawing any clear dividing line between the religious and the political spheres. From the Churches' point of view, one of the most important factors in this relationship was their need to remain part of the cultural mainstream in order to retain cultural power.

THE MAINSTREAM ROLE OF THE PCI AND THE DRC

We have already seen how the PCI was left in no doubt that the British government wanted it to adopt the role of 'persuader' with regard to the Joint Framework Documents. This was undoubtedly because the government viewed both the PCI and the Church of Ireland as denominations which formed part of the Protestant cultural mainstream in Northern Ireland. Moreover, these denominations were particularly influential in defining and promulgating the values by which most Protestants lived their lives. This is not to say that all Protestants would have agreed with their church's stand on issues of personal morality. Nevertheless, the denominations' views remained important as cultural reference points on such matters. For example, the PCI put a great deal of emphasis on the desirability of stable family life and this was reflected in the extent to which family relationships remained far more important to most Protestants in Northern Ireland than they would have been to people in Britain.

The DRC played a similar role within the Afrikaner community in South Africa. However, the influence of the churches was not limited to the private sphere. By helping to define the values which underpin society, an institution inevitably has an impact on the public as well as the private sphere. The ability of the church to sway public opinion was clearly in Nelson Mandela's mind when he held talks with senior figures in the DRC in April 1993, at the meeting referred to in the previous chapter.

At that meeting, Mandela expressed the hope that the DRC would act as an agent of reconciliation between those of its members who were fearful of change and those who were pressing for reform. Indeed, comments made to me after the meeting by the ANC's media spokesperson, Carl Niehaus, suggested that the party felt the DRC could be doing much more to encourage its people to accept change:

> It [the DRC] can convey a message of tolerance and peace but we're very concerned that the Church shouldn't get involved in party political pronouncements. In the past they have [made such pronouncements] all the time. The DRC was really promoting National Party policy and defining it. The ANC's position is clear. We want to see it stop. They say they have. We're not convinced. They still need to have a clearer position on the sin of apartheid and it's necessary for the DRC to take a more significant and leading role in uniting the different [DRC] churches.

However, while Mr Niehaus sounded as if his party had the upper hand in its relationship with the DRC, it needed the DRC as much as the Church needed the ANC at that particular point in time. In order to realise the goal of black majority rule and to ensure that it worked, it was essential to gain and to keep the tacit support of the key actors within the Afrikaans mainstream. Mandela cemented this reciprocal relationship in a highly symbolic way in October 1994, by addressing the DRC's General Synod at his own request.

Mandela told the delegates that apartheid had been the most serious denial of the basic value of human beings perpetrated in history. At the same time, he also praised the Church for its role in helping to bring about a change in attitudes.[1] One senior Church figure told me the speech was a very emotional moment, with many of the more 'conservative' ministers and elders clearly moved by the occasion.[2]

The wishes of Mr Niehaus were also fulfilled, to some extent, at this Synod. Another important guest was Dr Beyers Naudé who, as we have seen, had previously been ostracised by the Church for his stand over apartheid. In stark contrast to the treatment he had received in the past, he was given a standing ovation by the delegates. The incoming Moderator, Revd Freek Swanepoel, apologised to Dr Naudé for the way in which the Church had dealt with him in former times. Dr Naudé said the DRC had come full circle and that the 'The book on apartheid is now firmly closed.'[3] The Synod also confirmed its intention to merge with the DRC's sister churches.

However, while the ANC and the British government evidently saw the value of the DRC and the PCI respectively in helping them to achieve political change, neither Church was likely to be accorded the automatic status within the new political order that they had previously been granted as *volkskerks*. As we saw in Chapter One, the DRC had enjoyed such a close relationship with the National Party government that the Church was sometimes dubbed 'the National Party at prayer'. However, once black majority rule was in place, the new South African government would be anxious to appeal to as wide a constituency as possible and was most unlikely to ally itself too closely with any particular church.

While the British government clearly considered the PCI to be of potential use in 1995, the government had never accorded the Church the significance in decision-making which it had been accustomed to under the unionist regime at Stormont, as Chapter 1 has illustrated. Thus, while the PCI retained ethnoreligious capital within the Protestant mainstream during the mid-1990s, that capital had already been devalued in its general dealings with the British government. During this period, Northern Ireland was becoming a more secular society without the 'Protestant ethos' which had once coloured the way in which social life was ordered; Sunday trading was now permitted and the PCI was concerned about falling numbers in many of its

Belfast churches. In the pluralistic mainstream which would underpin the new political order, it seemed unlikely that the Church would be able to secure a position of significance purely through its religious credentials. Like the DRC, it would have to convert its ethnoreligious capital into more straightforward symbolic or cultural capital. In order to achieve this, both Churches needed to be seen to be in tune with the prevailing values and discourses of the emerging political and cultural mainstream.

DISCOURSES OF CHANGE VERSUS DISCOURSES OF CONTINUITY

This required a delicate process of negotiation between pressure from church members who still adhered to the traditional values of their ethnic group, and pressure from the advocates of change, both inside and outside the denomination. Some of the official statements which resulted from this process were highly ambiguous. One classic example of this was the DRC's position on apartheid as outlined in *Church and Society* in 1990:

> The Dutch Reformed Church had not sufficiently perceived that apartheid as a system had inter alia in its struggle against integration also received an ideological and ethnocentric basis. The right and freedom to remain true to one's own cultural heritage, was extended to become a political ideology of apartheid as a system for the protection of the white minority's own interests to the detriment of others ...
>
> ... Apartheid began to function in such a way that the largest part of the population of the country experienced it as an oppressive system which through the forced separation of peoples was in reality favouring one group wrongfully above the others ...
>
> Any system which in practice functions in this way, is unacceptable in the light of Scripture and the Christian conscience and must be rejected as sinful. Any attempt by a church to try to defend such a system biblically and ethically, must be seen as a serious fallacy, that is to say it is in conflict with the Bible.[4]

For critics such as Carl Niehaus, this statement was not direct enough. It could be interpreted as a criticism of apartheid *per se* but, equally, it could be seen as criticising apartheid only inasmuch as it actually resulted in oppression. In other words, the statement could be read as supporting the philosophy of 'separate development' which the creators of apartheid originally espoused. By stating its position in this ambiguous way, what the DRC could be sure of was that it would minimise opposition from those within the Church who still supported apartheid.

The ambiguity of the statement was highlighted by the confusion with which it was met when it was included in a pilot questionnaire for this study. Many interviewees simply could not understand what it was trying to say. In the end, a much briefer summary was devised. This took into account the fact that, since the publication of *Church and Society* in 1990, 'official' statements made on behalf of the Church had stated explicitly that apartheid was 'sinful'. Thus, the wording used for the purposes of this study seemed to represent, as closely as possible, the formal position of the Church in 1993, namely 'apartheid is an oppressive system and must be rejected as sinful'. This position did not receive wholehearted support from either the postal survey respondents or the fieldwork interviewees. While 71 per cent of the ministers agreed with this statement, it was supported by only 47 per cent of the lay respondents to the postal survey.

In the fieldwork congregations, three-fifths of the interviewees in Louis Trichardt, and roughly half the interviewees in Queenswood and Wespoort approved of the statement. There was undoubtedly still a measure of ambiguity surrounding the Church's stance on the subject, however; one of the smaller Afrikaans-speaking churches had urged the DRC not to 'demonise' those who designed apartheid by suggesting their intentions were evil. This sentiment seemed to be shared by a number of interviewees in Queenswood, perhaps because many would have been involved at a relatively senior level in helping to maintain apartheid or would have been among the many teachers and lecturers who promulgated the supposed virtues of the system. In most other respects, however, the evidence from this study suggested that DRC members in Northern Transvaal were in broad agreement with the Church's public stance on a number of potentially controversial issues. A majority in each congregation agreed with the DRC's position on political rights, human rights, equal pay and detention without trial.[5] In Louis Trichardt, only a third of the interview sample agreed with the Church's position that migrant or seasonal labour (a system which keeps family members apart for long periods of time) should be eliminated as far as possible, whereas a majority in the other two congregations were in favour of this proposition. This is doubtless explained by the fact that many farmers in the Louis Trichardt area would use such labour themselves.

As we noted in Chapter 1, both churches had made 'confessional' statements indicating some responsibility on their part for the problems which had arisen in each territory. However, this publicly expressed sense of guilt was not shared by many of those whose views were canvassed. In the DRC, a majority in each of the fieldwork congregations did not agree with the following statement: 'Members of the Dutch Reformed Church should be prepared to admit to their part in the creation of the current situation of conflict in South Africa.'

This was taken from a statement made by the DRC's General Synod in 1990 which called on Church members to 'admit to their part in the current situation of conflict in South Africa.'[6] This call is echoed in a 'confession' made in *Presbyterian Principles and Political Witness in Northern Ireland* which reads:

> Mission in Ireland must always be our first and immediate task, but mission has been seriously hindered by the unhappy divisions of Irish society, both North and South. We confess that we have not done all that we should to break down those barriers.[7]

A similar statement was put to both the PCI postal and fieldwork respondents. It read 'The Presbyterian Church has not done enough to break down the divisions between Protestants and Roman Catholics in Northern Ireland.' In the case of the postal survey respondents, the data suggested that a substantial body of clerical and lay opinion in the Church believed it had nothing to 'confess' in this regard. Almost half the session clerks and two-fifths of the ministers disagreed with this statement. There was less opposition from the fieldwork respondents; roughly a third of both the Seaview and Newtownhamilton samples opposed the statement, while a fifth of the Stormont interviewees did not support it.

There was a greater measure of dissension from the 'official' or public line on potentially controversial issues in the PCI than in the DRC. Both clerical and lay respondents to the PCI postal survey were asked for their reactions to another statement which was designed to represent 'official' Church thinking. This read:

> Local councillors in Northern Ireland should work alongside all legally elected representatives, including Sinn Fein politicians (even

if the IRA continues its campaign of violence and Sinn Fein refuses to condemn the IRA's actions).

This statement was taken from the position on this issue outlined in *Presbyterian Principles*.[8] Roughly three-quarters of the session clerks and two-thirds of the ministers were opposed to this statement. A majority of each of the fieldwork samples also disagreed with it. There was a similar level of opposition from the fieldwork samples to the following statement, taken from a suggestion made in the submission by the PCI's Church and Government Committee to the Opsahl Commission, which examined political options for Northern Ireland:

> If an appointed second chamber (like the House of Lords) was set up alongside an elected assembly in Northern Ireland, that second chamber could include people from the Republic of Ireland.[9]

There is little doubt, then, that neither of these views could be said to represent those held by many grassroots members of the PCI. Revd John Dickinson, of Seaview, believed history was partly to blame for Church statements which did not represent the views of the majority of the membership:

> It's just like everything else. The Church is subject to fashion and the current fashion in some circles in Presbyterianism is to hark back to the fact that, at certain stages in Irish history, Irish Presbyterianism was relatively liberal in its outlook ... A lot of the ideas that do come out from the General Board statements you read kind of try to reflect that idea – that somewhere there's a liberal buried inside the Presbyterian Church – it's only a matter of resurrecting him somehow or other and everything will be wonderful. But it's not like that – the Church has always had divided views. There always was and still is a liberal element inside Irish Presbyterianism, but the predominant element is unionist and British and conservative.

COMMUNICATION BETWEEN HIERARCHY AND LAITY

It would certainly seem that many lay members of both churches remained unaware of the content of those statements and documents which did not attract significant publicity within the news media. Church publications would seem to be one obvious way in which positions on various issues, such as those looked at above, could have been disseminated to members. However, very few interviewees had read documents such as *Church and Society* or *Presbyterian Principles* which contained key policy statements. The PCI had a monthly magazine, *Presbyterian Herald*, which appeared to be subscribed to fairly widely within the fieldwork congregations, but which rarely carried articles on political issues or 'current affairs'. In contrast, the DRC's weekly newspaper, *Die Kerkbode*, did carry many statements, interviews and editorials which reflected the views of the church leadership on topical issues. However, it reached only a relatively small proportion of respondents in Queenswood and Louis Trichardt, and was not taken by any interviewees in Wespoort.

Even when statements or actions by church figures were reported in the wider media, they failed to make an impression on all church members. To try to obtain some idea of the extent of awareness at the grassroots of the activities of senior figures in the respective churches, the fieldwork interviewees were asked whether they knew about meetings between leading churchmen and politicians which were regarded as potentially 'controversial' at the time. DRC interviewees were asked if they were aware that a meeting between the Church and Mandela had taken place in April 1993, just a few months before the fieldwork interviews. Just over half the respondents in Wespoort were unaware that such a meeting had happened, although it had been publicised in the media and in *Die Kerkbode* at the time. Most interviewees in the other two DRC congregations had heard about it. Nevertheless, two-fifths of the respondents in Louis Trichardt and one-third in Queenswood said they were not aware of it.

The PCI interviewees were asked a similar question about a series of unofficial meetings which had taken place in 1992 between two leading members of the Church and representatives of Sinn Fein to ask the latter to use their influence to stop the IRA campaign of violence.[10] Most interviewees in each of the PCI congregations said they had heard of these meetings. However, two-fifths of the interviewees in both Seaview and Newtownhamilton, and one fifth of the respondents in Stormont said they were unaware that the meetings had taken place. Again, there had been publicity about the meetings at the time, although in this case a much longer period had elapsed between the meetings and the interviews.

Both sets of figures suggest that a substantial minority of members remained unaware of what was going on in the denomination outside their local congregation. This was particularly evident in the urban working-class and rural congregations. When this is combined with the relative lack of access to published information from church sources on the views of leading figures and key committees on political and topical issues, one can only conclude that many members of both Churches relied on their ministers to inform them of such matters. This meant the clergy had a crucial gatekeeping and mediating role in disseminating and interpreting church policies to the laity.

CLERGY AND POLITICS

Church sermons provided the main opportunity for ministers to address such issues in front of their flocks. Clergymen in both the postal survey samples were asked how often they had talked about political issues, or issues of social and economic injustice, in their sermons in the previous six months. In both the DRC and PCI samples, 40 per cent said they had addressed these issues at least four times. Only 11 per cent in each denomination had not alluded to such matters at all.

About a third of the DRC clergymen said they did feel constrained in what they said in their sermons by fear of disapproval from either their congregation or members of their church council.[11] One argument a number of ministers put forward was that there was a danger of alienating members of the congregation who might eventually come round to accepting change. As one put it:

> There's a very thin line between politics and the church, and I think if you test that line too quickly and try to get people to see they've been wrong all these years ... you'd lose a lot of people who, in two years' time, would be willing to look at the situation with different eyes.

One of the two ministers in Louis Trichardt, Gerhardus Botha, said he believed people would simply leave the church if he talked about political issues in a specific manner – for example, by criticising the AWB:

> They [the congregation members] would go over to [the APK church] and ... I can't speak to them anymore. So, I try to say things but in a way that the people will start to think. And then, maybe in a month's time, they will be back and then there will be an opportunity to say something again and so forth. Otherwise, if they leave, they're gone, and then I don't have any influence on them.

However, some in the Church felt it was important for a minister to adopt a prophetic role and not to be afraid of taking a lead. Professor Pieter Meiring said ministers should not take refuge in very general statements that did not make their meaning clear:

> I think it is very human for a minister not to be too specific because it may create problems. But the Gospel creates problems and Jesus himself – when he preached, not everyone was happy with his preaching, but he proceeded with it. And I think there is a challenge to a minister, to bring the Gospel in such a way that it really has everything to do with the realities of South Africa and knowing that he will have to antagonise people who don't like that message, because they are happy with the way things are ... Knowingly antagonising some people, but doing it in such a way that he takes the congregation with him, and that they come to understand why he does it, and that they trust him for doing it. And I think that, in many congregations, people are *longing* for the minister to be more clear and more specific.

Only one in ten ministers in Northern Ireland said they felt constrained by the thought of opposition from members of their congregation or kirk session.[12] David Moore, the Assistant Minister at Stormont, felt it was vital to deal with political issues:

> It's so much part of our lives here – like it or lump it. I am not of the idea that we have to mention it every week – and I think we want to avoid a party political stance, even by implication. But the Gospel has implications for all of our life. Now, there's quite a strain in Christian thinking which says 'I don't want to be involved in politics – politics is a dirty business. Come out from among them and be separate.' Well, that's just illogical – it can't happen. We're in the midst of the world, and we have to be responsible citizens – so politics is there, but it's in its place. It's not my job to be a political orator.

Revd Moore sent me examples of his own sermons in which he felt he had dealt with political issues. In a letter accompanying the sermons, he commented:

> In a sense sermons condemning 'the system' get nowhere, because 'the system' can always be seen as 'them not us' by our listeners. Rather than vague generalisations what we need is to address the individual, and ask them 'How is *your* Christian discipleship?' In

matching this personal line with the Scriptures then people begin to change and our country starts to be healed 'from the grassroots' where the real problem lies.

One of the sermons was entitled 'Meekness' and Revd Moore said it reflected his 'underlying approach to our troubles'. Yet, on reading the text, I found it hard to see how any listener would have interpreted it as such. It was an eloquent and persuasive speech about the value of practising meekness in society and in our personal lives. However, the only specific reference to Northern Ireland noted that Ulster Protestants were not renowned worldwide for their meekness. The sermon suggested this might be because it was a virtue which Protestants tended to ignore.

The ambiguous nature of the 'political' content of sermons was reflected in the differing views expressed by a congregation's members over whether their minister did address such issues. For example, although both the clergymen at Stormont said they did comment on political issues in their sermons, a quarter of the interviewees in this congregation believed their ministers did not address such matters. It was evident from the fieldwork interviews that a minister's concept of 'talking about politics' was not always the same as a member of his flock. In many cases, interviewees confidently asserted that their minister never talked about politics, when he had told me otherwise. There seemed to be two reasons for this disparity. One was the ambiguity of many sermon texts where generalisations can be interpreted in different ways. The other was that people often appeared to hear what they want to hear. This became evident when data from the fieldwork surveys was analysed in detail. The analysis suggested that those who felt ministers *should* speak about such issues were more likely to believe that their own minister actually did than those who were opposed to preaching on political issues.[13]

Nevertheless, Stormont was the one congregation where a number of people did feel that their ministers' comments on political issues had influenced their views. One-fifth of the interviewees said they had been swayed by comments on political issues which one of the ministers had made in a sermon. One in eight said they had been influenced by a reference to political issues which their minister had made during an individual discussion with them. The latter method was one which a number of clergymen felt was preferable to speaking too explicitly on such issues in sermons. Individual discussions normally took place during visits to members' homes, which ministers in both Churches were expected to make from time to time. In general, ministers only discussed political issues if they were raised by the congregation member. However, Stormont was the only congregation where this method appeared to have had an impact. Hardly anyone in the other congregations in the PCI and the DRC felt they had been influenced by such conversations. Moreover, few felt they had been persuaded by any references to political issues in sermons. The degree of influence over attitudes possessed by clergymen was very hard to measure, however. One of the problems was that people generally only felt they had been influenced if they had actually changed their mind on an issue as a result of hearing a sermon or taking part in a discussion. Many people said any views expressed by their minister tended to reflect their own.

An attempt was also made to investigate the social status of ministers in the fieldwork congregations in the eyes of their members. Interviewees were asked the following question:

In your view is the local DRC/Presbyterian minister:
1. The most important person in your local community
2. One of the most important people in your local community
3. No more or less important than many other people in the local community
4. Less important than many other people in the local community

The results are given in Figure 6.1.

As can be seen, almost two-thirds of the Stormont sample rated their ministers as among the most important members of the community, although few rated either of them as the most significant. By contrast, two-fifths of the Wespoort sample felt that their ministers were the most important people in the local community. Despite the fact that few felt that the clergy influenced their views on political issues, a

Figure 6.1 Status of clergy. Figures on the left axis show percentages who chose each of the possible responses.

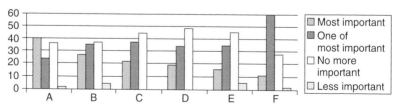

A = Wespoort, B = Seaview, C = Newtownhamilton, D = Queenswood, E = Louis Trichardt, F = Stormont

large minority of the Wespoort sample seemed to have a deferential attitude towards the ministers. This also applied to a slightly lesser degree in Seaview where a quarter of the interview sample rated the minister as the most important individual in the local area. The high status accorded to clergymen in these working-class congregations is a subject to which we shall return in Chapter 8.

THE DISCOURSE OF SEPARATION BETWEEN CHURCH AND POLITICS

The relationship of the church to the political sphere is one which is keenly debated throughout western Christianity. On the one hand, 'separationists' argue that the domains of the church and state should remain entirely distinct and that one should not attempt to interfere with the running of the other. On the other hand, 'transformationists' believe that religious principles should affect all the actions of religious believers.[14]

The discourse of separation was particularly strong in the South African congregations. Some people seemed to repeat 'church and politics should not mix' as if it were a mantra. Undoubtedly, the DRC's involvement in advocating apartheid was a big influence. Those who were opposed to apartheid were often uncomfortable about the DRC's previous support for it. Those who were not opposed to it had a tendency to lump it in with 'politics' as a generally controversial and unspiritual field to be avoided by the church at all costs. One woman in Louis Trichardt who was opposed in principle to apartheid, nevertheless felt it was not something to dwell on:

> ... unfortunately, it's been done and it's passed, but to harp on, it aggravates people and it makes it very difficult. If I listen to people like Tutu [the former Archbishop Desmond Tutu], they get very emotional and they tend to bring politics into everything they're having a sermon on. I agree they [blacks] were disadvantaged. It should never have happened. But I'm very frightened about the church and politics under one umbrella – some of the Afrikaner people get so emotional and they walk out.

Many PCI members and some clergy also took a separationist line. Again, 'church and politics' had an uncomfortable association for some. While many people in the DRC equated 'church and politics' with apartheid, 'church and politics' in the PCI was sometimes equated with the Free Presbyterian founder and DUP leader, Ian Paisley. As a woman in Stormont put it:

> I think it's spiritual matters that a minister should be concerned with and not politics. A minister should leave politics to the politicians. Paisley brings politics into the pulpit, but I think it's good to have politicians who are Christians and bring something of that into their work.

Another woman who cited Paisley as a bad example of mixing politics and preaching, took the same view. 'I think it's okay to have views and so on,' she said, 'but the spiritual side is the key one. It's what people read into what they [ministers] say – and I think we're there to hear the word of God, not political issues.'

The discourse of separation between church and politics clearly had an important influence in both denominations. As with the discourse of alienation, it constructed politics as something which was dirty. Politics was painted as being beneath the more elevated, holier concerns of the spiritual sphere. Yet, I would argue that what this discourse actually provided in practice was simply another means by which church members could ignore their own relationship to politics and could deny responsibility for what was going on in the political sphere.

This discourse also conveniently side-stepped the issue of what actually constitutes 'politics'. The word 'political' was frequently viewed as synonymous with the word 'controversial'. It was clearly seen as being tied up with the painful loss of status and power which both Afrikaners and Ulster Protestants were experiencing. However, if one is to view a certain subject-area as being 'out of bounds' for the church, it is necessary to draw a demarcation line over which one should not step. It is through examining the different ways in which that line was constructed that one can come to understand better why many clergy and laity were so keen to delineate a firm boundary between the religious and political spheres.

Many clergymen in both churches told me that they were much happier talking about government policy on moral issues, such as gambling, in their sermons than about issues related to the political changes which were taking place. Yet, both are 'political' in the sense that they affect the way in which society is ordered. It could be argued that the church would be expected to speak out on moral issues which are traditionally seen as part of its domain. However, some ministers admitted that the main reason they preferred to deal with the former rather than the latter was the fact that pronouncements on moral issues, whether or not congregation members agreed with them, did not result in the hostility which comments on political change could arouse. Ron Savage in Stormont said he did not shrink from dealing with political issues in the broader sense, but he did feel it was easier to deal with moral issues:

> I think it is easier in that you're aware that, if you're addressing political issues, people are much more touchy. And, you know, I'm also aware when I'm talking about political issues in a sermon, that there's a greater hush comes over the congregation. They listen much more attentively but, equally, I'm much more careful in how I word things and I would certainly script those bits very carefully.

Dr Savage faced another problem in addressing political issues. One means by which ministers can structure their sermons is by using a lectionary, which prescribes a pre-set programme of Bible readings throughout the year. For a non-chuchgoing outsider such as myself, this seemed a curiously rigid system which created a disjunction between the ever-changing 'real' world and the fixed, stable world of the Bible. Both the Queenswood and Stormont congregations used such a programme. However, ministers were divided as to whether the lectionary actually did constrain them in terms of addressing topical issues. Daniel van Zyl, in the Queenswood congregation, was quite adamant that it did:

> We haven't got a free hand to preach what we like. Our whole programme for preaching and Bible study is planned a year ahead. By doing that, we are certain our point of departure is the Scripture and not my hobby-horse – just preaching conversion the whole time or political issues the whole time or social issues the whole time. We try and bring the whole spectrum of the Scripture, of the Bible.
>
> ... It's useless to take a text in the Bible and to go and hang whatever you want to say on that text ... If you want to be loyal, as a minister, to the word of God and to God, and to say 'the Lord says', you've got to say what the Bible says – not more or less.

However, one of his colleagues in Queenswood, Petrus van der Merwe, took a different point of view. He saw the lectionary as a flexible tool with which one could examine current issues:

> Some of the topics ... are fixed but, within your topic, you have a very wide range, you know, where you can address certain issues

that turn up during the week. So my topic for this Sunday, for instance, is the trouble which David had with his son Solomon … and one of the issues can be that people are getting so fearful like David in his relationship with Solomon. Why? … So you know you have a beautiful scenario [which is like the one] a South African family is in at the moment, and you sort of react and bring the message what [*sic*] God told them. So, we have a topic but there's room enough to bring in the daily problems.

Ron Savage in Stormont was an advocate of addressing political issues in sermons. However, he shared Dr van Zyl's concerns about the dangers of flexibility:

> I'm always wary of that [ministers choosing their own topics] because, if you move away from the set lectionary, you can find yourself riding your own particular hobby-horse. The lectionary is a good discipline to work through the Christian year and through topics which have been set from time immemorial.

However, he attributed the need to stick to the lectionary as the reason that he had spoken about an alleged case of wrongful imprisonment which many unionists were concerned about (the UDR Four) but had not addressed a similar case which had been a focus of campaigning for nationalists (the Birmingham Six). He explained why he had dealt with the UDR Four case:

> It just happened to be that that was in the newspapers that particular week when I was doing something about it … the application of Christianity to social issues, and that was one of the ones [examples] I picked up. Some of the others I picked up were about housing and care of the elderly.

I asked him is there was any particular reason that he had not addressed an issue like the Birmingham Six. He paused for a long time before replying:

> I suppose the reason I wouldn't have addressed it directly is that the preaching tends to come out of scripture passages and the issues they raise and, unless the set scripture for the week, unless its interpretation would coincide with one of the topical happenings, I might not necessarily pick it up and look for a scripture so I could preach about the Birmingham Six.

It was hard not to suspect that the risk of offending his congregation had not played at least a subconscious role. For those ministers who were prepared to speak about political issues, there was another demarcation line between the 'acceptable' and the 'unacceptable'. This was the line between 'politics' and 'party politics'. Every clergyman I spoke to was anxious to ensure that they were not seen to advocate or criticise any particular political party. Again, however, the term 'party politics' was a relative one. In Queenswood, the ministers had an agreement not to identify any parties in their sermons. However, Phillippus Loots admitted he would talk about communists because there were none in his congregation. Indeed, as noted earlier, communism was vilified by many clergymen and members within the DRC. *Church and Society* states that 'the church must testify against Marxism, communism, totalitarianism, racism, integrationism and all other unchristian ideologies'.[15]

Yet many blacks supported the South African Communist Party (SACP). Was the DRC not being 'party political' in opposing the ideology which underpinned the SACP? The reference in the above statement to 'integrationism' is somewhat curious but was presumably included to appease those who feared that the Church was moving too quickly towards racially mixed worship, a subject which we shall examine in greater detail in the next chapter. Once more, it also illustrates the way in which the DRC attempted to negotiate between the discourse of continuity and the discourse of change. Racism was condemned but, for those who still supported a degree of insitutionalised racism in the form of 'separate development', 'integrationism' was also criticised. I suspect that the reference to totalitarianism was also included to 'balance' the reference to Marxism and communism.

CONCLUSION

It is clear that both Nelson Mandela and the British government believed major denominations wielded considerable cultural power among their laity and that they could act as agents of change. Yet, as we have seen, members were often divided over the merits of policy statements and proposals put forward by their churches. Moreover, they were unlikely to be aware of such statements if they were not reported in the news media or disseminated by their minister. Even media publicity about controversial events involving their church quite often failed to make an impact. Thus, clergymen had a significant role as both gatekeepers and mediators in the internal communication of denominational policies.

As we have seen, relatively few lay members felt they had been directly influenced by anything their minister had said on topical issues. References to such issues in sermons were often of a general nature. Furthermore, there was evidence that church members tended to hear what they wanted to hear in sermons; if they did not approve of clergymen referring to politics in sermons, they were less likely to believe that their minister did comment on such issues than those who felt sermons should encompass politics.

One could interpret these findings as suggesting that the impact of the church on the attitudes of its members was negligible. However, the process of 'attitude change' is much more complex than this. The views which people articulate about various issues can easily change, depending on the particular circumstances in which they are speaking and on the shifting social climate. In this sense, it is really more valuable to analyse the process of 'attitude change' in terms of the circulation of different discourses.[16] We have already discussed how both the DRC and the PCI could be seen as arenas on which was being played out a contest between discourses of change and discourses of continuity. Documents such as *Church and Society* and *Presbyterian Principles* put down important markers on what might best be seen as the discursive 'maps' which framed the parameters of these contests. Yet, these church statements were also products of those very ideological struggles; hence their sometimes tortured ambiguity.

In particular, the discursive markers provided by such documents undoubtedly had an impact on general religious and moral discourses within the churches. This is important because, in both denominations, many clergy and laity made a clear distinction between the spheres of religion and politics. This discourse of separation between church and politics echoed the discourse of alienation in constructing politics as something inferior and in providing a means by which clergy and laity could avoid any sense of responsibility for events in the political sphere. Yet, the comments of those who espoused the discourse of separation clearly show how the dividing line between 'church' and 'politics' or between 'acceptable' and 'unacceptable' references to politics was a matter of contingency and interpretation. 'Politics' is a relative term. In reality, politics embraces all aspects of our lives. However, in many cases, acknowledgement of that fact would have removed the barrier by which people could protect themselves from the uncomfortable changes taking place, and from the imbalances of power which had led to those changes.

Thus, church leaders and clergy may, at times, have overestimated the immediate impact of church statements on a denomination's members. Yet, historically, both the DRC and the PCI had played a central role in the respective public spheres of their particular ethnic group. Moreover, they were clearly still regarded as potentially significant agents of change by those political interests which were driving forward the process of political change. Both denominations were eager to secure their place in the new mainstream which was being constructed as that process took place. At the same time, they were certainly sensitive to the concerns of their members, even if that membership was less aware of what was happening at General Assembly and Synod level than one might have assumed. Given the fact that both churches had faced the departure of members in the past, they felt under considerable pressure to bear in mind the interests of their own flocks, many of whom regarded change with suspicion and fear. After all, churches are symbols of *continuity*, particularly during periods of rapid transition or transformation.

Ministers played a key role in this delicate process of negotiating competing discourses, perspectives and interests. In effect, much of the cultural power of the church was devolved to them, albeit within parameters which were defined by the 'hierarchies' of each denomination. As we shall see in the next chapter, the minister was also crucial in determining whether or not his congregation was involved in efforts to improve relations between the groups at the centre of both conflicts.

7 The Church as 'Conciliator': The Difficult Task of Bridge-Building

Revd Jan van den Berg took a sip of his tea and smiled with enthusiasm as he gave me his view of race relations in Queenswood. 'When I do my visits with my members and I talk with them about the black woman who's working in their house,' he began. 'Really, it warms my heart when I see the lovely understanding between the white people and the black people who are working for them ... how they try to help them, how they give them money to help their children go to school.'

He paused and leaned forward to ensure I appreciated his point. 'You know, we see on the television the hate between the black and white people. But there's many examples which don't appear on TV because it's not news where there's a lovely understanding between people.'

I suspected that Revd Jan van den Berg, a courteous but punctilious man in his fifties, thought that I shared the mistaken international preconception that all South African whites were bad people. We were taking tea, prepared and served by his black maid, in the minister's tastefully decorated front room. His elegant but, by white middle-class standards, reasonably modest home had a reassuring air of comfort and stability which befitted a minister who had served his congregation for seventeen years.

It was a world away from the barren, bleak environment of the townships and impoverished settlements where most of Queenswood's maids lived or had their families. This world was one which Queenswood's white residents were only just beginning to get acquainted with. Seven months before my interview with him, Revd van den Berg and his wife had actually visited their maid's home in the 'black' district of Hammanskraal, north of Pretoria. He claimed many members of his congregation had done likewise, although this was not evident from my interviews with them. However, it was clear that those who prided themselves on having a social conscience were

142

making it their business to talk to their maids about their living conditions, something which would have been almost unthinkable a few years previously.

Yet, Revd van den Berg's comments were a reminder of the nature of the relationship between black and white. In both Queenswood and Louis Trichardt, most interviewees employed black people in their homes. Just under half of the Wespoort respondents had a black employee in their home. This meant that, for many white people, much of the contact they had with blacks was in the form of the master–servant relationship. They did not interact on an equal basis.

This was one legacy of apartheid. Another was the racial segregation of residential areas and workplaces. Hammanskraal was some sixty kilometres from Queenswood – about an hour's drive. In order to get there, Queenswood residents had to make a special effort. In any case, as I was often warned, black settlements were perceived as hostile places where whites were in danger of getting attacked – 'better to stay well away' most white residents of Pretoria told themselves, although there was relatively little violence in any of the townships surrounding Pretoria while I was carrying out my research.

However, while the world knows about racial segregation in South Africa, it is less well known that there is a very high degree of residential segregation along religious lines in Northern Ireland. Data from Northern Ireland's 1991 government population census showed that approximately half the province's population were living in areas where more than 90 per cent of the residents were either Protestant or Catholic.[1] The authors of a detailed analysis of data from the 1981 census concluded that:

> the majority of Northern Ireland towns are strongly segregated. Moreover, the towns with the less intense levels of dominance [by either Protestants or Catholics] are almost all small towns, so the urban population of the province is heavily concentrated into those towns that are strongly segregated.[2]

Indeed, many interviewees in both the Belfast congregations said they had no Catholic neighbours living close to them. Nearly half the respondents in Seaview and a third of those in Stormont said there were no Catholic residents in their street or immediate vicinity. Newtownhamilton was more integrated in terms of residential patterns although, as we shall see, this did not necessarily mean that cross-community relations were any better than in the other congregations.

Not surprisingly, the degree of residential segregation between whites and blacks was much higher than this in the three congregations in South Africa. Black South Africans were only just beginning to move into the white residential areas from which these congregations drew their members. Some twenty black families had recently bought or rented houses in Louis Trichardt. When the first family arrived, they were greeted by a mob of angry stone-throwers. Although such displays of open hostility had subsided, animosity certainly continued to be present at a less visible level.

One recent new arrival, Pieter Malgas, recounted his grim experiences of racism. Mr Malgas had moved up to Louis Trichardt from the Cape to take up a senior administrative post in the nearby University of Venda. He had gone up ahead of his family who were still in the Cape while he tried to find a house for them, and to reserve school places for his children.

This latter task was not proving easy. His children had always been educated in Afrikaans-medium schools, as that was the family's first language. There were few schools teaching in Afrikaans in Venda, so he decided to make enquiries at three all-white schools in Louis Trichardt. Mr Malgas was not encouraged by the response he got from the school principals. 'Two said something like "As far as I'm concerned you're welcome, but the attitudes here are still very prejudiced", while a third said they would have to consult the school's Board of Management,' he told me. 'From that basic reaction, I decided I wouldn't like to expose my children to negative racial attitudes.'

There had been other examples of enforced racial segregation. The hotel in which he was staying had three bars. It was quite evident that two were unofficially reserved for whites while the other one was where blacks were expected to drink. Mr Malgas had also been saddened to find that one doctor's waiting room had been arranged in such a way that all the whites sat on one side, while all the blacks sat on the other. However, he had not come across one of the less visible but most telling vestiges of apartheid which remained in Louis Trichardt. According to the news editor of the town's local paper, most of the workplace toilets in the town were still racially segregated.[3]

To the best of my knowledge, no factory or office in Northern Ireland has religiously segregated washrooms! However, in a more general sense, interviewees in the Northern Ireland congregation did not seem to have any greater opportunity to mix with Catholics at work than did their counterparts in the South African congregations to mix with blacks. In both cases, between one-third and one-half of each interview sample said they had either black or Catholic colleagues at work or in their place of study.

On the other hand, a majority of each of the Northern Ireland samples said they had Catholic friends who were not employees, colleagues, neighbours or relatives. The proportion ranged from three-quarters of the Stormont interviewees to just over half of the Newtownhamilton respondents. Most of those with Catholic friends said they invited them into their homes, although such visits tended to be occasional rather than regular affairs. Most did not generally discuss either religion or politics with their Catholic friends or acquaintances. In the South African congregations, such inter-ethnic social mixing was still relatively rare and only a small proportion of interviewees in each congregation said they had black friends who were not employees, colleagues or neighbours.

REACHING OUT

Lack of contact was undoubtedly one of the main reasons for the negative attitudes towards blacks and Catholics respectively which have been discussed in earlier chapters. At an official level, both the PCI and the DRC recognised that this was a problem and encouraged congregations to initiate schemes which would bring the different communities together. The DRC was the more explicit of the two Churches in this regard. *Church and Society* states:

> It is of the greatest importance that congregations should strive for a closer unity between the members and congregations of the Dutch Reformed Church family. Church councils ought to take the initiative in this matter.[4]

While *Presbyterian Principles* did not allude directly to the need for cross-community action by its congregations, the 1994 PCI General Assembly received a report from the Church's Peace and Peacemaking Committee which stated that the Church should 'provide resources and encouragement to enable congregations to move forward at the local level in the field of inter-community relations.'[5] The following year, the General Assembly asked kirk sessions to appoint 'peacemaking agents' to take concrete steps to work towards peace and to improve cross-community relationships.[6]

Stormont was the only one of the three PCI fieldwork congregations which had tried to promote cross-community activity among its members. Its most ambitious scheme had been an intergroup project which brought together younger members of the congregation with their counterparts from a Catholic church near Andersonstown in West Belfast. This was centred around two residential weekends, at which teenagers discussed their situations and their views of each other. One young person, who was at both the weekends, said they did help to dispel some myths:

> I wasn't bigoted or anything. But, there was always doubt in the mind that 'Oh, maybe they [Catholics] are different a bit.' Because I wasn't close friends with any and I didn't have many contacts with them. But after, we got together with them – not through the church – but we got together to talk and I just realised they were normal people ... they're not different at all.

He had particularly enjoyed a cross-community weekend at a leisure park in the north-west of England which had also been organised by Stormont. This visit had focused on having fun rather than any structured discussions:

> I thought it was better – you're just friendly towards each other and there's no pressure. 'Cos there's pressure put into the first two [discussion-based] weekends, 'cos you were made to join in the groups and you were half Catholic and half Protestant, while the weekend just past, you were just going by yourself and got to know everyone by yourself.

However, while several friendships and a couple of romances resulted from these get-togethers, most of them did not last long. Andersonstown and Stormont are several miles apart and there is no direct link by public transport. Both the romances and most of the friendships petered out due to the hassle involved in travelling and making arrangements to meet. There was also some opposition from parents who did not like children travelling to a nationalist district which was synonymous in Protestant eyes with republican violence. Moreover, both the Protestant and Catholic participants were taunted by their peers for taking part in the scheme.

The Catholic congregation involved in the scheme attracted many middle-class families. Stormont's Assistant Minister, David Moore, admitted this meant the young Protestants involved were getting a rather 'protected' view of West Belfast. 'There's a question-mark over whether two middle-class groups getting together is what it's all about', he said ruefully. 'We did it like that so we weren't overcoming a lot of barriers – there were enough barriers to start with.'

Revd Moore said it would be wonderful, in theory, if the congregation could link up with a working-class congregation in West Belfast. However, he felt it would be difficult to make such a move without appearing patronising. Within the DRC, however, such a concern was rarely evident. A colonialist mentality still coloured much of the inter-racial work which was undertaken within the Church. The world view which informed this approach was essentially one in which educated and 'civilised' whites lent a charitable hand to their black inferiors.

'MISSION' EFFORTS AND THE DISCOURSE OF COLONIALISM

The reader may recall the comments made by one congregation member who had been involved in a project initiated by the Queenswood congregation to build a church for a black congregation. Christo Meyer felt very strongly that the paternalistic attitude of whites had led to a passive mentality from blacks involved in this particular project:[7]

> You tried to organise work parties where a group of us got out and we tried to get them to come and join us with putting up fencing and that sort of thing. And it ended up that two or three of *them* came and *twenty* of us came! And, if you tried to get them to do something independently, it just never came to anything. So, in the end, you had to take over and you had to organise everything one-sidedly ... I tried to give them the example that, if you pick up something, you use two fingers. If you lose any one of the two, you cannot pick it up. But they just didn't grasp the concept. They are so used to relying on the whites ... It's a nice church and they are thankful for it and they accepted it and everything else, but they wouldn't, from their own side, do a lot to improve the situation there.

However, the charitable efforts of the Queenswood congregation were all predicated on the assumption that whites had a great deal to teach blacks, and not vice versa. In common with many congregations, Queenswood had begun classes in useful 'life-skills' for black maids. Around twenty women attended a class in dressmaking, and programmes in reading and writing were also planned. However, there were no similar programmes by which white women could learn skills from their black counterparts, or even learn more about their experiences and culture. As with the whole ideology of apartheid, the underlying ethos was one of whites 'civilising' the blacks.

This was certainly not an attitude confined to the Dutch Reformed Church. I vividly recall being shown around a hostel which housed black migrant workers in a township just outside Johannesburg which had seen some of the fiercest clashes between supporters of the ANC and Zulu supporters of Inkatha. My guides were a white Anglican clergyman and his wife. The clergyman had gained enormous respect for his unstinting efforts to mediate between the two sides. However, while the minister thought nothing of getting out of bed at two in the morning to go and sort out a violent dispute, his wife had the air of someone who would have been far happier in a sedate country parish in England.

The couple led me round one of the grim hostels. The men's rooms were situated along tall, dark corridors. Anything up to four men shared a dormitory, which was equipped only with the most basic of furniture. As we entered to inspect one of these rooms, the minister's wife stopped and let out a cry of pleasure. 'Oh, now haven't you made your bed *so* neatly?' she exclaimed. The poor young man responsible for this showpiece of domesticity smiled politely. Perhaps he was used to being complimented as if he was a small child, but I winced with embarrassment.

Within the DRC, the same attitude was also evident in the way in which congregations charitably provided facilities for worship for black domestic staff working locally. The Queenswood congregation had made available various different buildings for this purpose. Firstly, they came up with a member's private garage. Not surprisingly, this proved too small. Then they found a much larger outbuilding on a smallholding owned by another member. However, recently the plot had been rented out to tenants who said they did not want blacks on the land. As a result of this, Queenswood had offered black worshippers the use of the church hall.

For outsiders such as myself, the obvious question was 'Why not let them have the church?' According to one of the congregation's elders, when the issue of such provision was first raised, the garage and then the outbuilding had been chosen because some members of the church council had not wanted black people using any church buildings. One of the ministers admitted to me that this may well have been the case. However, another minister, Revd van den Berg, insisted that the latest decision to use the church hall, rather than the church, was not made for reasons of prejudice:

> I think it's more for practical reasons. The church hall, we don't use as much as the church itself on Sundays and I think they will agree and they will be satisfied to use the church hall … and we think it will be more practical for them.

> Q: In what way?

> Because it's smaller. The church can hold a thousand people and there aren't very many of our black people attending the services and we think the church hall could be more comfortable for them.

To be fair, Queenswood did use the church hall for one of its two Sunday morning services for its own members. However, one minister in the 'black' Dutch Reformed Church in Africa (DRCA) – said he had preached in a number of white areas in Pretoria and had never been offered the use of a church:

> In the olden days, we used to hold services in garages … Now they want to abolish the 'garage service'. Now they allow us to go to the hall … My experience is [that the reason why] we can't use the church but only the hall is because the hall's used for everything. In other words, our services isn't so much respected as in our place here [i.e. the black district where he ministered]. That's why they give us the hall rather than the church. White people don't want to go into a church where black people have been sitting.

The provision of the types of support outlined above all fell under the heading of 'mission work' in the DRC. Yet, this had clear connotations of the white colonial missionaries who brought Christianity to the 'natives', in the belief that western Christianity was superior to indigenous religions. When I returned to South Africa for a brief visit in 1995, two years after I carried out my research, I discovered that there was a move within the Church to try to drop the 'mission' label. The Church's former Director of Ecumenical Affairs and Information, Professor Meiring, told me that black and coloured DRC congregations had made it clear that they regarded themselves as churches, 'not the mission field'.

By that point, Queenswood had decided to rename its 'mission committee' the 'expansion committee' because its activities would be designed to expand the view of congregation members. One of the ministers, Dr Loots, told me that the decision had been taken because 'There's something of a stigma attached to the word "missionary" as if we do the missionary work and all the black people must be people who need to be evangelised.' Thus, by 1995, attitudes within the DRC were beginning to change. However, it was clearly going to take a long time for the resonances of colonialist discourse to disappear.

WORSHIP AS A 'BOUNDARY MARKER'

In theory, there was nothing to stop black domestic workers from joining the normal Sunday morning service. Prior to 1986, individual church councils were allowed to decide whether or not they wished to permit 'non-whites' to join the congregation. While there had been no formal declaration of a change of policy, I was told that the publication of *Church and Society* in 1986 and its acceptance by the General Synod meant that church councils could no longer turn down an application for membership on the basis of race. This is not spelled out explicitly in the 1990 version of *Church and Society* but it does say: 'Membership of all Dutch Reformed congregations are [*sic*] open to any believer who accepts the confession of this church.'[8] It also states that 'public worship and other gatherings are open to all visitors who desire to listen to the Word in fellowship with other believers.'[9]

The Church was also committed to move towards integration with its sister 'black', 'coloured' and 'Indian' churches. The 'black' and 'coloured' Churches (the DRCA and the DRMC, respectively) joined together in April 1994, to become the Uniting Reformed Church in Southern Africa (URCSA). The use of the word 'uniting' was quite deliberate – they said they would only call themselves the 'United' church once the other two sister churches had joined with them.

However, when I carried out my interviews in 1993, there was considerable opposition within the DRC to this idea, particularly among clergy. Respondents in both the postal and fieldwork samples were asked for their reaction to the following statement:

> The Dutch Reformed family of churches should work towards becoming a racially integrated church in an integrated society.[10]

45 per cent of the ministers who responded to the postal survey disagreed with this statement. Indeed, one-fifth said they 'strongly disagreed'. About a third of the lay respondents – all members of their congregation's ruling body, the church council – took a similar view.

There was less opposition from interviewees in the fieldwork congregations, although two-fifths of the respondents in Louis Trichardt and a third of the Queenswood interviewees said they did not agree with this statement. One minister who opposed the idea was Revd Jan Barnard in Wespoort. The reasons he gave again show the influence of the colonialist discourse that still permeated the DRC:

> In church and school, you have a culture that you strive to keep and to improve. You can't integrate – church and school are two places where I want to live out my own culture … But we can't say 'no' because we've got other races that also want to be lifted up and I'm not against it – to help them in getting on in life – but I'm not going to force myself down … We should take hands – but I just feel, in school and church, you can't afford it, it's impossible.

The assumption that white culture was superior to black culture can be seen clearly in Revd Barnard's remarks. Indeed, he went on to tell me that, as a member of a local school board, he had voted against allowing members of other races into that school because he feared that 'standards' would fall.

With feelings on the issue clearly running high in the Church, the DRC hierarchy was treading carefully in its approach to the question of integration. One major issue of contention within the DRC was the degree of integration which would take place. Church leaders did not envisage that white congregations would be forced to worship with black ones, a move which they clearly judged as unacceptable to many white congregations.

One of the main arguments of those opposed to mixed worship was that there were irreconcilable differences in culture. Again, this was clearly predicated on the assumption that white Afrikaans culture was superior to black ways of doing things. It centred around the perceived difference in the manner in which whites and blacks worshipped. While whites liked to sing hymns to the accompaniment of an organ, the opponents argued, blacks preferred to sing unaccompanied. While whites were relatively unemotional, blacks liked to move about and clap their hands. Worst of all, while whites turned up on time for services, blacks allegedly turned up late and felt no need to stick to a prescribed time-limit for a service.

One black minister conceded that these differences did exist, although he pointed out that blacks often turned up late because they did not have cars and had to walk to church, sometimes from a long distance. However, he did not feel that such distinctions posed an insurmountable hurdle to worshipping together. 'It's easy to over-come,' he told me. 'It can't be a problem which divides us until Jesus returns. We can work together and meet together and worship together. It won't be easy at first but, if you keep doing it, it'll be all right.'

A white minister in the DRCA agreed with these sentiments. 'You can make an issue out of anything,' he said. 'If people are filled with the Holy Spirit, it's not a problem. The black people are just more extrovert and emotional whereas the white people are more reserved ... I foresee that, in the future, it'll be the norm.'

Indeed, some 'white' DRC congregations in Northern Transvaal were beginning to experiment with less formal styles of worship that appealed more to younger people. Certainly, the differences seemed to be relative rather than absolute. The other argument against mixed worship revolved around language. As we have already seen, many Afrikaners held their language very dear; they were not prepared to worship in another language, or even to listen to an Afrikaans translation from another tongue. One member of the Queenswood congregation explained why he felt strongly about the issue, although as he spoke, it was evident he was almost arguing against himself:

> It is easier to read your Bible in your own language and pray in your own language and have your sermon delivered in your own language. It will have a bigger effect on me than if I had to have it maybe said in French and had an interpreter. I mean you are impressed by hearing someone delivering a sermon in another language, sometimes you get ... Okay, let's take English. You get nuances you don't pick up in Afrikaans. It is like reading the Bible in Greek, for instance. To understand exactly what the original meaning of the word was and then by hearing it in English, you might get a different colour to a certain interpretation, but normally you lose by getting it in another language ... you lose some of the quality, you always lose some of the quality.

> Q: Even with an interpreter?

> Even with an interpreter, because the interpreter got [*sic*] to make an impromptu translation which is never the same quality as the original was.

What most whites who took this line seemed to forget was that interpreters were used in the DRCA to a certain extent. In many rural areas, where DRCA ministers were overstretched, white lay preachers helped out by taking services. These lay assistants generally required interpreters as most could not speak the indigenous language. This anomaly was never mentioned by any of the DRC clergy or members that I interviewed; it did not seem to have occurred to them although many would have been aware of the use of interpreters in their 'sister' Church. It appeared to be a case of one law for the whites and another for the blacks.

The fact that these arguments over cultural difference and language were voiced so strongly had much less to do with logic, however, than with the need for a collective sense of identity. For so long, Afrikaners in the DRC had worshipped among themselves. The act of worship was, in effect, a boundary marker between blacks and white Afrikaners and, indeed, between Afrikaners and English-speaking whites. It 'flagged' the collective ethnic identity of Church members. For some, such as Revd Barnard, it also clearly served to reinforce a superior sense of collective self *vis-à-vis* the 'inferior' Other.

In the PCI in Northern Ireland, there was just as much opposition to the notion of joint Protestant–Catholic worship. Again, the act of worship was a boundary marker. However, in this case, the divide was along religious lines. Those who opposed joint worship did so on theological grounds, which they espoused with every bit as much as passion as those Afrikaners who were set against interracial worship on cultural and linguistic grounds. While many Presbyterians aware of my research told me that there was a *qualitative* difference between theological and cultural objections to mixed worship, the effect was the same. Such objections show how the actual act of worship took on a central significance as a means of constructing and reinforcing a sense of collective identity relative to the Other, whose members could not partake of the same worship. This symbolic demarcation had an impact that went far beyond the act of worship, however. It played a central role in structuring the discourse and attitudes which shaped broader efforts to improve cross-community relations within both Churches.

JOINING TOGETHER

The strength of orthodox theological conviction within the Presbyterian Church could be seen in the General Assembly's decision in 1993 to reject a proposal to examine the possibility of removing references to the Pope as 'the Anti-Christ' from the Westminster

Confession of Faith, which was adhered to by the Church and which all new ministers and elders had to sign. The suggestion had followed a decision by the Presbyterian Church in Scotland to take out these references, which many Catholics, not surprisingly, found offensive.[11] The decision of the PCI General Assembly not to do likewise was taken in private session, so there is no public record of the debate. However, as a former moderator, Dr John Dunlop, observes, it is clear that a 'linguistic expression of a belief system … formulated in the light of the issues which raged at the time when it was written in the 1640s, when the Reformation and Counter-Reformation struggles were being carried on in the nation states of Europe' still has a major influence on Presbyterian discourse and thinking.[12]

The strength of feeling surrounding the act of worship is seen in another General Assembly decision taken in the same year. The Assembly rejected part of a resolution which had called for the promotion of joint worship and witness. However, it accepted a resolution which urged the Church to 'engage in more positive and meaningful inter-Church relationships and activities wherever possible, *with due regard to our Church's doctrinal standards*.'[13]

Revd John Dickinson, of Seaview, was one of those who would not partake of joint worship. He summed up what, for him and many other Presbyterians, was the nub of the problem:

> The Roman Catholic system tends to suggest that what makes a good Christian is someone who follows, as far as humanly possible, what the Church tells you to follow. And that, by being related to the Church, you are related to Christ. Whereas, I guess the Protestant outlook is exactly the opposite – the most important relationship is firstly to Christ and secondly to the Church. And that's where the problem lies between us … now, that's compounded in Northern Ireland by a whole set of other factors which have got to do with politics and history and so on, which is most unfortunate. But you can't get around that.

Another PCI clergyman who was opposed to joint worship was the Moderator of the PCI in 1994–5, Dr David McGaughey. He told me why, as a minister in his own congregation, he took this stance. His comments sum up another fundamental objection to worshipping with Catholics that many Presbyterians have:

> I believe that the church of Rome is a Church which is in error and I personally believe that they would very largely preach that salvation is through the seven Sacraments which are administered.

Within the Reformed Church, to which I belong, we believe that salvation is through the grace of God, but *faith* plays a major part in the person who responds to the grace of God. So, it's through faith that we are saved in the grace of God, whereas the Roman Catholic Church would teach that it is through the Sacraments that one is saved. I think there is that difference and, because of that differ- ence, I find it hard at times to have that cooperation and to have that fellowship which you're talking about.

In both the PCI and the DRC in Northern Transvaal, only a minority of congregations provided occasional opportunities for joint worship; a fifth of the PCI ministers and a quarter of the DRC ministers who responded to the postal survey said such opportunities were available in their congregation 'from time to time'. Not surprisingly, there was greater opportunity for cross-community activity of a more general nature. One-third of the ministers who took part in the Northern Ireland postal survey said their congregation provided some opportunity for members to meet Catholics to help try to improve cross-community rela- tions. In Northern Transvaal, nearly half the ministers who responded to the postal survey said their congregation provided some opportunity to meet black South Africans in an effort to improve race relations.

However, the response to the above question gives an indication only of some sort of contact – in practice that contact may have been occasional and superficial. To provide an indication of the level of potentially more meaningful contact, respondents were also asked whether their congregations provided any opportunity for members to meet blacks/Catholics and to discuss what traditionally were seen as controversial issues (in the case of the questionnaire for Presbyterian ministers, this referred to social and political rather than theological issues). Although few congregations in either territory were engaged in such projects, they were more popular in Northern Transvaal with one in five of DRC ministers reporting that such opportunities were available in their congregations, compared with one in ten in Northern Ireland.

It was a commonly voiced view in both Churches that many minis- ters were held back from attempting cross-community initiatives by the likelihood of opposition from their congregations. John Dickinson, for example, said there was little appetite for cross-community activity within his congregation:

Most of the people, most of the core group [the most committed members], those people would hold no animosity to their Roman

Catholic neighbours and so on, but they would all be very strongly unionist and they would feel justifiably aggrieved, I would imagine, at some of the things that have happened over the last while and at the attitudes and political aspirations of their Roman Catholic neighbours. And all those sort of things create problems and that spills over into church life inevitably. I mean, the church is a part of its community and it's very difficult, just the same as it's very difficult for the Roman Catholic Church to appear to be anything other than nationalist.

Revd Hendrik Lambrechts, in Wespoort, took a similar view with regard to the reaction he would get from his church council if he tried to initiate any interracial meetings:

They will never grant me permission to do it. For me, it's an academic question because they won't do it. You know, quite a lot of these people are very conservative in this area. They are not outspoken about it, so you don't always know what political party they join, but if I look at when the municipal election was here, quite a lot of them voted for the CP [Conservative Party] ... And, you know, the way they talk. They don't talk about blacks, you know, they talk about kaffirs and things like that. Then you get the message – the type of language they use. Sometimes, they don't even vote for the CP, but they still talk about kaffirs.

Indeed, his colleague, Revd Barnard, told me that about a dozen people had left the congregation in protest after a theology student staying in Danville organised an unofficial meeting between church members and some black people living in the area. Yet, despite this incident and the fear of similar problems in other congregations, a majority in each of the DRC and PCI fieldwork congregations claimed to support congregational involvement in intergroup initiatives. Both the fieldwork and the postal survey respondents were asked for their reaction to three types of initiative on the part of congregations: intergroup meetings designed to enable congregation members to meet blacks and Catholics respectively, intergroup meetings at which discussion on issues which tended to divide each group took place, and occasional joint services of worship.[14]

As can be seen from Figure 7.1, at least half the interviewees in each of the congregations supported congregational involvement in intergroup efforts, including those which involved talking about divisive issues. In Stormont and Seaview, the proportion was much higher.

Figure 7.1 Support for cross-community efforts. A = Stormont; B = Seaview; C = Newtownhamilton; D = Queenswood; E = Wespoort; F = Louis Trichardt. Figures on the left axis show percentages who chose 'agree' or 'strongly agree' in response to the relevant statements.

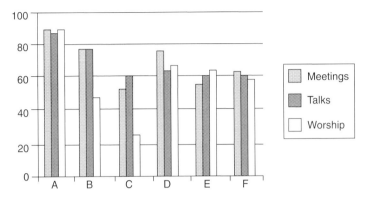

Even in Wespoort, three-fifths of the interview sample claimed to favour such initiatives. One man in Wespoort said:

> I think it's very important, especially in this area here ... I think the education has something to do with it ... When you talk to a black man, you don't know his culture, so some of the white men start screaming at him or hitting him.

Another man in Seaview voiced similar views:

> The way it is at the minute, it's going to take us to do something. This is the only way we're going to get round it. We won't get round it politically. It's only the Roman Catholic and the Protestant people that can get round these troubles.

These comments were echoed by many other interviewees. However, there was less support for such initiatives among the PCI clergy and session clerks who took part in the postal survey. Just two-fifths of the ministers and a third of the session clerks favoured cross-community meetings, with or without a discussion element. There was an even lower level of support for occasional services of mixed worship; just 22 per cent of ministers and 16 per cent of session clerks felt that congregations should hold such events.

Between three-fifths and a third of each of the DRC fieldwork samples supported the idea that congregations should hold occasional interracial services. An even higher proportion in each of the congregations said they would be prepared to attend such a service. Most also said they would be prepared to continue attending services if a few black people joined their congregation, and that they would be prepared to be a member of a racially integrated DRC congregation if the service was held in Afrikaans or an interpreter was provided.

There was slightly less enthusiasm among the DRC ministers and lay postal survey respondents for any move towards integrated worship. We have already seen that nearly half the ministers did not support moves towards a fully racially integrated Church within the DRC family of churches. Just over half supported the idea that congregations should organise occasional services of joint worship. This option was favoured by 47 per cent of the lay respondents. There was greater support for the 'meetings' and 'talks' statements, which were favoured by around two-thirds of the ministers and a slightly lower proportion of the lay respondents.

Thus, in both cases, ministers and lay members of their congregation's ruling body displayed less enthusiasm for mixed worship than did the interviewees in the fieldwork congregations. In the PCI, they were also less supportive of congregational involvement in intergroup contact schemes. One possible reason for the relative enthusiasm of the fieldwork interviewees may have been the fact that they would not be responsible for organising events; it is easy to support a particular initiative if the work is done by somebody else!

THE ROLE OF THE MINISTER

Certainly, the above figures suggest that some congregations were not participating in intergroup contact initiatives because the minister had chosen not to go down such a route. Conversely, one could argue that the minister could play a vital role if he wished to get such a scheme underway. This was certainly the view of some people in the Louis Trichardt congregation. One leading member of the congregation's Mission Committee told me of plans they had to enable young people from the congregation to meet members of a black DRCA congregation. Initially, the white youngsters would be involved in helping to repair one of the DRCA churches. She told me that this project had only got off the ground due to the efforts of Revd Christo Barnard, who had recently arrived as an assistant minister in the congregation. She claimed the other two ministers had previously been 'too busy to be bothered'. She felt the involvement of a minister was important because of the influence he carried within the congregation:

> You know the people respect the minister. When he tells them something, they are more apt to believe it than they would be to believe me. Because, to them, he is the messenger of God. So, if he speaks to them, surely it would be a more powerful message.

When I asked ministers individually why they did not do more to actively promote intergroup contact, several clergymen mentioned lack of time as a problem. While this is only an impressionistic view, it did appear that DRC ministers had a heavier workload than their PCI counterparts. For example, DRC ministers were expected to visit every household in their congregation, or the part of the congregation for which they were responsible, once a year. While household visits were considered to be part of a clergyman's duties in the PCI, there was no stipulation as to how frequent these should be. In the Northern Ireland postal survey, those clergymen who said their congregation was not participating in any intergroup initiatives were asked to give the main reason why this was so. As can be seen from Table 7.1, lack of time was only cited by a few ministers. Neither did opposition from the kirk session or fear of opposition from the congregation appear to be a major factor. The single most common reason put forward was opposition to the idea in principle.

Table 7.1 'What would you say is the main reason that you are not carrying out any joint activities with Roman Catholics at the moment?' Replies by PCI ministers to the question

I am opposed to the idea in principle	17
There's no interest in such efforts among the congregation	12
My kirk session is opposed to the idea in principle	3
I don't have the time to organise such projects	3
I'd be worried about opposition in the congregation	2
The idea hadn't occurred to us	0
Our congregation has tried such a project/projects in the past but it/they weren't successful	0
Other reply	24
Total	61

Indeed, analysis of the postal survey data strongly suggested that the personal views of ministers were a major factor in determining whether or not a congregation was engaged in intergroup activities. In the case of each of the three types of intergroup activity covered in the postal questionnaire (that is, joint meetings, joint discussions and joint services), the responses of the ministers with regard to their views on the desirability of that activity were crosstabulated with their response to the relevant question on whether their congregation was engaged in such activities. In each instance, the chi-squared statistical test produced a result that was statistically significant. In each case, congregations were more likely to provide such opportunities where their minister favoured such an initiative.[15]

Several of the ministers in the fieldwork congregations also testified to the influence they had within their church council or kirk session. In Louis Trichardt, the assistant minister, Christo Barnard, said church council members were in awe of the ministers, but that the ministers had to take some responsibility for this situation:

> It all depends on the openness we have towards people. If I have this aura around me that you're not capable of criticising me, you would most definitely not criticise me and then you would gossip behind my back, won't you? Because you have to have an outlet for your feelings and, if you can't have me as your outlet, I'm afraid you get other people. And that's why I say, as well, that is definitely not democratic, and the people are not capable, preachers in general are not capable to handle that criticism.

Perhaps not surprisingly, when I put this criticism to one of the ministers, he retorted that the council had been dominated by certain members, rather than the ministers. Another minister who felt clergymen were potentially powerful figures was John Dickinson in Seaview. Revd Dickinson said that, while there were certain forceful individuals in his kirk session, he still felt he wielded the most influence and that the same would apply to most kirk sessions:

> The nature of the Presbyterian system is such that it needs someone to coordinate it. Too many cooks spoil the broth and therefore you can't have everybody doing their own thing. So, therefore, somebody's got to provide coordination and, basically, the minister does that. And you do it on the basis of a gentleman's agreement. And the gentleman's agreement is that sessions, by and large, are fairly willing to let the minister have a degree of latitude.

And to say, 'well, we may not be totally enamoured with this, but, he wants to do it, so we'll go along with it' type of thing would be fairly common …

I've always found that, where you're pretty upfront and you tell people what you want to do, and why you want to do it, and you seek to persuade them, and if you see you're not persuading them, you back off, it usually works quite well.

In Newtownhamilton, one local community worker, Anne Murray, who had helped set up intergroup facilities in a local community centre, said she felt clergymen had a great deal of potential influence. The group she was involved with had succeeded in starting up and maintaining a cross-community playgroup and a cross-community senior citizens' club, although not without a considerable amount of persuasion and patience in the beginning. Ms Murray told me she felt local clergy should be actively encouraging the congregation to participate in such efforts:

> I find they [Revd Maurice Wade and the local priest] are not particularly interested [in cross-community work]. And I think their attitude then rubs off on some of their congregation. You know, one person's personality can make an awful difference. You know, I feel if they were there to say 'Come on, let's make a bit of an effort with this' … I'm not saying by any means they don't want it. I'm not sure they know how to handle it … I just don't think they understand exactly what community relations are – maybe they're frightened of it to a certain extent. And one doesn't like to be seen to be first. I'm quite sure that the Presbyterian minister would be afraid to say 'Come on, let's go out and play with the Catholics' – or vice versa. It's a matter of taking a lead and I don't think you're going to find them [clergy who would do that] in a small town like Newtown.

EVANGELICALISM AND CROSS-COMMUNITY PROJECTS

However, Maurice Wade had tried to initiate contact between members of his own congregation and Catholics. The efforts had not proved successful and there appeared to be one very obvious reason for this. His congregation's initiative was an evangelical one, based on the 'mission' notion of spreading the word to those who remained in ignorance of it and on the notion of the *individual's* conversion to Christianity. As the reader may recall from Revd Dickinson's comments above, this approach touches on what many Presbyterians see as a fundamental theological divide between Protestantism and Catholicism.

Maurice Wade told me that he had tried to start a joint Protestant–Catholic discussion group focusing on theological issues. However, when he suggested it to the local priest, Father A. F. MacCourt, the latter said there was not enough interest in the idea from his own congregation. When I asked Maurice Wade whether he saw the main purpose of the proposed discussion group as being to try to improve relations between Protestants and Catholics or to further his evangelical aims, he replied:

> Well, I have to be honest and say that my bottom line is to further my evangelical aims. That's the bottom line but within that I certainly believe that those sort of discussions would help the two communities understand each other and I think if you understand, at least there's the hope of some sort of friendship and less possibilities for mistrust.

Although Father MacCourt did not say this evangelical approach concerned him, he did say he felt joint theological discussions were phoney because the Protestant and Catholic theologies were simply incompatible. In fact, in 1992, the Newtownhamilton congregation had organised an 'evangelical outreach' and had invited Catholics in the town. Only one turned up. The elder who set up that outreach conceded that cross-community activities of an evangelical nature might make Catholics think all the Protestants wanted to do was convert them. However, he said it was the only type of activity his congregation could contemplate. 'From a church point of view, we want to spread the word of God and, if the church doesn't have some evangelical teaching in the events we've organised, we're not getting our aims across,' he explained.

The PCI's Moderator, Dr David McGaughey, was himself a committed evangelical. He conceded that there was a conflict of interest between this approach and initiating cross-community work within the Church:

> I think that a good number of Presbyterian ministers would recognise the Roman Catholic Church as a church, but a church in error. They would believe that folks within the Roman Catholic Church need to be born again, need to be saved, and, since they believe that, they are quite convinced that they have a mission to Roman

Catholics in the area, and would be ever seeking to reach out to them with what they would see as the truth.

Now, that causes a conflict because, if you are indeed reaching out to people in such a group, you're drawing them into the group that you minister in. And, obviously, there is a conflict there.

The parallels between the attitudes inculcated by the colonialist discourse of 'mission' within the DRC, and the discourse of evangelicalism within the PCI seemed quite striking. Both Dr McGaughey and Revd Wade believed it was possible to be a Catholic and a Christian – if you had been 'saved'. However, a few interviewees referred to all Catholics as 'non-Christian'. For example, one woman from Seaview, who was fervently evangelical in her views, quoted the Bible in explaining why she was opposed to mixed marriage: 'Be ye not unequally yoked together with unbelievers.' Another member of the same congregation said 'It's a different religion [Catholicism] – I don't even think of it as a religion.'

Most interviewees were not as blunt in their comments as that. Dr McGaughey did not believe that the evangelical approach encouraged Protestants to see Catholics as heathens. However, his comments do point to the fundamental conflict he had acknowledged between reaching out to understand 'the other side' and reaching out to convert them:

We, for instance, have a Footsteps coffee bar. We have a little place in Kilkeel and that's open on four or five nights a week.[16] And the Roman Catholics would actually come into that. And we would have four or five workers there each night. And they would just bid them welcome, they would play games together – and just try to befriend them ... I don't think any of them have been saved yet – and they've been working there for two years. But, at least, there's a place open where they can come and talk and have a cup of coffee or what have you.

Q: But, is the bottom line to try to save them?

Well, to be fair, I think eventually they hope that, as they would show them love and compassion and understanding, that they would save them – but not to *Protestantism*, I think that's the important thing – but [that they] will bring them to *Christ*. I think this is the sad thing, that so many Protestants are not what I would term 'Biblical Christians', and those same workers would have exactly the same love for the Protestant children who are also outside Christ.

INTERGROUP INITIATIVES AND APATHY

Despite the fact that a majority of those in each fieldwork congregation had supported church involvement in intergroup schemes, only a
small proportion of church members were involved in such programmes, where they existed. The chairperson of Louis Trichardt's
Mission Committee, Antoinette van Graan, said that only seven
members of her 1200-strong congregation were active in the work of
the mission committee:

> Most people say they just haven't got time ... I get the impression –
> because I've only been here for five years – that, in their hearts, you
> know, they believe in mission work, but what will their friends say if
> they see that they are sort of involved in missionary work? Because,
> you know, in the light of politics ...
>
> Q: And do some people associate mission work with politics?
>
> Yes. A lot.
>
> Q: In what way?
>
> You know, the people from the far right wing – they don't want
> apartheid to end and they feel that everything is moving to us
> working together and getting together and *that* they are opposed to
> very strongly. So, politics are [*sic*], in a way, involved.

In Stormont, some interviewees said they had not been aware that
there were any opportunities for cross-community contact. Ron
Savage said young people were much more enthusiastic about such
schemes than older members of the congregation:

> The young people are pretty much all involved – the ones in the
> [youth] groups anyway – they are all involved. In a sense, it's
> because it's part of their programme. As one of the girls giving a
> report in the church one Sunday said, 'If all the adults could do the
> kind of things we've done and were interested enough to do them,
> not only would this area be very different but so would the whole of
> Northern Ireland.' So the young people themselves perceive that
> they are all enthusiastic and involved, and only a fraction of the
> adults.
>
> Q: Why do you think this is?
>
> I think they just don't have the age-old prejudices and built-in mem-
> ories that their grandparents had, and perhaps also they led quite a

sheltered existence in this area – there's not a lot of threat here really.

Dr Savage admitted another factor was the type of programmes offered. One means of meeting Catholics was through joint Bible study groups. Yet, the congregation's own Bible study group attracted at most only about thirty people. The Queenswood congregation could also attend joint services on three Sunday evenings each year. Around a hundred people generally went along. From the point of view of other churches which participated, Sunday evening was the most mutually convenient time. However, Dr Savage said that Sunday evening had never been a popular time for Presbyterian worship, so such services were unlikely to attract large numbers.

One person who had attended the joint Bible study groups had stopped going because he felt they achieved very little. 'There's an awful lot of waffle and it doesn't really get anywhere,' he said. 'What do they waffle about?' I asked him. 'Well, in our [the congregation's own] discussion group it's "Well, what do you think this passage means? And what do you think this passage means? And what do think this passage means?", he elaborated. 'In the ones I've been to in the other [joint] group, it's about trying to be nice to each other, and there's only so much you can say. They're not actually *doing* anything as such.'

CONCLUSION

There is a fundamental contradiction between the role of the church as conciliator and the role of the church as a *volkskerk*. While both Churches officially encouraged congregational involvement in inter-group contact schemes, most PCI congregations in Northern Ireland and many DRC congregations in Northern Transvaal did not partici-pate in such programmes. The main factor determining congrega-tional involvement in such schemes appeared to be the attitudes of ministers, despite a decentralised decision-making system in both churches which, in theory, allowed the laity a major say in running their local church.

Attitudes towards church participation in intergroup schemes were shaped by a number of factors. One of the most important was the extent of opposition to interracial worship in the DRC and to joint Protestant/Catholic worship in the PCI. Clearly, there was an import-ant qualitative difference between the theological objections put forward by anti-ecumenists in the PCI and the cultural problems cited by those who opposed interracial worship in the DRC. However, from a sociological point of view, the effect was the same in that it meant, in both cases, the act of worship functioned as an important symbolic ethnic boundary marker.

In this sense, the church was operating as a *volkskerk*. Moreover, the approach towards cross-community work within both Churches was shaped, to some extent, by discourses which emphasised the superiority of Afrikaners, on the one hand, and Protestants, on the other, *vis-à-vis* the inferior Other. In the DRC, the colonialist discourse of mission coloured the approach to intergroup contact and ensured that there was an underlying assumption that whites could 'civilise' blacks and that there was little or nothing that whites could learn from blacks. In the PCI, the discourse of evangelicalism seemed to encourage an attitude among some church members that Protestants were superior to Catholics, although evangelicals make a distinction between Christians, who have been 'saved', and non-Christians who have not. Some clergymen who adhered to this discourse could only approach any cross-community contact with the aim in mind of attempting to 'save' those who participated. Clearly, this was hardly an attitude likely to endear Catholics who were quite happy with their own religion.

Intergroup contact schemes were more common in urban rather than rural areas, and attitudes towards the ethnic Other generally seemed to be more open in city than in country congregations. When one is examining the prevalence of certain discourses, it is easy to gloss over the significance of differences in location. It is to these differences that I wish to turn in the next chapter.

8 Different Worlds: Rural–Urban and Social Class Divisions

My abiding memory of Newtownhamilton is of huge farm kitchens with stone floors, an old-fashioned stove, a plain kitchen table – and very little else. As a town-dweller whose experience of country dwellings was limited to picturesque bed and breakfasts, I had expected tasteful interiors with curtains and tablecloths in attractive cotton prints, dried flowers in hanging baskets and beautifully preserved antiques. A few farmhouses lived up to my naïve expectations, but many looked as if they had not been decorated for years and had no more furniture than was absolutely essential for the functioning of domestic life on a farm.

When I told friends who had been brought up in the country, they smiled with amusement and recognition. Yes, they confirmed, interior design was not a big preoccupation among practical farm folk – and why should it be? Why indeed? My urban bourgeois values were very different from those of the farmers of Newtownhamilton who, during the summer months in which I interviewed them, were often out on the land for twelve hours a day. Many of the farmhouses had been handed down through the generations and had changed little in decades. Their parents and grandparents had been preoccupied with making a living rather than creating a lifestyle, and they were no different.

The culture shock which I experienced was an education for me in the difference between rural and urban ways of living, particularly between the lives of country-dwellers on relatively low incomes and middle-class urbanites such as myself. It was a difference which was reflected time and again in the results of my research; the rural–urban divide was one of the most profound – and possibly the most profound – intra-ethnic boundary in both Northern Transvaal and Northern Ireland. Moreover, there were striking similarities between the rural areas, on the one hand, and the urban areas, on the other, in both territories.

We tend to take for granted that we are members of certain communities. Yet, given that we will never meet all the members of most of the groupings we identify with, these are but imagined communi-ties.[1] For these communities to have an aura of reality, it is necessary to construct perimeters around them. We have seen already how both the Churches in this study contributed to that process of creating and reinforcing boundaries in a number of ways, particularly through the act of worship. We have also seen how passions over the act of worship revolved around *religious* distinctiveness in Northern Ireland and perceived *cultural* difference in the DRC. These distinctions mir-rored the fault-lines of identity around which the ethnic conflicts in each territory were structured.

This process of boundary-making went on in other ways besides the act of worship in each of the fieldwork congregations. It was con-ducted in the most intense manner in both the rural fieldwork congre-gations, especially in Newtownhamilton. Newtownhamilton was the only one of the six congregations where there was a fairly large measure of residential integration across the ethnic divide. My suspi-cion was, therefore, that this contributed to a need to work that much harder at keeping the symbolic, imaginary boundaries in place.

BOUNDARY-MAKING IN THE RURAL CONGREGATIONS

Land has always been very important in Ireland, north and south. It represents the staking-out of territory, identity and power. In the country, the individual and collective soul is woven into the land. In Northern Ireland, it has also become an emblem of the wider ethnic conflict. Battles may no longer be fought over it but an economic stand-off continues to simmer between Protestant and Catholic. All over Northern Ireland, one hears tales of the reluctance of Protestants to sell land to Catholics and vice versa. To the best of my knowledge, no research has ever been carried out on this subject and the extent of this invisible barrier remains the source of much speculation.

This economic barrier certainly existed in Newtownhamilton. Just over two-thirds of those interviewed said they would not sell land to a Catholic. Some said they were simply worried about what their Protestant neighbours would think and feared retribution or being cold-shouldered. As one farmer and leading member of the church's congregational committee put it:

Land has a different meaning from property in the Ulster Protestant's mind. My family would turn their backs on me if I did sell the farm to a Roman Catholic, and the whole society would turn their backs on me – it wouldn't be fair on my family.

For others, however, it was a matter of personal principle. 'I'd just rather they [Catholics] didn't have it. I think they get enough in this country,' one woman told me in a matter of fact of voice. 'It would be another bit of Northern Ireland away to the Roman Catholics – that's the way I look at it,' said a farmer, while another explained, 'It's just the way I was made … It seems to be the thing in this area [for the Catholics] to grab the Protestant land.'

A few people claimed the local Orange lodge did not allow Protestants to sell land to Catholics, but this was denied by the former master of the local lodge. He said the lodge preferred to see Protestant land sold to another Protestant but that this was not always possible. He was adamant that any members who did sell land to Catholics would not be ostracised by their peers, although he said they might have to put up with a bit of teasing.

Some Presbyterians in Newtownhamilton also contended that Catholics would not sell land to them, a fact readily acknowledged by the local priest. Father MacCourt told me:

Catholics never had that much. They were dispossessed by the British plantation of Ulster – driven off their land … For a Catholic to get land, it's a great achievement and he's more inclined to hold onto it when he gets it.

This acute awareness of history and its painful consequences was echoed in many interviews I carried out in Newtownhamilton. Memories here ran back a long way. Many Protestants referred to one incident in which IRA gunmen ran into a meeting of the local Orange lodge just outside the town and started shooting. Four people were killed and another seven injured. Although the attack took place in the mid-1970s, it had remained etched indelibly on the collective memory. It clearly contributed to a deep distrust of Catholics among many local Protestants. As Revd Maurice Wade put it, 'They feel that, even though Roman Catholics may not fully support the IRA, that there might be some sort of sympathy towards them … and they feel the best way to deal with the difference is just to stay clear.'

This distrust was illustrated in the strength of opposition towards both religiously mixed marriage and integrated education among congregation members. Three-fifths of the Newtownhamilton interviewees said they disapproved of mixed marriage. A higher proportion

cited theological reasons than was the case in the other two PCI congregations, although several voiced both theological and cultural concerns. One woman said, 'Theologically, both Protestants and Roman
Catholics believe in something completely different, and they have different cultural backgrounds. It's difficult enough to hold a marriage
together without starting off with all those problems.' Maurice Wade
shared her concerns, although his principal distinction was between
what he termed 'Christians' and 'non-Christians':

> I wouldn't marry a person who says they are Christian to one who
> says they are not. I've never married a couple, one from a
> Protestant background, one from a Catholic background. I've
> spoken to two persons about it but they had to get married in a
> Roman Catholic church. In principle, I have no problem with it but
> I see, perhaps, difficulties arising. For example what church will
> they affiliate themselves to? Will one party go to one and the other
> to the other? What happens when children come along? What
> about education?

The issue of integrated education was another matter on which many
Presbyterians in Newtownhamilton had strong views. In all three PCI
congregations, interviewees were asked for their reaction to the following statement: 'I would like to see an education system in which
most Protestant and Roman Catholic children are able to attend
school together.' In Stormont, all but two of the 47 interviewees
agreed with the statement, with almost half saying they strongly
agreed. Most of the Seaview respondents also supported it, with four
people saying they did not accept it. However, in Newtownhamilton,
just under half agreed with the statement, while a third of the interviewees said they disagreed.

One of the reasons given for opposition to integrated education was
a fear that mixed education might result in mixed marriage. One
woman, referring to her young daughter, said, 'I certainly wouldn't be
keen on a mixed school. I wouldn't be keen that she [her daughter]
would have an opportunity to marry into another religion.' Another
woman expressed similar worries, 'I just wouldn't like it. If you let
them all mix together, you'd have Protestants marrying Catholics and
Catholics marrying Protestants, and if they're separated, they'll not do
that.'

These comments articulate very clearly what both mixed marriage
and integrated education represented to many Presbyterians in
Newtownhamilton. Both these practices could have started dissolving

the boundaries between Protestant and Catholic, and revealing the fact that each was not so very different after all. Pierre van den Berghe has spelt out the threat that both ethnic and racial inter-marriage pose to ethnic distinctiveness:

> racial groups can survive only as long as interbreeding remains rela-tively infrequent. Three or four generations of 25 per cent or more exogamy typically erode both racial and ethnic boundaries, and lead to the formation of new ethnic groups. Both race and ethnicity are *not* immutable, but their mutability is a function of exogamy over several generations.[2]

The fear of the dissolution of ethnic boundaries was evident in all three DRC congregations, although it was most acute in Louis Trichardt, where more than four-fifths of the interviewees said they disapproved of racially mixed marriages, with three-fifths voicing strong disapproval. More than two-thirds in each of the other two DRC congregations were also opposed to the idea. The reasons given were not dissimilar from those expressed in Newtownhamilton:

> God made us separate, white and black. If he'd wanted us to get married, he'd have made us all the same. [Police officer – Louis Trichardt]
>
> Let me tell you that, if you do that [marry someone from another race], you have to break your back making that marriage work. While you're in love, it's very easy to say 'I'll compromise' but after-wards, it is not as easy as that. You must remember culture is man and man is culture. [University lecturer – Queenswood]

The strength of opposition to mixed marriage in the rural fieldwork congregations in Northern Ireland and Northern Transvaal reflected a pattern that was also evident in the postal survey and fieldwork responses to other questions. Within both the postal survey and fieldwork samples, there was a correlation between geographical area and attitude towards mixed marriage, with rural respondents more likely to disapprove of mixed marriage than their urban counterparts.[3] In many cases, rural respondents were also more likely than their urban counterparts to disapprove of intergroup activities and joint worship.

The strong sense of continuity and shared history which was evident in both Newtownhamilton and Louis Trichardt was clearly an import-ant factor in shaping the discourses expressed in these congregations. In both cases, that historical narrative was one of settlers staking out territory and of violent clashes with 'natives'. Both towns were, in fact, named after settlers. Newtownhamilton was named after a Scottish settler called Hamilton, who was given a grant of land in the district. According to a local historian, one of the two army barracks in the area during this period was run by another Scottish settler, John Johnston, who was paid by the English every time he beheaded a Catholic 'rebel'.[4]

Louis Trichardt was named after a well-known Voortrekker leader whose trek party camped in the area in 1836. A great deal of violence preceded permanent white settlement in the area. Having established a sizeable settlement by the middle of the century, the colonists were driven back south by the Venda in 1867. The land was reclaimed by the settlers in 1898 when a military commando of 2000 soldiers was sent up to the area. Its members chased the Venda chief to what is now Zimbabwe, and routed the capital of Venda which, at that time, was positioned on the striking Hanglip mountain which towers over Louis Trichardt.[5]

In both Louis Trichardt and Newtownhamilton, one could feel the continued presence of history in a much more vivid way than was the case in the urban congregations. The Orange Order, which had originated in a skirmish not far from Newtownhamilton, remained a focal point of social life and of collective identity in the district. In Louis Trichardt, the rush of interest in both the Volksfront and the AWB, with their use of Voortrekker symbolism and mythology, brought history back to life in an uncomfortable guise. Just before I left the town, having completed my research, its inhabitants were treated to an ugly reminder of what the AWB stood for. Armed AWB members, their faces grim and defiant, positioned themselves outside the town's schools. They said they were there in case striking teachers from neighbouring black schools tried to 'invade' the local white schools. In fact, there had never been any such threat. The teachers had planned to march through the town, but the council refused permission for their protest and it was called off. Nevertheless, the uniformed AWB demonstrators remained outside the school gates for some two hours in what was presumably intended to be a 'show of force'.

Alan Finlayson has argued that nationalist ideologies discursively position people so that they see themselves as a member of that nation.[6] He contends that these nationalisms achieve their power through the coherence and interrelatedness of their different elements. In the case of Ulster loyalist discourse, these elements comprise a sense of national identity, the Protestant religion, a belief in democracy and freedom, and an antipathy towards Catholicism and the Irish Republic. Each of these elements 'evokes another and "operates as a symbol of the others"'.[7] Thus, according to Finlayson, the discourse *positions* the individual as someone who identifies with Ulster heritage and Protestant religion, is antipathetic towards Catholicism and the Irish Republic, and supports loyalist political rhetoric.

In both Newtownhamilton and Louis Trichardt, one could see this sort of interrelationship working at a subtle *symbolic* level of meaning. Each of the symbolic elements of Protestant and Afrikaner identity, respectively, was alive and was imbued with meaning by many of the interviewees. In many cases, their antipathy towards the ethnic Other ran deep. In the urban congregations, on the other hand, the symbolic elements of identity did not hold the same dynamic and coherent quality. In Wespoort and Seaview, there was less participation than in the rural congregations in the rituals surrounding both civil and denominational religion. In the middle-class congregations, many interviewees expressed disgust at the use of civil religion symbols for 'political' ends. Moreover, in Stormont, there was a not inconsiderable degree of opposition to links between the PCI and the Orange Order, with many interviewees believing that clergymen should not belong to the Order. A number of members of this congregation also expressed antipathy towards the man once held to be the hero of the Protestant working class, Ian Paisley. At the same time, however, far from wholeheartedly embracing political change, many interviewees in both Stormont and Queenswood viewed the future with apprehension.

Thus, the symbolic elements of both Protestantism and Afrikanerdom did not seem to form a neat, discursive whole in the urban congregations in the manner suggested by Finlayson. On the other hand, the rural congregations did manifest greater coherence in the meaning their members attached to the symbolic and discursive aspects of their collective identity. This coherence seemed to be due, at least in part, to the strong sense of historical continuity which existed in both Louis Trichardt and Newtownhamilton. There was a reawakening of the 'unease' which Jennifer Todd referred to and which the first settlers must have felt when they reached these areas.[8] It must also be remembered that there was a much greater degree of residential integration in Newtownhamilton than in the other two PCI congregations. This may well have enhanced the significance of other, more symbolic means of constituting the boundary between Catholic and Protestant.

ACCOMMODATING TO THE MAINSTREAM

The nature of intergroup relations in a particular area was only one factor which a minister had to gauge when he arrived in a new congregation. In both the DRC and the PCI, ministers had rarely grown up in the locality which they served. They were outsiders and thus had to adapt to their congregation and their locality. The ability to do this successfully was clearly regarded as an essential attribute by those ministers I interviewed. In the case of both Churches, the establishment of good relations with one's kirk session or church council was obviously a priority. This body represented the 'cultural mainstream' within the congregation. In rural areas, such individuals would also be likely to form an important part of the mainstream within the local district.

While one of the Louis Trichardt ministers, Revd Harm Bonnema, had lived in the town for some years, his colleague, Revd Gerhardus Botha, was a relative newcomer. This also applied to Maurice Wade in Newtownhamilton. Both these 'outsiders' had found they had had to compromise their principles in some respects. The reader will recall that Maurice Wade had felt it would not be prudent to upset the applecart by taking a stand on the fact that the Orange Order held a biannual service in his church, despite his opposition to the Order. Nevertheless, he had taken a firm line on the need to declare oneself 'saved' in order to become a communicant member of the church. This had not gone down well with everyone in his congregation or kirk session.

Certain interviewees said they had stopped going to church because of Maurice Wade's 'born-again' stance. Revd Wade himself admitted that most of his kirk session would be happy with a less rigorous approach to the rule. However, he said they knew his position when they called him to minister to the congregation. Two elders described him as inflexible. One said 'He has a mind of his own ... Sometimes it's out of accord with the kirk session.' The minister rejected the charge that he was inflexible, but he felt the elders were too reticent about speaking their mind at kirk session meetings. 'Countrymen are very quick to let you make the decisions and then, when something goes wrong, they're very quick to remind you that it's your decision and not theirs,' he told me, with a wry smile.

Gerhardus Botha certainly felt that ordinary members of his congregation in Louis Trichardt were not particularly forthright:

> In the [Orange] Free State [where he had previously served as a minister], we had a few guys from the right wing, but at least they'd

come and speak to you afterwards about something you'd said. Here, I think they listen and decide you're a liberal and they just don't come any more ...

From the first day, people want to know where you stand and you try not to let the people know whether you stand to the left or the right, because then you lose those people and the chance to preach the Word is gone. I wouldn't mind if people said I was on one side, but it would make your life in the town not so easy.

Revd Botha had only been in Louis Trichardt for a year. However, he said he had felt a shift in his own attitudes during that time, as if the collective sense of threat among whites had seeped into his blood:

Although ... I believe everyone has a place, and I believe in democracy, I'm more afraid than I was in the Free State. It's really something one feels. I don't *want* to feel like that but it is really so. The place one is in and the people one meets has [*sic*] made a small shift in my attitudes.

I'm not afraid of losing out. But I believe I understand the people more. I understand some of the right-wing people. They make up 50 per cent of the congregation ... They pay me! I'd rather be in the Free State again rather than here because I don' t want to be a part of a town that is so aggressive and so right-wing.

The experiences of Revd Botha and Revd Wade suggest that there is pressure on rural ministers to accommodate to the cultural mainstream at a local level. If they do not, they will continue to be regarded as 'outsiders' which is what seemed to have happened, to some extent, in the case of Revd Wade. This pressure to adapt stems from the significance of the local district as an 'imagined community' in the minds of its inhabitants. Many of the members of Newtownhamilton congregation rarely travelled beyond two larger towns in County Armagh, which were both about twenty minutes' drive away. The boundaries of their world were drawn around the local rural district. The cities of Belfast and Pretoria were seen and hence portrayed by the residents of Newtownhamilton and Louis Trichardt respectively, as the 'imagined Other'. These cities were places which were experienced largely through the medium of television. They were places full of change and flux, a world away from the slower pace of life in rural areas.

There was a strong contrast between these rural congregations and the middle-class congregations of Queenswood and Stormont. Both these congregations contained some of the senior civil servants involved in implementing the political changes taking place. Although interviewees would have identified to some extent with the suburb they lived in, their most significant 'imagined community' was a wider one which encompassed Northern Ireland, on the one hand, and South Africa, on the other. Although the prime concern of many members of both these congregations was undoubtedly the micro-community of their own families, it was in these congregations that many interviewees took a 'politically correct' pride in describing them-selves as 'Northern Irish' or 'South African'. These were individuals who sensed the shifting flow of the cultural mainstream and were adjusting accordingly. While they were already adapting to changes that many of them saw as inevitable, church members in the rural con-gregations were clinging to symbols of continuity, such as the church and civil religion. Yet, this was often out of fear because many of them also saw change as inevitable.

The ministers in both Stormont and Queenswood were important local figures in this process of change. We have seen that the ministers in Stormont did appear to have influenced the attitudes of a number of their members. Yet, their eye was on the cultural mainstream at a wider level than that of their immediate locality. While the ministers in the rural congregations had to negotiate with the 'mainstream' at a local level, in an effort to remain part of it, ministers in both Stormont and Queenswood, like many in their congregations, were positioning themselves to become part of the wider new mainstream that was evolving from political change.

THE WORKING-CLASS CONGREGATIONS

In many ways, the contrast between the working-class and middle-class congregations in both Belfast and Pretoria was just as marked as that between the rural and urban districts. This was especially evident in Pretoria. The Wespoort congregation was at the edge of a sprawling industrial area which stretched out to the west of the city. It was on the other side of the city from the more comfortable suburbs in the north and east. Many of those who lived in the suburbs had never been to this humbler part of town. While the poverty here did not begin to compare to that of the black townships, life was far from easy for those without jobs or on medical pensions.

The proportion of interviewees who were out of work in the Wespoort sample indicated an unemployment rate of about 9 per cent in the congregation. In general, those without jobs were able to find work within six months. Thus, unemployment was a relatively short-term phenomenon. However, many others were on minimal medical pensions as a result of being declared unfit for work. The church distributed food parcels to those in need in the Wespoort congregation, a phenomenon unheard of in Northern Ireland where direct government welfare assistance was more generous.

Like the rural congregations, there was a sense in Wespoort of a self-contained community, partly because a major road cut the district off from the main part of the residential area in West Pretoria. This was less true of Seaview which, geographically, merged into the rest of North Belfast and seemed to lack any particular focal point for the community. While the district of Danville in the Wespoort congregation had one main shopping area, for example, Seaview simply had small shops scattered here and there.

In Seaview, the proportion of interviewees without jobs indicated an unemployment rate in the congregation of 17 per cent. Moreover, a number of those interviewed had either been unemployed recently or feared they would be out of work again in the near future. Unemployment also tended to be a more long-term phenomenon than was the case in Wespoort. However, those without jobs were able to draw on a more generous level of welfare assistance than that provided by the South African government. The local congregation did not provide any help for the unemployed, although it did offer a programme of support for elderly congregation members.

Yet, while there was not the same sense of a firm geographical boundary as in Wespoort or the rural congregations, many interviewees in Seaview clearly drew a firm mental line between themselves and the world of politics, feeling there was little they could do to influence the political decisions which affected their lives. This attitude was also very evident in Wespoort and in both the rural congregations. Among some of the Seaview and Wespoort interviewees, there was also an attitude of the church as an Other within their midst; something rather intimidating or awe-inspiring. Clergymen were regarded as individuals who had a relatively high social standing. As noted in Chapter 6, two-fifths of the Wespoort sample and a quarter of the Seaview sample rated their clergymen as the most important people in their local community. Some church members said they were put off attending by the formality or by the fact that they felt expected to wear smart clothes. Both these congregations had lower rates of attendance than any of the other fieldwork congregations. In the context of Britain, Grace Davie has argued that this does not mean that such individuals are not religious, merely that they express their religiosity in different ways:

> The discrepancy between believing and belonging, for example, is at its sharpest in urban working-class areas, and above all in the inner city. Here belief persists (albeit in a depressed form), but the expected reluctance to practise religion is compounded by a further factor, a mistrust of institutional life of whatever kind, the churches included ... In a middle-class environment people are more likely to make conscious choices about both belief and practice; if they do one, they do the other. In contrast, in a working-class environment (where levels of education are lower) there is, apparently, no need to put belief into institutional or liturgical practice. Indeed, it could be argued that the reverse is true; in many urban areas, churchgoing is seen as at best unnecessary and at worst hypocritical.[9]

In both Louis Trichardt and Newtownhamilton, on the other hand, there was a greater feeling of involvement with the church, although there was a sense in which the ministers were seen as the Other, particularly in Newtownhamilton. In Newtownhamilton, the congregation was clearly divided over Revd Wade's evangelical approach; those who were not of his persuasion could be very contemptuous of those who were. Here, then, was another boundary which formed part of the process by which people constructed their sense of identity.

CONCLUSION

The tendency to define ourselves in terms of what we are not runs deep in western culture. Research carried out by Robert Wuthnow has suggested that both religious liberals and conservatives in the United States constitute their sense of identity, at least in part, from the negative image they have of the other grouping.[10] While it is clear that negative images of the Catholic and black Other respectively played a major part in the process of identity formation for most of the Afrikaners and Protestants interviewed for this study, it is also evident that each drew on a wide range of Others in order to carry out this process. Boundary lines were drawn not only between Protestants and Catholics, Afrikaners and blacks, but also between different groups within Afrikanerdom and Protestantism, between individuals and certain institutions which claimed to represent them, and between individuals and the 'political' meanings attached to certain civil religion symbols.

In response to the rapid changes taking place and to the loss of collective status and power, many individuals seemed to draw these lines ever more firmly, perhaps in a bid to feel more secure. In rural congregations, there was a firm sense of continuity with the past and a strong identification with both denominational religion and the symbols of civil religion. In the middle-class congregations, interviewees operated within a wider imagined community and there was an evident wish among many to secure a place as part of the new liberal mainstream that was emerging in both territories. This distinction had an impact on the way in which ministers negotiated their relationship with their congregation. In rural areas, it was essential to integrate into the local mainstream, while in middle-class urban districts, ministers seemed more anxious to be involved in the cultural mainstream at a wider level.

Conclusion

The preceding chapter has reminded us of the complex nature of the constitution and reconstitution of ethnic identity. In this book, I have tried to delineate some of the processes involved in the collective imagining of ethnicity where the balance of political power is shifting away from a once-dominant ethnic group. In this final chapter, I want to draw together these different threads and to consider their applicability to other situations.

At the beginning of this study, I talked about the act of collective worship as a means by which identity is 'flagged'. Where ethnic and religious boundaries coincide, as in the two case studies we have examined here, going to church reminds the worshipper of their ethnic identity. This process can occur in a very mundane way. However, where these ethnic boundaries provide the framework for the structures around which one group is able to enjoy a dominant position, the act of worship takes on a particular kind of symbolic significance. We saw how passions were aroused within both the PCI and the DRC over the issue of religiously mixed worship, on the one hand, and racially mixed worship, on the other. In these cases, worship represented both the symbolisation and the institutionalisation of these ethnic boundaries. While political changes were threatening the security of these perimeters for both Afrikaners and Ulster Protestants, their churches provided sacred spaces where these boundaries remained relatively intact.

Afrikaners and Ulster Protestants had both enjoyed the power to *define* the boundary between themselves and the Other by enshrining it either in law or in widely followed discriminatory practices. For Afrikaners, this power was wielded in the form of the inhumane institution of apartheid. In Northern Ireland, the former unionist government at Stormont had allowed religious discrimination to flourish. It had also presided over a 'British' region where the British constitutional claim was contested by a large minority of the inhabitants. This contested constitutional link continued to be underwritten by the British government under Direct Rule, thus privileging the right of unionists to define their identity over the right of nationalists to do likewise.

CIVIL RELIGION

As we have seen, by the early 1990s, shifts in the balance of political power were threatening the ability of both Afrikaners and Ulster Protestants to continue to define the boundaries of collective identity. During the period which we have examined, the imminent loss of that power gave added significance to discursive, symbolic and ritualistic means of constituting both identity and status. In Northern Ireland, this was particularly evident in the violent conflict which erupted during the mid-1990s over the annual Orange Order parade from Drumcree Church. Here the ritual balance of power, in the form of the parade, became a symbolic indicator of the *real* balance of power between unionists and nationalists. In deciding whether unionists or nationalists would be appeased, the British state (ostensibly through the RUC and, more recently, the Parades Commission) was choosing which community retained the upper hand in defining national identity.

The controversy highlighted the symbolic relationship between the main Protestant churches and the Orange Order which, until this time, had been of mutual benefit to both institutions, in that the Protestant churches enhanced their traditional image as *volkskerks*, while the Orange Order gained in terms of its credibility and symbolic weight. This relationship was played out through the use of churches by the Orange Order for special services and the willingness of ministers to preach at those services. Just under three-quarters of the Presbyterian ministers who responded to the postal survey said that their church was used for such services and that they preached at them. In 1997 and 1998, church leaders in both the PCI and the Church of Ireland issued statements which differed in content but essentially urged the Orangemen at Drumcree to behave in a considerate and sensitive manner. This appeared to be an attempt by both Church hierarchies to distance themselves from the uncompromising stand being taken by the Orange Order over Drumcree. Clearly, there was an acute conflict of interest between the professed role of both Churches as conciliators and bridge-builders, and the symbolic identification of these denominations with an organisation whose activities resulted in violence of the type seen at Drumcree.

In the Afrikaner case, the relationship between denominational and civil religion was a slightly more complicated one. The institutionalised, but highly secretive, form of civil religion – the Broederbond – had had very close links with the DRC. However, during the early

1990s, the Church distanced itself from the Bond and the Bond itself underwent a transformation in a bid to accommodate itself to the 'new South Africa'. A symbolically significant relationship still survived between the DRC and another aspect of Afrikaner civil religion. This centred on the services of worship conducted on the Day of the Vow, a symbolic commemoration of a victory by white settlers over Zulus; not surprisingly, this annual ritual deeply offended many black South Africans. The Church's involvement in this commemoration enhanced the symbolic and moral authority of the ritual. The Day of the Vow was a public holiday and, in this sense, it was an 'institution'. It institutionalised a pool of civil religion symbols and represented an attempt by the National Party government to foster a sense of collective pride among Afrikaners.

However, the evidence from the fieldwork conducted for this study suggested interest in the Day of the Vow and other strands of Afrikaner culture was diminishing. The changes within the Broederbond, referred to above, indicated an organisation which was experiencing a crisis of both identity and purpose. Many Afrikaners I spoke to felt that the Bond's influence had waned not only within the DRC but also in other sectors of society. An umbrella Afrikaner cultural organisation, the FAK, which seemed to have close links with the Bond, failed to capture the imagination of the Afrikaner public when it attempted to launch a new version of the mobilisation of Afrikaner nationalist sentiment which had first taken place in the 1930s and 1940s. What did inspire allegiance from Afrikaners, particularly in rural and urban working-class areas, was the use of the symbols of Afrikaner civil religion to push a right-wing political message which was opposed to black majority rule throughout South Africa and which insisted that Afrikaners should have their own *volkstaat*.

Both the Afrikaner Volksfront and the AWB, the two most prominent right-wing groups during 1993, achieved far more media attention and clearly attracted much greater active interest from Afrikaners than either the Bond or the FAK. The Volksfront and the AWB played a major role in defining the parameters of public debate in South Africa by providing a symbolic reminder of the potential for violent mass action by whites. However, they were relatively new groups which quickly faded from prominence once black majority rule was implemented.[1]

By contrast, the Orange Order was almost two hundred years old. Through the hundreds of parades it organised across Northern

Ireland every year, it retained the ability to spatially constrain social life in a manner which had a direct, and often deeply resented, impact on many nationalists. Its parades represented the symbolic reconstitution both of the ethnic boundary between Protestants and Catholics, and of the privileged status of Protestants over Catholics. While 'blood and thunder' bands and loyalist paramilitary groups did contest the definitional authority of the Orange Order over civil religion symbols, Ulster Protestant civil religion still remained institutionalised in one monolithic entity which had no exact parallel in South Africa.

As we have seen, among both Afrikaners and Ulster Protestants, there was stronger support for groups which utilised civil religion in rural than in urban areas. The links between the Churches and civil religion were also closer in rural areas. While four-fifths of rural clergymen in the PCI preached at Orange Order services, only just over half of their counterparts in urban congregations presided over such events. Likewise, in the DRC in Northern Transvaal, rural ministers were more likely than urban clergymen to preach at Day of the Vow services.

IDENTITY AND DISCOURSE

In South Africa, the rhetoric employed by the political groups which drew on civil religion mythology appealed especially to those fearful of losing their land or their jobs once black majority rule was in place. Afrikaners, in particular, exhibited signs of the 'unease' *vis-à-vis* the 'natives' which Jennifer Todd discerned in many Ulster Protestants.[2] There was an evident desire among the Afrikaners I interviewed to dominate in discourse where they could no longer dominate in practice; many talked in terms which assumed that blacks were far less 'civilised' than whites. This colonialist mentality was reinforced by the widespread use of the term 'mission work' within the DRC to describe any activities involving blacks.

The discourse of 'mission' assumed that the religious and cultural practices of whites were superior to those of the 'natives'. Likewise, the discourse of 'evangelicalism', espoused by many within the PCI, assumed a superior set of religious beliefs to those of their 'non-Christian' neighbours. While this discourse did not appear to rule out the possibility of Catholics being 'saved' and 'born again' as Christians, it seemed to encourage a mind-set which saw Protestants as superior to Catholics. However, it also drew a demarcation line between Presbyterians who had been 'saved' and their less fortunate brothers and sisters who had not undergone this experience. The insistence of some clergymen that Presbyterians should make a declaration that they had been 'saved' before becoming full members of the Church had created resentment in a number of congregations. In Newtownhamilton, for example, many interviewees seemed to draw part of their sense of identity from comparing themselves to the type of Presbyterian – evangelical or non-evangelical – which they were *not*.

This is one illustration of the complex way in which identity is formed in relation to a number of Others, some of which will be external to ethnic boundaries, but some of which will lie within it. The symbolic and institutionalised versions of the external ethnic Other acted as objects onto which both Ulster Protestants and Afrikaners could project their fear of the future and of change. These negative signifiers, such as the Catholic Church and the ANC, seemed to activate or reactivate the motivational power of positive signifiers of ethnic identity, such as the Orange Order and Voortrekker symbolism.

Thus, the collective identities of both Afrikaners and Ulster Protestants were constituted in relation to what they were *not*. At the same time, members of each group constructed internal boundaries which were also important in terms of creating a sense of identity. Thus, many middle-class Afrikaners in Queenswood defined themselves as *not* being Volksfront or AWB supporters. Many members of the Stormont congregation criticised the Orange Order for being too political or for having lost its original character; they defined themselves as *not* a supporter of the Order. The same process of internal delineation of boundaries could also be seen with regard to the political sphere. Many Afrikaners and Ulster Presbyterians clearly drew a firm mental line between themselves and the political sphere, which they felt powerless to influence. This articulation of alienation from the political process was clearly an important discursive means of coping with the enormity of the political changes on the horizon. It enabled interviewees to tell themselves that they were in no way responsible for what was going on. In many cases, it also articulated a quite genuine sense of powerlessness. Presbyterians, in particular, often seemed to take a positive pride in their disdain for the world of politics.

In both Churches, there existed a discourse of separation between the religious and political spheres. This was not a universal discourse but it mirrored the discourse of political alienation in providing a means by which church members and clergymen could draw a mental boundary between the sacred space provided by the church and the secular, murky world of politics. This line was often drawn in a way which permitted what were traditionally viewed as 'moral issues' to be discussed in a church setting; 'politics' essentially consisted of those issues which were at the heart of the ethnic conflicts within each territory and were thus too 'sensitive' to discuss.

THE CHURCH AS PART OF THE MAINSTREAM

The reality is that it is impossible to separate religion from politics and it is impossible to draw a firm dividing line between the religious and the secular spheres. At the beginning of this book, I discussed how the church derived much of its cultural power from being part of the cultural mainstream of the ethnic group with which it was associated. As the balance of political power began to shift, the framework for a new mainstream began to emerge and, in both cases, the churches positioned themselves so they might become part of the new political and cultural order.

While other elites within both ethnic groups had accorded a certain amount of authority on its own terms to denominational religion, the emerging mainstreams were more secular and pluralistic in ethos. This meant that the churches needed to convert ethnoreligious capital into cultural or symbolic capital by ensuring that the discourses they articulated were in tune with the predominant discourses of the new mainstream.

Thus, many of the official pronouncements of the church were based on discourses of change which advocated greater openness and cooperation with the ethnic Other, and a willingness to accept political compromises. However, these liberal attitudes were not necessarily shared by the clergy and laity, many of whom clung to discourses of continuity; of preserving the *status quo*. The contest between these two types of discourse was played out most dramatically in the DRC over the issue of apartheid. Having advocated apartheid for decades, the Church switched its position in the mid-1980s, finally declaring in 1990 that apartheid had been practised in an oppressive and 'sinful' way. The results of this study suggest that some clergy and many laity in the DRC did not share this revised view.

The clergy were key figures in the contest between competing discourses over issues such as apartheid. Relatively few church members read the type of church publication which contained pronouncements on political and social issues. Even wider publicity in the news media did not appear to reach all church members. Thus, the clergy were important as gatekeepers and mediators in the process of communication between the 'hierarchy' and the grassroots.

The clergy also played an important role in negotiating the conflict of interest which both the DRC and the PCI faced between their traditional role as *volkskerks* and their self-proclaimed role as conciliators. Both Churches encouraged congregations to participate in intergroup activities designed to improve understanding between different ethnic groups. However, many congregations were not involved in such schemes and many clergy were not enthusiastic about such programmes.

The role of the clergy was crucial in this respect; the evidence from the study suggested that there was a strong link between the willingness of a congregation's minister to become involved in such schemes, and the participation or otherwise of a congregation in intergroup initiatives. This is interesting given that the organisational structure of both Churches was designed in such a way that a great deal of potential power was devolved to the laity at congregational level. Congregations were run by bodies in which, theoretically, the minister was on an equal footing with the lay members. However, in practice, these bodies often deferred to the minister and looked to him for leadership. Thus, while the organisational structure permitted power to be shared between clergy and laity, in practice, the religious capital possessed by the clergy enabled them to occupy a dominant position of influence within the congregation.

The extent to which interviewees articulated a sense of alienation with regard to politics suggests that they were as willing to accord symbolic authority to politicians as they were to their clergy. In other words, there was a readiness to cede power to elites within the ethnic group. For the clergy, this provided those who supported intergroup initiatives with potentially greater freedom to attempt such schemes than some of them appeared to realise. In the political sphere, it enabled politicians to enact change relatively swiftly without fear of mass rebellion by Afrikaners, on the one hand, or Ulster Protestants, on the other.

This willingness to defer to elite groups also helped to ensure that the constitution of a new cultural mainstream in each case could be based around 'rules' of membership defined by those with political, economic and cultural power. Given the manner in which power shifted during the period examined in both cases, the process of defining the new mainstream was one of constant struggle and negotiation. However, it was a contest confined to elite groupings; it did not involve ordinary citizens in an active and meaningful way. One of the contributing factors to this pattern was undoubtedly the discourse of alienation which certainly influenced the way in which Afrikaners and Ulster Protestants approached politics, and doubtless shaped the attitudes of other groups in these territories as well.

The exact configuration of the membership and discourse of the cultural mainstream reflected the views of the powerful rather than the powerless. This is, of course, exactly how hegemony operates. This begs the question as to whether hegemony is able to establish its hold more successfully in times of rapid change than during periods of stability. We have seen that, for many people, the discourse of alienation represented a means of helping them to cope with transition. This would suggest that, during periods of upheaval, powerful mainstream interests do indeed have greater scope for enacting and managing change at a collective level because of the strategies for dealing with change at an individual level which many people adopt.

BROADER IMPLICATIONS

The above hypothesis clearly has relevance to many ethnic conflict situations. However, in Chapter 3 it was observed that a culture of political alienation may well have developed among Afrikaners and Ulster Protestants much earlier than the period of change on which we have focused. This may help to explain why these respective ethnic conflicts lasted so long; if ordinary Afrikaners and Ulster Protestants erected a discursive barrier between themselves and their political leaders during the era of apartheid in South Africa and the period of the Troubles in Northern Ireland, there would have been little pressure on their political representatives to try to achieve a settlement. Thus, one could argue that the existence of a discourse of alienation may contribute towards resolution of ethnic conflict but it may also help to explain why that conflict is sustained.

It must also be remembered that the demarcation line between the dominant group and the symbolic Other seemed to run much deeper in *rural* than in *urban* areas. The collective ethnic memory and sense of continuity was much stronger in the rural districts examined in this study. This meant that the symbolic aspects of ethnic identity, when combined together, were more meaningful to rural inhabitants. The imagined community within which they existed had narrow boundaries in geographic terms but flexible perimeters in temporal terms; those boundaries extended back into a reconstituted past which helped to provide a meaningful context for the signifiers of ethnicity.

Therefore, the social processes which form part of ethnic conflict may play themselves out in very different ways in different types of locale. Likewise, as we have observed above, boundaries are drawn up *within* ethnic groups as well as around them; certain symbolic signifiers which are said to form a focus for group identification may also function as the symbolic Other *against* which some group members constitute their sense of identity. This means one needs to be wary of generalising about any group involved in such a struggle and to be conscious of the complexity of the discursive and symbolic processes involved.

Clearly, the role of both the DRC and the PCI during the period of change examined in this book arose out of very specific sets of historical circumstances. It is important, however, to remember that these were mainstream Protestant denominations, not fundamentalist sects. A worshipper from one of the major Protestant churches in the United States or Britain would not feel out of place in either of these denominations. These two case-studies demonstrate the capacity for mainstream religion to play a key role in ethnic conflict. It is misleading to assume, as many westerners seem to do at present, that only 'extremist' religious groups play an active part in ethnic conflict.

Mainstream denominations, like fundamentalist sects, contain various symbolic and ritualistic signifiers which can be imbued with different meanings. We have examined the symbolic significance of the act of worship in both the DRC and the PCI. I have argued that, where religious and ethnic boundaries converge, participation in the act of worship quietly flags one's ethnic as well as religious identity. However, the act of worship can become a marker of much greater importance when those boundaries are under threat. This applies just as much to conventional denominational forms of religion as to more radical religious sects.

The role of religion is always contingent on many different factors. In examining Ulster Protestants and Afrikaners, it is easy for 'modern liberals' around the world to see both these ethnic groups as Others which are very different from themselves. The truth is that they are not so different at all and that, if liberal-minded readers had grown up as Afrikaners under apartheid or as Protestants during the Troubles, they might well espouse some of the more unsavoury views quoted in this book. Likewise, the need to retain symbolic authority within a collectivity means mainstream religion has an awesome capacity to be a force which promotes oppression and conflict, just as much as it has the capacity to be a force for positive change.

Notes and References

Introduction

1. See Cash, John Daniel (1996) *Identity, Ideology and Conflict: The Structuration of Politics in Northern Ireland* (Cambridge: Cambridge University Press) and Billig, Michael (1995) *Banal Nationalism* (London: Sage).
2. See, for example, Juergensmeyer, Mark (1993) *The New Cold War? Religious Nationalism Confronts the Secular State* (Berkeley: University of California Press) and Kepel, Gilles (1994) *The Revenge of God: The Resurgence of Islam, Christianity and Judaism in the Modern World* (trans. Alan Braley) (Cambridge: Polity Press).
3. This term was inspired by the use of the term 'mainstream' or 'mainline' religion, which seems to me to generally mean the denominations or religious groups which form part of the cultural mainstream of a particular nation or community. See especially Roof, Wade Clark and McKinney, William (1987) *American Mainline Religion: Its Changing Shape and Future* (New Brunswick: Rutgers University Press).
4. I use 'clergymen' throughout this text to refer to those I interviewed and those who responded to the postal surveys I conducted (see Chapters 2 and 3). Quite simply, this is because they were all men. Both the DRC and the PCI permit women to become ministers. While the PCI did have some female ministers when I conducted my research in Northern Ireland in 1994, there were no female clergy in the DRC's Northern Transvaal Regional Synod, which covered the area where I carried out my research in South Africa, during the period in which I carried it out in 1993. I am told that ministers are never referred to as 'clergymen' within the PCI. However, I am afraid I have opted to use both 'clergymen' and ministers as the use of only one term could prove rather monotonous for the reader.
5. Smith, A. D. (1986) *The Ethnic Origins of Nations* (Oxford: Blackwell).
6. De Vos, George A. and Romanucci-Ross, Lola (1995) 'Ethnic Identity: A Psychocultural Perspective', in Romanucci-Ross, Lola and De Vos, George A. (eds) *Ethnic Identity: Creation, Conflict and Accommodation*, 3rd edn (Walnut Creek: Altamira Press) p. 357.
7. Stavenhagen makes this general point about the successful mobilisation of ethnic sentiment. See Stavenhagen, Rodolfo (1996) *Ethnic Conflicts and the Nation-State* (Basingstoke: Macmillan).
8. Smith, op. cit., pp. 22–30.
9. Barth, Fredrik (1969) 'Introduction', in Barth, Fredrik (ed.) *Ethnic Groups and Boundaries: The Social Organization of Culture Difference* (London: George Allen & Unwin), pp. 9–38.

190

10. See Jenkins, Richard (1997) *Rethinking Ethnicity: Arguments and Explorations* (London: Sage).
11. Billig, op. cit.
12. Anderson, Benedict (1991) *Imagined Communities: Reflections on the Origins and Spread of Nationalism* Revised edition (London: Verso).
13. Jarman, Neil (1997) *Material Conflicts: Parades and Visual Displays in Northern Ireland* (Oxford: Berg).
14. Ibid., p. 261.
15. Jarman's book discusses the more frequent Orange Order and other loyalist band parades which take place throughout the summer, as well as similar republican parades. The more regular parades could be seen as serving the function of flagging identity in a manner less mundane than simple attendance at church and yet more routine than the annual Twelfth parades.
16. See Smith, op. cit., and Smith, A. D. (1995) *Nations and Nationalism in a Global Era* (Cambridge: Polity Press).
17. See notes 25 and 27 below. John B. Thompson also makes a useful distinction between different types of power in Thompson, John B. (1995) *The Media and Modernity: A Social Theory of the Media* (Cambridge: Polity Press).
18. Smith, *The Ethnic Origins of Nations*.
19. Smith, *Nations and Nationalism in a Global Era*.
20. See Bourdieu, Pierre (1991) 'Genesis and Structure of the Religious Field', *Comparative Social Research*, vol. 13, pp. 1–44.
21. See Smith, *The Ethnic Origins of Nations*.
22. Ibid.
23. See Bellah, Robert (1967) 'Civil Religion in America', *Daedalus*, vol. 96, no. 1, pp. 1–21.
24. Ian Paisley is the leader of the Democratic Unionist Party, the more hardline of the two main unionist parties. David Trimble is the leader of the largest unionist party, the Ulster Unionist Party.
25. See Bourdieu, Pierre (1991) (ed. John B. Thompson) *Language and Symbolic Power* (Cambridge: Polity Press with Blackwell).
26. The concept of hegemony is drawn from the work of Antonio Gramsci. See Gramsci, Antonio (1971) *Selections from the Prison Notebooks* (New York: International Publishers).
27. For the sake of simplicity, I do not make a distinction in this text between symbolic and cultural capital or power. However, Pierre Bourdieu does make a useful differentiation between symbolic capital, which is the ability to command authority, deference etc., and cultural capital, which relates to cultural competences, such as educational level, artistic ability. The accumulation of cultural capital is likely to enhance one's symbolic capital and, hence, symbolic power. See Bourdieu, Pierre (1993) (ed. Randal Johnson; trans. various) *The Field of Cultural Production* (Cambridge: Polity Press).
28. This phenomenon is discussed by Margaret Wetherell and Jonathan Potter in Wetherell, Margaret and Potter, Jonathan (1992) *Mapping the Language of Racism: Discourse and the Legitimation of Exploitation* (New York: Harvester Wheatsheaf).

29.   See Amir, Yehuda (1976) 'The Role of Intergroup Contact in the Change of Prejudice and Ethnic Relations', in Katz, P. A. (ed.) *Towards the Elimination of Racism* (New York: Pergamon Press).

30.   Aletta Norval has stressed the significance of the internal logic of apartheid discourse as a factor which helps to explain why so many Afrikaners readily accepted it. See Norval, Aletta (1996) *Deconstructing Apartheid Discourse* (London: Verso).

31.   See van Dijk, Teun A. (1993) *Elite Discourse and Racism* (Newbury Park: Sage).

32.   Two of the most important investigations of the 'fundamentalist' and 'evangelical' aspects of Ulster Protestantism include Bruce, Steve (1989) *God Save Ulster! The Religion and Politics of Paisleyism* (Oxford University Press) and Wright, Frank (1973) 'Protestant Ideology and Politics in Ulster', *European Journal of Sociology*, vol. 14, no. 2, pp. 213–80. See Cochrane, Feargal (1997) *Unionist Politics and the Politics of Unionism since the Anglo-Irish Agreement* (Cork University Press) for a critique of Bruce's thesis and a review of other critical comments on his work.

1   Under Siege

1.   See Todd, Jennifer (1994) 'History and Structure in Loyalist Ideology: The Possibilities of Ideological Change', *Irish Journal of Sociology*, vol. 4, pp. 67–79, and Clayton, Pamela (1996) *Enemies and Passing Friends: Settler Ideologies in Twentieth Century Ulster* (London: Pluto Press). Clayton maintains that Ulster Protestants can still be viewed as settlers because they 'constitute a group which is seen to be distinct and which maintains status closure and a relatively powerful position *vis-à-vis* indigenes who present at least a latent threat to this supremacy ...' (p. 34).

2.   *Irish Times*, 22.11.95.

3.   For much more sophisticated expositions of the argument against the comparison, see Brewer, John D. (1992) 'Sectarianism and Racism, and Their Parallels and Differences', *Ethnic and Racial Studies*, vol. 15, no. 3, pp. 352–64, and Smith, M. G. (1986) 'Pluralism, Race and Ethnicity in Selected African Countries', Rex, John and Mason, David (eds) *Theories of Race and Ethnic Relations* (Cambridge University Press) pp. 187–225.

4.   See Miles, Robert (1993) *Racism After 'Race Relations'* (London: Routledge).

5.   Mason, David (1986) 'Introduction. Controversies and Continuities in Race and Ethnic Relations Theory', in Rex and Mason, op. cit., p. 8.

6.   No statistics are available on the subject of religious conversion in Northern Ireland, therefore the conclusion is based on my own view which has been kindly corroborated by David Stevens, of the Irish Council of Churches. A survey by Paul Compton and John Coward suggests that approximately 40 per cent of mixed marriages in Northern Ireland involve a change of religious denomination by one of the partners. See Compton, Paul A. and Coward, John (1989) *Fertility and Family Planning in Northern Ireland* (Aldershot: Avebury), p. 191. The

rate of mixed marriage varies in different parts of Northern Ireland. Gillian Robinson cites figures which suggest that, in 1990, while almost 20 per cent of marriages in the Down and Connor Catholic diocese (which covers Belfast) were mixed, only 9 per cent in the Derry diocese and 4 per cent in the Armagh diocese were mixed marriages. See Robinson, Gillian (1992) *Cross-Community Marriage in Northern Ireland* (Belfast: Centre for Social Research, Queen's University) p. 11.

7. See, for example, Robinson, op. cit., p. 1.
8. See ibid., p. 3.
9. See Northern Ireland Statistics and Research Agency (1996) *1994 Labour Force Survey Religion Report* (Belfast: NISRA) p. 9. Its figures suggest that Catholic men are twice as likely to be unemployed as Protestant men. The Catholic/Protestant ratio for the likelihood of unemployment for both sexes is 1.9:1.
10. Analysis of data from the 1991 Northern Ireland Census suggests that roughly half of all households in Northern Ireland are in areas which are either more than 90 per cent Catholic or more than 90 per cent Protestant. A further 17 per cent of households are in areas where either Catholics or Protestants account for between 80 per cent and 90 per cent of the population. See Northern Ireland Statistics and Research Agency (1997) *Focus on Northern Ireland: A Statistical Profile* (London: The Stationery Office) p. 45.
11. The following sources were drawn on in compiling this brief history of Afrikaner nationalism: Butler, Jeffrey (1989) 'Afrikaner Women and the Creation of Ethnicity in a Small South African Town, 1902–1950', in Vail, Leroy (ed.) *The Creation of Tribalism in Southern Africa* (London: James Currey) pp. 55–81; Davenport, T. R. H. (1987) *South Africa: A Modern History*, 3rd edn (Basingstoke: Macmillan); De Gruchy, John W. (1986) *The Church Struggle in South Africa*, 2nd edn (London: Collins); Giliomee, Hermann (1989) 'The Communal Nature of the South African Conflict', Giliomee, Hermann and Schlemmer, Lawrence (eds) *Negotiating South Africa's Future* (Basingstoke: Macmillan) pp. 114–29; Leach, Graham (1990) *The Afrikaners: Their Last Great Trek* (London: Mandarin); Louw, P. Eric (1994) 'Shifting Patterns of Political Discourse in the New South Africa', *Critical Studies in Mass Communication*, vol. 11, pp. 22–53; Moodie, T. Dunbar (1975) *The Rise of Afrikanerdom: Power, Apartheid and the Afrikaner Civil Religion* (Berkeley: University of California Press); O'Meara, Dan (1983) *Volkscapitalisme: Class, Capital and Ideology in the Development of Afrikaner Nationalism, 1934–1948* (Cambridge University Press); Serfontein, J. H. P. (1982) *Apartheid Change and the NG Kerk* (Emmarentia, SA: Taurus); Worden, Nigel (1994) *The Making of Modern South Africa: Conquest, Segregation and Apartheid* (Oxford: Blackwell).
12. Moodie, op. cit., p. 181.
13. De Gruchy, op. cit., p. 30.
14. O'Meara, op. cit., p. 64.
15. Ibid.

16. Ibid., p. 165.
17. Giliomee, Hermann (1987) 'Afrikaner Nationalism, 1870–2001', in Fischer, Alan and Albeldas, Michel (eds) *A Question of Survival: Conversations with Key South Africans* (Johannesburg: Jonathan Ball Publishers), p. 17.
18. See DRC (1997) *The Story of the Dutch Reformed Church's Journey with Apartheid, 1960–1994: A Testimony and Confession* (English extract from the Afrikaans document) (Wellington: Hugenote-Uitgewers).
19. See Bosch, D. J. (1984) 'The Roots and Fruits of Afrikaner Civil Religion', in Hofmeyer, J. W. and Vorster, W. S. (eds) *New Faces of Africa: Essays in Honour of Ben (Barend Jacobus) Marais* (Pretoria: University of South Africa) pp. 14–35.
20. See Ngcokovane, Cecil (1989) *Demons of Apartheid: A Moral and Ethical Analysis of the N. G. K., N. P. and Broederbond's Justification of Apartheid* (Braamfontein: Skotaville Publishers). The DRC's admission of its own lobbying activities after 1948 is contained in DRC, op. cit.
21. See DRC, op. cit.; Giliomee, Hermann (1994) '"Survival in Justice": An Afrikaner Debate over Apartheid', *Comparative Studies in Society and History*, vol. 36, no. 3, pp. 527–48; and Leach, op. cit.
22. See DRC, op. cit., and Walshe, Peter (1983) *Church Versus State: The Case of the Christian Institute* (London: Hurst).
23. The WARC readmitted the DRC as a member in October 1998 after the DRC's General Synod accepted a resolution which stated that the fundamental nature of apartheid was wrong.
24. In addition to works already cited, this section draws on the following texts: Lapping, Brian (1987) [1986] *Apartheid: A History* (London: Paladin Grafton Books) and Sparks, Allister (1994) *Tomorrow Is Another Country: The Inside Story of South Africa's Negotiated Revolution* (Johannesburg: Struik Book Distributors).
25. Quoted in Leach, op. cit., pp. 188–9.
26. DRC (1990) *Church and Society 1990: A Testimony of the Dutch Reformed Church (Ned Geref Kerk)* (Bloemfontein: General Synodical Commission), pp. 39–40.
27. DRC, *Church and Society 1990*, p. 18.
28. It should be noted that the DRC has since gone much further. See note 23. It has also published a self-critical report on its stance towards apartheid (DRC *The Story of the Dutch Reformed Church's Journey*). The document states that the Church 'did not always maintain the desirable critical distance from the government' and that the DRC 'was concerned for the survival of the Afrikaners and did not always pay the same attention to the desperate circumstances endured by other people from day to day' (ibid., p. 36). It goes on to say:

   > The church must acknowledge to its members, old and young, that the guidance given by ecclesiastical assemblies in respect of societal matters over the past decades was sometimes sadly lacking. For that we are deeply and sincerely sorry. (Ibid., p. 36)

29. Cited in Sparks, op. cit., p. 74
30. Leach, op. cit., p. 204.

31. Dr Mike Smuts, Moderator of the DRC's Northern Transvaal Regional Synod, in correspondence with the author.

32. See Villa-Vicencio, Charles (1991) 'Piety and Politics', *Africa Report*, January–February 1991, pp. 47–9.

33. Louw, op. cit., p. 41.

34. *The Economist*, 4.7.87; *DRC News* (1990), vol. 15, no. 1, p. 13.

35. This figure is an approximate one based on a percentage figure supplied in *Demographic Statistics 1993*, published by the South African government using 1991 Census data, and from further information supplied by the government's Central Statistical Service.

36. This section draws on the following sources: Akenson, Donald Harman (1992) *God's Peoples: Covenant and Land in South Africa, Israel and Ulster* (Ithaca and London: Cornell University Press); Bardon, Jonathan (1992) *A History of Ulster* (Belfast: Blackstaff); Buckland, Patrick (1981) *A History of Northern Ireland* (Dublin: Gill & Macmillan); Foster, R. F. (1988) *Modern Ireland 1600–1972* (Harmondsworth: Allen Lane); Gray, Tony (1972) *The Orange Order* (London: Bodley Head) and Miller, David (1978) *Queen's Rebels: Ulster Loyalism in Historical Perspective* (Dublin: Gill & Macmillan).

37. Historians differ over the role that the Scots played in this plantation. Akenson cites A. T. Q. Stewart as asserting that the greater part of the immigration of Scottish settlers was due to a widespread move across the water by many who settled independently of the official plantations. However, Jonathan Bardon's detailed and persuasive account suggests that the Scots made a significant contribution to the British colonial project in the north of Ireland. He provides many examples of the enthusiastic role they played.

38. Hempton, David (1996) *Religion and Political Culture in Britain and Ireland: From the Glorious Revolution to the Decline of Empire* (Cambridge University Press) p. 93. With regard to Bohemia, Hempton states that its entire Protestant gentry class was expropriated.

39. Akenson, op. cit., p. 111. Roy Foster disputes what he calls the 'image of the romantic woodkerne preying on colonists from woods and mountains', as he says many native Irish farmers stayed on in planted areas as tenants but on extremely insecure terms. Nevertheless, he acknowledges their 'resentment was no less heartfelt, and the fear of displacement no less present'. See Foster, op. cit., p. 64.

40. Akenson, op. cit., p. 115.

41. Akenson, op. cit., p. 116.

42. Miller, op. cit., p. 116. Miller refers to the clergymen as army chaplains.

43. See Dunlop, John (1995) *A Precarious Belonging: Presbyterians and the Conflict in Ireland* (Belfast: Blackstaff).

44. Gray, op. cit., p. 57.

45. Miller, op. cit., p. 52.

46. Gray, op. cit., p. 81.

47. Miller, op. cit., p. 56.

48. Gray, op. cit., p. 87.

49. Wright, Frank (1973) 'Protestant Ideology and Politics in Ulster', *European Journal of Sociology*, vol. 14, no. 2, pp. 213–80.

50. See Buckland, op. cit., pp. 6–16, for a concise summary of the British government's unsuccessful attempts to implement Home Rule, prior to Partition, and the unionist campaign against the proposals.
51. See Bardon, op. cit., p. 439.
52. Holmes, R. F. G. (1990) 'The General Assembly and Politics' in Holmes, R. F. G. and Knox, R. Buick (eds) *The General Assembly of the Presbyterian Church in Ireland 1840–1990: A Celebration of Presbyterian Witness During 150 Years* (Coleraine: PCI) pp. 175–6, citing *Witness*, 2 June 1914.
53. Buckland, op. cit., p. 20.
54. Holmes, op. cit., p. 177, citing *Irish Presbyterian, XXIX*, p. 117.
55. See Akenson, Donald (1973) *Education and Enmity: The Control of Schooling in Northern Ireland 1920–50* (Newton Abbot: David & Charles). Also Jones, Stewart (1986) *Irish Presbyterianism and Unionism in the Context of the Creation and Development of the Northern Ireland State* (unpublished thesis presented as part of Master's degree, Belfast: Queen's University).
56. Jones, op. cit., p. 75.
57. Ibid., p. 179.
58. Wallace, Martin (1971) *Northern Ireland: 50 Years of Self-Government* (Newton Abbot: David & Charles) p. 120.
59. See Whyte, John (1991) *Interpreting Northern Ireland* (Oxford: Clarendon Press) pp. 164–9 for a discussion on differing views on the extent of discrimination.
60. PCI (1967) *General Assembly Annual Reports* (Belfast: PCI) p. 127.
61. See Dunlop, op. cit., p. 57.
62. PCI, Church and Government Committee (1993) *Presbyterian Principles and Political Witness in Northern Ireland* (Belfast: PCI) p. 15.
63. Ibid., p. 7.
64. Ibid., p. 13.
65. PCI General Board statement made in February 1972, in PCI (1972) *The Northern Ireland Situation: A Selection of Church Statements* (Belfast: PCI) p. 7.
66. Jones, op. cit., p. 153.
67. See Bardon, op. cit., pp. 405–6.
68. Norval, Aletta J. (1996) *Deconstructing Apartheid Discourse* (London: Verso) p. 95.
69. Todd, op. cit., p. 70. Todd is referring to those who adhere to a loyalist political oulook (see note 6, Chapter 2 with regard to a definition of loyalism). The settler theme is also explored by Pamela Clayton in Clayton, op. cit.
70. Akenson, *God's Peoples*. Another proponent of this argument is David Martin. See Martin, David (1997) *Does Christianity Cause War?* (Oxford: Clarendon Press).
71. Miller, op. cit.
72. See van Jaarsveld, F. A. (1977) 'The Afrikaner's Idea of His Calling and Mission in South African History', *Journal of Theology for Southern Africa*, vol. 19, pp. 16–28.
73. See Dunlop, op. cit., p. 15.

74. See Bruce, Steve (1986) *God Save Ulster! The Religion and Politics of Paisleyism* (Oxford: Clarendon Press) and Gallagher, Eric and Worrall, Stanley (1982) *Christians in Ulster 1968–1980* (Oxford University Press).
75. See Dunlop, op. cit., pp. 15–16 and Bruce, op. cit., p. 179.
76. Dunlop, op. cit., p. 16.
77. See Wuthnow, Robert (1989) [1988] *The Restructuring of American Religion* (Princeton University Press) and Wuthnow, Robert (1989) *The Struggle for America's Soul: Evangelicals, Liberals and Secularism* (Grand Rapids, Michigan: William B. Eerdmans).
78. The term 'curator' is used in a similar but not identical fashion by Buckley and Kenney. They identify active participants in churches and cultural organisations as 'curators' of the activities and belief-systems of an ethnic group. See Buckley, Anthony and Mary Kenney (1995) *Negotiating Identity: Rhetoric, Metaphor, and Social Drama in Northern Ireland* (Washington: Smithsonian Institute Press).

2   Setting the Scene

1. See Sparks, Allister (1994) *Tomorrow is Another Country: The Inside Story of South Africa's Negotiated Revolution* (Sandton, South Africa: Struik Book Distributors).
2. Ibid.
3. As South Africa is in the southern hemisphere, its winter season is during the months which would constitute summer in the northern hemisphere.
4. In each of these congregations, I carried out between 47 and 50 semi-structured interviews with a random sample of congregation members. These interviews were supplemented with some informal open-ended interviews with ministers and certain other individuals chosen for specific reasons. Full anonymity and confidentiality were guaranteed to all participants, other than those who were happy to be identified. In each case, the ministers in these congregations gave kind permission for the names of the congregations and their own names to be used.
5. 'Homelands' were nominally independent states within South Africa which were reserved for black settlement and which formed a key part of the administrative structure of apartheid.
6. Paramilitaries who associate themselves with unionist political aims have always been referred to as 'loyalist' rather than 'unionist', presumably to disassociate themselves from the unionist parties which condemn paramilitary violence. The term 'loyalist' remains ill-defined. However, it tends to be associated with working-class unionist political culture. It is often used to connote those shades of unionism which are least willing to compromise on political principles and/or possess a willingness to use violence to achieve unionist aims. Todd sees loyalism as a self-contained political culture, which has only a secondary allegiance to Britain. See Todd, Jennifer (1987) 'Two Traditions in Unionist Political Culture', *Irish Political Studies*, vol. 2, pp. 1–26. See also Cochrane, Feargal (1997) *Unionist Politics and the Politics of Unionism*, Cork University Press, ch. 2.

7. See Bruce, Steve (1994) *The Edge of the Union: The Ulster Loyalist Vision* (Oxford University Press) pp. 92–4.
8. Despite its name, Second Newtownhamilton was the main Presbyterian congregation in the town.
9. The initials UVF here refer to one of the main loyalist paramilitary groups, the Ulster Volunteer Force, which uses the same name as the UVF which fought Home Rule.
10. See Bruce, Steve and Alderdice, Fiona (1993) 'Religious Belief and Behaviour', in Stringer, Peter and Robinson, Gillian (eds), *Social Attitudes in Northern Ireland: The Third Report 1992-3* (Belfast: Blackstaff Press) pp. 5–20, and Stevens, David (1995) 'A Profile of Irish Religion', in *1995 Annual Report of the Irish Council of Churches* (Belfast: Irish Council of Churches) pp. 15–30.
11. See PCI (1994) *General Assembly Annual Reports* (Belfast: PCI) p. 175.
12. Davie, Grace (1994) *Religion in Britain Since 1945: Believing Without Belonging* (Oxford: Blackwell).

3   Fear, Insecurity and Alienation

1. This information was given to me by a local archaeologist, Sydney Miller.
2. Pieter De Wet is a pseudonym.
3. Keane, Fergal (1996) *Letter to Daniel: Despatches from the Heart* (London: BBC Books/Penguin) pp. 103–4.
4. In each cases, interviewees were asked for their response to the following two statements: 'I feel my own future is very uncertain,' and 'I feel my own future is much more uncertain than it used to be.' They were given five possible options for their response: 'strongly agree', 'agree', 'neither agree nor disagree', 'disagree' or 'strongly disagree'.
5. In order to measure each individual's sense of collective threat, interviewees were asked for their response to the following statement: 'I feel the rights of Ulster Protestants are under threat' or 'I feel the rights of white South Africans are under threat'. The possible responses offered were identical to those noted in Note 4. A Sense of Threat Scale was then constructed for each congregation. Points were allocated in the following way: 'strongly agree' = 2 points, 'agree' = 1 point, 'neither agree nor disagree'/'don't know' = 0 points, 'disagree' = –1 point and 'strongly disagree' = –2 points. In each case, the figure for the percentage which gave each response was multiplied by the number of points for that response. The resulting figures are given in Table 3A.1.

Table 3A.1   Sense of threat scale (minimum points = –200 and maximum points = 200)

Stormont	20	Queenswood	35
Seaview	61	Wespoort	68
Newtownhamilton	51	Louis Trichardt	64

6. Todd, Jennifer (1994) 'History and Structure in Loyalist Ideology: The Possibilities of Ideological Change', *Irish Journal of Sociology*, vol. 4, p. 70.
7. Divorce has been legalised in the Republic of Ireland since this comment was made.
8. This comment was made by Dr Johann Olivier at the Human Sciences Research Council in Pretoria, in an interview with the author. However, Dr Olivier felt that the culture was changing and that Afrikaners were beginning to question political decisions made in their name.
9. In order to examine this hypothesis and other possible correlations between variables, the three samples from each territory were amalgamated into two larger categories (PCI congregations and DRC congregations) and cross-tabulations were carried out within each of these amalgamated samples. These cross-tabulations were collapsed where necessary in order to ensure a sufficiently large frequency in each cell. The chi-squared statistic was then used to examine hypotheses concerning possible links between variables. Throughout this book, relationships between variables are noted where they proved to be significant at the 0.05 level, except where reference is made to a 'weak' relationship, in which case the correlation was significant at more than the 0.05 level. However, it must be borne in mind that these aggregated samples cannot be held to be a representative sample of the wider memberships of either church. Therefore, the relationships found can only be held to be indicative, suggesting that any hypotheses they do support may be worthy of further investigation. (This qualification does not apply to the postal survey samples which were random samples, of the group they were selected from.) The reference in the text to 'manual' and 'non-manual' refers to a categorisation that was used with regard to the occupation of the person deemed to be the chief breadwinner in their household.
10. See Edwards, John (1995) *Affirmative Action in a Sectarian Society: Fair Employment Policy in Northern Ireland* (Aldershot: Avebury).
11. When interviews were carried out, all interviewees were given a copy of the questionnaire on which the interview was based. The words 'equally suitable' were underlined in the PCI questionnaire because, after the earlier South African fieldwork was conducted, it was felt that not all the DRC interviewees had taken in the significance of these words. Clearly, this may have affected the comparative response to the question.
12. It should be noted that the category 'agree' also includes those who put 'strongly agree', the category 'neither' includes those who put 'neither agree nor disagree' or 'don't know', while the category 'disagree' also includes those who put 'strongly disagree'.
13. Jan Venter is a pseudonym.
14. Helena is a pseudonym.
15. In his Forward to the FEC's 1996/97 Annual Report, the Commission's Chairman, Bob Cooper, says 'there is no evidence whatsoever to support the contention that progress for Catholics has resulted in Protestants now experiencing disadvantage' (Fair Employment

Commission for Northern Ireland (1997) *Eighth Annual Report 1996/7* (Belfast: FEC)).

16. This statement was used by Dean R. Hoge to measure 'racial integration' in a study of attitudes in the United Presbyterian Church in the United States. See Hoge, Dean R. (1976) *Division in the Protestant House: The Basic Reasons Behind Intra-Church Conflicts* (Philadelphia: Westminster Press), p. 147.

17. See van Dijk, Teun A. (1997) 'Political Discourse and Racism: Describing Others in Western Parliaments' in Riggins, Stephen Harold (ed.) *The Language and Politics of Exclusion: Others in Discourse* (Thousand Oaks, CA: Sage), pp. 31–64, and van Dijk, Teun A. (1993) *Elite Discourse and Racism* (Newbury Park, CA: Sage).

18. van Dijk, 'Political Discourse and Racism', p. 37.

19. Christo Meyer is a pseudonym.

20. For an analysis of data on identity from the Northern Ireland Social Attitude surveys and a review of similar data from other surveys, see Trew, Karen (1996) 'National Identity' in Breen, Richard, Devine, Paula, and Dowds, Lizanne (eds) *Social Attitudes in Northern Ireland: The Fifth Report 1995–6* (Belfast: Appletree Press), pp. 140–52. Trew does include an analysis of the data based on location and social class. However, none of these surveys has given respondents the specific option of calling themselves 'Protestant'.

4 Civil Religion

1. See Sparks, Allister (1994) *Tomorrow is Another Country: The Inside Story of South Africa's Negotiated Revolution* (Sandton, South Africa: Struik Book Distributors) pp. 200–1.

2. See *The Citizen*, 20.5.93.

3. Quoted in Sparks, Allister, op. cit., p. 200. In July 1993, Viljoen did make a speech at a rally in Pietersburg in which he told his supporters to arm themselves for self-defence. However, he reacted angrily to the media's focus on this statement and said the real theme of the speech was the danger of conflict, and the need for a peaceful resolution of the country's devisions (*The Star*, 24.7.93).

4. Interview with author.

5. Anton Van Zyl, news editor of *Die Zoutpansberger*.

6. See Jarman, Neil (1997) *Material Conflicts: Parades and Visual Displays in Northern Ireland* (Oxford: Berg). Jarman notes that, while the image of King Billy when used in Orange Order parades signifies a *keeper* of civil and religious liberties, on loyalist paramilitary murals in Protestant working-class estates, it is used to signify 'a man who was prepared to *fight* for his faith' (p. 256 – my italics).

7. Bell, Desmond (1990) *Acts of Union: Youth Culture and Sectarianism in Northern Ireland* (Basingstoke: Macmillan).

8. Ibid., p. 100.

9. Jarman, Neil and Bryan, Dominic (1996) *Parade and Protest: A Discussion of Parading Disputes in Northern Ireland* (Coleraine: Centre for the Study of Conflict, University of Ulster) p. 13.

10. Interviewees were asked what, if anything, they considered to be the main significance of the Twelfth. They were asked to pick one of four options: 'It's an important religious day;' 'It's an opportunity to celebrate one's identity and heritage as a Protestant;' 'It's not a particularly important day as far as I'm concerned,' or 'Other', where none of the first three statements represented their view.
11. Quoted in ibid., p. 62.
12. See ibid., pp. 61–3.
13. Quoted in *Irish News*, 8.7.96, p. 1.
14. Quoted in *News Letter*, 13.12.96, p. 2.
15. *Irish News*, 25.7.97.
16. *Irish News*, 11.7.97.
17. If one includes those votes cast for three UUP representatives who opposed the Agreement, anti-Agreement unionist candidates attracted approximately 210 000 votes as opposed to pro-Agreement unionist candidates who attracted approximately 191 000. See Frank Millar 'Pressures on Trimble Present Strong Challenge to Sinn Fein', *Irish Times*, 29.6.98.
18. Quoted in *Irish Times*, 1.7.98.
19. Gellner, Ernest (1992) *Postmodernism, Reason and Religion* (London: Routledge) p. 91.
20. Jarman, op. cit., p. 94.

5   The Church as *Volkskerk*

1. *Irish Times*, 6.8.96.
2. *Orange Standard*, July 1997, p. 1.
3. Jarman, Neil (1997) *Material Conflicts: Parades and Visual Displays in Northern Ireland* (Oxford: Berg) p. 172.
4. See Bourdieu, Pierre (1991) 'Genesis and Structure of the Religious Field,' *Comparative Social Research*, vol. 13, pp. 1–44.
5. The postal survey was conducted in 1994. Questionnaires were sent to a random sample of one third of PCI ministers in Northern Ireland. 82 (75%) ministers responded. Ministers were asked to pass on a separate questionnaire to the Clerk of Session (or the Clerk of Session of their largest congregation where the minister was responsible for more than one). The Clerk of Session is the leading lay officer in a congregation's ruling body, the kirk session. 64 (58%) of the Clerks of Session responded to the survey.
6. Congregations were categorised as 'urban' if they were in Belfast or Derry or the outskirts of either of these cities. All other congregations were categorised as 'rural'.
7. These statistics were supplied by Revd Martin Smyth who was then Grand Master of the Orange Order. According to him, there were approximately the same number of Church of Ireland clergymen in the Grand Lodge.
8. *Orange Standard*, March 1990, p. 8.
9. Interview with the author, 13.11.92.
10. From PCI Press Release issued on 4.7.97.

11. PCI *General Assembly Annual Reports 1996* (Belfast: PCI) p. 30.
12. PCI *General Assembly Annual Reports 1997* (Belfast: PCI) pp. 18–20.
13. Quoted in *Irish Times*, 13.7.98.
14. Ibid.
15. Ibid.
16. *Irish Times*, 15.7.98.
17. *News Letter*, 22.7.98.
18. Quoted in *Irish Times*, 15.7.98.
19. *Irish Times*, 27.7.98.
20. Serfontein, J. H. P. (1982) *Apartheid Change and the NG Kerk* (Emmarentia, South Africa: Taurus) p. 94.
21. Ibid., p. 105.
22. This information was supplied by Professor Flip van der Watt, who was a member of the Bond's Executive at the time of the interview and a former Moderator of the Northern Transvaal Regional Synod.
23. Interview with the author.
24. *Die Kerkbode*, 26.2.93.
25. See, for example, Montgomery, Graham G. W. and Whitten, J. Richard (1995) *The Order on Parade* (Grand Orange Lodge of Ireland Education Committee), and Kennedy, Billy (ed.) (1990) *A Celebration: 1690–1990 The Orange Institution* (Grand Orange Lodge of Ireland).
26. Quoted in *Die Kerkbode*, 25.6.93.
27. *Die Kerkbode*, 2.7.93.
28. *Die Kerkbode*, 11.6.93.
29. A postal survey questionnaire, translated into Afrikaans, was sent to one minister in each of the 128 congregations in the Northern Transvaal Regional Synod. In order to examine lay opinion, ministers were also asked to pass on a separate questionnaire to a leading member of each congregation's ruling body, the church council. These councils have two categories of members – elders and deacons – and each council has an elected Chief Elder and Chief Deacon. Ministers were asked to pass on the questionnaire to one of these two officers, as stipulated. This stipulation was made on a random basis. Thus, half the ministers were asked to give the questionnaire to a Chief Elder while the other half were asked to give it to their Chief Deacon. Responses were obtained from 81 (63%) of the ministers and 74 (58%) of the elders and deacons.
30. Dr Eames is quoted in the *Irish News*, 10.9.94. Dr McGaughey is quoted in the *Irish News*, 1.9.94.
31. *Belfast Telegraph*, 24.10.94.
32. PCI Church and Government Committee (1994) *Press Statement*, 15.9.94. The Anglo-Irish Agreement was signed by the then British Prime Minister, Margaret Thatcher, and the then Taoiseach, Garret FitzGerald, on 15 November 1985. Its significance lay in the fact that it provided formal mechanisms by which the Irish and British governments could consult with each other on matters concerning Northern Ireland. The move greatly angered unionists, who saw it as a means by which the Irish government could 'interfere' in Northern Ireland affairs.

33. PCI (1995) *Report of the Church and Government Committee to the General Board on the Framework Documents* (Belfast: PCI).
34. *News Letter*, 5.6.95.
35. *Orange Standard*, September 1993, p. 8.
36. *Orange Standard*, July 1990, p. 1.

6 Church and Politics

1. *DRC News*, vol. 19, no. 1, 1995.
2. An account of the occasion was provided by Professor Pieter Meiring in an interview with the author in July 1995.
3. Ibid.
4. DRC (1990) *Church and Society 1990: A Testimony of the Dutch Reformed Church (Ned Geref Kerk)* (Bloemfontein: General Synodical Commission) pp. 39–40.
5. The following statements or summaries of statements made by the DRC were used in the fieldwork interview schedule (the statement on human rights was also used in both postal surveys):

> A. 'Withholding political rights from any section of the population cannot be justified.'
> B. 'All people are entitled to certain basic human rights, regardless of how they behave.'
> C. 'Workers are entitled to equal wages for equal work and work performance (that is, productivity and quality of work), regardless of their race.'
> D. 'Detention without trial should only be practised in extreme cases under sufficient control, so that application of the measures should always be beyond reproach.'
> E. 'Migrant labour (also known as contract or seasonal labour) should be eliminated as far as possible or at least restricted to a minimum because of its disruptive effects on people's lives.'

 A majority of both the ministers and the lay respondents to the postal survey also agreed with the statement on human rights (the other statements were not included in the postal survey).
6. DRC (1990) *Handelinge van die Agste Vergadering van die Algemene Sinode van die Nederduitse Gereformeerde Kerk 1990* (Bloemfontein: N. G. Sendingpers) p. 492.
7. PCI, Church and Government Committee (1993) *Presbyterian Principles and Political Witness in Northern Ireland* (Belfast: PCI) p. 7.
8. Ibid., p. 19. The tenor of the statement used in the interviews was somewhat different from that in *Presbyterian Principles* which sympathised with councillors who did not wish to work with Sinn Fein but explained why they should. However, it was felt that that statement was too long as it stood to include in the questionnaire. The section in brackets was introduced after pilot testing suggested the statement would be too ambiguous otherwise.

9. The actual wording is contained in PCI, Church and Government Committee (1992) *From Conflict to Cooperation? A Submission* [to the Opsahl Commission] *from the Church and Government Committee of the General Board of the Presbyterian Church in Ireland*, p. 11. It reads:

> It may be that a second chamber of some kind with initiating, scrutiny and delaying powers would be helpful in a system of devolved responsibilities [in Northern Ireland]. To prevent this body being a mirror image of the elected chamber, it could be composed of experienced people nominated by a wide range of bodies within Northern Ireland.
>
> Relationships between the people of Northern Ireland and the Republic of Ireland are important. The precise nature of these relationships is a matter for political negotiation. It could be that the second chamber might be the place into which some input could be invited from people from the Republic of Ireland.
>
> A similar input might be invited from Northern Ireland people into the deliberations of the Senate in the Republic of Ireland.

10. The members of the PCI involved in these talks were Dr Jack Weir and Dr Godfrey Brown.
11. 30 per cent said they felt constrained by the possibility of disapproval from members of their congregation, while 27 per cent said they felt constrained by the possibility of disapproval from members of their church council.
12. 11 per cent said they felt constrained by the possibility of disapproval from members of their congregation, while 10 per cent said they felt constrained by the possibility of disapproval from members of their church council.
13. See Note 9, Chapter 3, for details of how the statistical analysis was carried out. In this case, the relationship between the relevant variables in both samples was significant at the 0.05 level.
14. See Hargrove, Barbara (1989) *The Sociology of Religion: Classical and Contemporary Approaches* 2nd edn (Arlington Heights, IL: Harlan Davidson).
15. DRC, *Church and Society 1990*, p. 30.
16. For a useful critique of the concept of 'attitude' measurement, see Potter, Simon and Wetherell, Margaret (1987) *Discourse and Social Psychology: Beyond Attitudes and Behaviour* (London: Sage). Also Wetherell, Margaret and Potter, Jonathan (1992) *Mapping the Language of Racism: Discourse and the Legitimation of Exploitation* (New York: Harvester Wheatsheaf).

7   The Church as 'Conciliator'

1. See Northern Ireland Statistics and Research Agency (1997) *Focus on Northern Ireland: A Statistical Profile* (London: The Stationery Office) p. 45.
2. Poole, Michael and Doherty, Paul (1996) *Ethnic Residential Segregation in Northern Ireland* (Coleraine: Centre for the Study of Conflict, University of Ulster) p. 235.

3. Information provided by Anton van Zyl, News Editor, *Die Zoutpansberger*, in interview with author.

4. DRC (1990) *Church and Society 1990: A Testimony of the Dutch Reformed Church (Ned Geref Kerk)* (Bloemfontein: General Synodical Commission) p. 36.

5. PCI (1994) *1994 General Assembly Annual Reports* (PCI: Belfast) p. 24.

6. PCI (1995) *1995 General Assembly Annual Reports* (PCI: Belfast) pp. 29–33.

7. Christo Meyer is a pseudonym.

8. DRC, op. cit., p. 35.

9. Ibid., p. 36.

10. This statement was adapted from one used by Hoge. See Hoge, Dean R. (1976) *Division in the Protestant House: The Basic Reasons behind Intra-Church Conflicts* (Philadelphia: Westminster Press), p. 146. The statement also clarified to which churches the phrase 'family of churches' referred.

11. *Irish News*, 7.6.93.

12. Dunlop, John (1995) *A Precarious Belonging: Presbyterians and the Conflict in Ireland* (Belfast: Blackstaff Press) p. 111.

13. *Irish News*, 6.6.93. Emphasis in italics has been added by the author.

14. Fieldwork and postal survey respondents were asked for their reaction to the following three statements:

   1. (PCI): Ministers and kirk sessions should organise opportunities for members of their congregations to get to meet Roman Catholics to help improve cross-community relations./ (DRC): Ministers and church councils should organise opportunities for members of their congregations to get to meet black people to help improve race relations.

   2. (PCI): Ministers and kirk sessions should organise opportunities for members of their congregations to meet Roman Catholics and to discuss frankly some of the issues which tend to divide Protestants and Roman Catholics in Northern Ireland (that is, social and political rather than theological issues)./ (DRC): Ministers and church councils should organise opportunities for members of their congregations to meet black people and to discuss frankly some of the issues which tend to divide black and white people in South Africa.

   3. (PCI): Presbyterian congregations should hold special joint services of worship with Roman Catholics from time to time./ (DRC): DRC congregations should hold special interracial services of worship from time to time.

15. This finding has to be treated with some caution in the case of the DRC, where many congregations had more than one minister. In Northern Ireland, however, each congregation only had one minister (although some also had an assistant minister and some shared a minister with other congregations). It should be noted that, in the PCI, congregations were more likely to hold occasional services of joint worship where the minister did not oppose it.

16. This was an inter-denominational initiative involving three Protestant churches.

8 Different Worlds

1. See Anderson, Benedict (1991) *Imagined Communities*, revised edn (London: Verso).
2. van den Berghe, Pierre (1995) 'Does Race Matter?', *Nations and Nationalism*, vol. 1, no. 3, p. 361.
3. However, it should be noted that the relationship between the relevant variables was not significant at the 0.05 level in every case.
4. This information was provided by Herbie Conlin, an amateur historian, in an interview with the author.
5. This information was provided by a local archaeologist, Sydney Miller, in an interview with the author.
6. Finlayson, Alan (1996) 'Nationalism as Ideological Interpellation: The Case of Ulster Loyalism', *Ethnic and Racial Studies*, vol. 19, no. 1, pp. 88–112.
7. Ibid., p. 104. Finlayson is dealing here with the way in which loyalist ideology influences those who identify with it. He does not suggest it is adhered to by the whole Protestant community.
8. Todd, Jennifer (1994) 'History and Structure in Loyalist Ideology: The Possibilities of Ideological Change', *Irish Journal of Sociology*, vol. 4, pp. 67–79.
9. Davie, Grace (1994) *Religion in Britain Since 1945: Believing Without Belonging* (Oxford: Blackwell) pp. 106–7.
10. Wuthnow, Robert (1996) 'Restructuring of American Religion: Further Evidence', *Sociological Inquiry*, vol. 66, no. 3, pp. 303–29.

Conclusion

1. The AWB was formed in 1976. See 'White South Africa: The Forgotten Tribe', *The Economist*, 23.12.95–5.1.96, pp. 59–61, and O'Loughlin, Edward 'Terre Blanche's AWB Awaits New Dawn of Bloodshed', *Irish Times*, 8.8.95, p. 7, on the demise of the white right wing.
2. Todd, Jennifer (1994) 'History and Structure in Loyalist Ideology: The Possibilities of Ideological Change', *Irish Journal of Sociology*, vol. 4, p. 70.

Select Bibliography

BOOKS AND JOURNAL ARTICLES

Akenson, Donald Harman (1992) *God's Peoples: Covenant and Land in South Africa, Israel and Ulster* (Ithaca and London: Cornell University Press).

Anderson, Benedict (1991) *Imagined Communities: Reflections on the Origins and Spread of Nationalism*, revised version (London: Verso).

Bardon, Jonathan (1992) *A History of Ulster* (Belfast: Blackstaff).

Barth, Fredrik (1969) 'Introduction', in Barth, Fredrik (ed.) *Ethnic Groups and Boundaries: The Social Organization of Culture Difference* (London: George Allen & Unwin) pp. 9–38.

Bell, Desmond (1990) *Acts of Union: Youth Culture and Sectarianism in Northern Ireland* (Basingstoke: Macmillan).

Bellah, Robert (1967) 'Civil Religion in America', *Daedalus*, vol. 96, no. 1, pp. 1–21.

Billig, Michael (1995) *Banal Nationalism* (London: Sage).

Bourdieu, Pierre (1991) 'Genesis and Structure of the Religious Field', *Comparative Social Research*, vol. 13, pp. 1–44.

Bourdieu, Pierre (1991) [ed. John B. Thompson] *Language and Symbolic Power* (Cambridge: Polity Press with Blackwell).

Bourdieu, Pierre (1993) [ed. Randal Johnson] [trans. various] *The Field of Cultural Production* (Cambridge: Polity Press).

Bruce, Steve (1989) *God Save Ulster! The Religion and Politics of Paisleyism* (Oxford: Oxford University Press).

Buckland, Patrick (1981) *A History of Northern Ireland* (Dublin: Gill & Macmillan).

Buckley, Anthony and Mary Kenney (1995) *Negotiating Identity: Rhetoric, Metaphor, and Social Drama in Northern Ireland* (Washington: Smithsonian Institute Press).

Cochrane, Feargal (1997) *Unionist Politics and the Politics of Unionism Since the Anglo-Irish Agreement* (Cork: Cork University Press).

Davenport, T. R. H. (1987) *South Africa: A Modern History*, 3rd edn (Basingstoke: Macmillan).

Davie, Grace (1994) *Religion in Britain Since 1945: Believing Without Belonging* (Oxford: Blackwell).

De Gruchy, John W. (1986) *The Church Struggle in South Africa*, 2nd edn (London: Collins).

Dunlop, John (1995) *A Precarious Belonging: Presbyterians and the Conflict in Ireland* (Belfast: Blackstaff).

Finlayson, Alan (1996) 'Nationalism as Ideological Interpellation: The Case of Ulster Loyalism', *Ethnic and Racial Studies*, vol. 19, no. 1, pp. 88–112.

Gellner, Ernest (1992) *Postmodernism, Reason and Religion* (London: Routledge).

207

Giliomee, Hermann (1989) 'The Communal Nature of the South African Conflict', in Giliomee, Hermann and Schlemmer, Lawrence (eds) *Negotiating South Africa's Future* (Basingstoke: Macmillan) pp. 114–29.

Gramsci, Antonio (1971) *Selections from the Prison Notebooks* (New York: International Publishers).

Gray, Tony (1972) *The Orange Order* (London: Bodley Head).

Hargrove, Barbara (1989) *The Sociology of Religion: Classical and Contemporary Approaches* 2nd edn (Arlington Heights, IL: Harlan Davidson).

Jarman, Neil (1997) *Material Conflicts: Parades and Visual Displays in Northern Ireland* (Oxford: Berg).

Jenkins, Richard (1997) *Rethinking Ethnicity: Arguments and Explorations* (London: Sage).

Keane, Fergal (1996) *Letter to Daniel: Despatches from the Heart* (London: BBC Books/Penguin).

Leach, Graham (1990) *The Afrikaners: Their Last Great Trek* (London: Mandarin).

Miller, David (1978) *Queen's Rebels: Ulster Loyalism in Historical Perspective* (Dublin: Gill & Macmillan).

Moodie, T. Dunbar (1975) *The Rise of Afrikanerdom: Power, Apartheid and the Afrikaner Civil Religion* (Berkeley: University of California Press).

Norval, Aletta (1996) *Deconstructing Apartheid Discourse* (London: Verso).

O'Meara, Dan (1983) *Volkscapitalisme: Class, Capital and Ideology in the Development of Afrikaner Nationalism, 1934–1948* (Cambridge: Cambridge University Press).

Potter, Simon and Wetherell, Margaret (1987) *Discourse and Social Psychology: Beyond Attitudes and Behaviour* (London: Sage).

Serfontein, J. H. P. (1982) *Apartheid Change and the NG Kerk* (Emmarentia, South Africa: Taurus).

Smith, A. D. (1986) *The Ethnic Origins of Nations* (Oxford: Blackwell).

Smith, A. D. (1995) *Nations and Nationalism in a Global Era* (Cambridge: Polity Press).

Sparks, Allister (1994) *Tomorrow is Another Country: The Inside Story of South Africa's Negotiated Revolution* (Johannesburg: Struik Book Distributors).

Thompson, John B. (1995) *The Media and Modernity: A Social Theory of the Media* (Cambridge: Polity Press).

Todd, Jennifer (1994) 'History and Structure in Loyalist Ideology: The Possibilities of Ideological Change', *Irish Journal of Sociology*, vol. 4, pp. 67–79.

van Dijk, Teun A. (1993) *Elite Discourse and Racism* (Newbury Park, CA: Sage).

van Jaarsveld, F. A. (1977) 'The Afrikaner's Idea of his Calling and Mission in South African History', *Journal of Theology for Southern Africa*, vol. 19, pp. 16–28.

Wetherell, Margaret and Potter, Jonathan (1992) *Mapping the Language of Racism: Discourse and the Legitimation of Exploitation* (New York: Harvester Wheatsheaf).

Wright, Frank (1973) 'Protestant Ideology and Politics in Ulster', *European Journal of Sociology*, vol. 14, no. 2, pp. 213–280.

Wuthnow, Robert (1989) [1988] *The Restructuring of American Religion* (Princeton, NJ: Princeton University Press).

Wuthnow, Robert (1989) *The Struggle for America's Soul: Evangelicals, Liberals and Secularism* (Grand Rapids, MI: William B. Eerdmans).

Wuthnow, Robert (1996) 'Restructuring of American Religion: Further Evidence', *Sociological Inquiry*, vol. 66, no. 3, pp. 303–29.

CHURCH DOCUMENTS

DRC (1990) *Church and Society 1990: A Testimony of the Dutch Reformed Church* (*Ned Geref Kerk*) (Bloemfontein: General Synodical Commission).

DRC (1997) *The Story of the Dutch Reformed Church's Journey with Apartheid, 1960–1994: A Testimony and Confession* (Wellington: Hugenote-Uitgewers).

PCI, Church and Government Committee (1993) *Presbyterian Principles and Political Witness in Northern Ireland* (Belfast: PCI).

Index

Note: for abbreviations used in subheadings please refer to page xi.

210